Other books by the author

Sports Injuries: A Self-help Guide
Knee Health: Problems, Prevention and Cure
Strokes and Head Injuries: A Guide for Patients,
    Families, Friends and Carers (with Mary Lynch)
Children and Sport: Fitness, Injuries and Diet

RUNNING
FITNESS AND INJURIES
A Self-Help Guide

Vivian Grisogono

JOHN MURRAY

First published in 1994
by John Murray (Publishers) Ltd.,
50 Albemarle Street, London W1X 4BD

A catalogue record for this book is available from the British Library

Readers are advised to seek professional help in any case of injury. The author and publishers cannot be held responsible for readers' injuries in any circumstances.

ISBN 0-7195-5064 5

Typeset in Sabon
Printed and bound in Great Britain by Butler & Tanner, Frome and London

This book is dedicated to Andrew and Mislav,
and to the Hash House Harriers, Zagreb

Contents

Acknowledgements   ix

1. Training, diet and injuries: time for a re-think   1
2. Look after yourself: fitness monitoring, warming-up and training   27
3. Running shoes and clothes   55
4. How to cope with injuries   71
5. Food intolerance and injuries   91
6. Bone problems   97
7. Foot injuries   113
8. Ankle injuries   131
9. Achilles tendon and calf muscle injuries   139
10. Shin problems   153
11. Knee joint problems   165
12. 'Runner's knee'   185
13. Hamstring injuries   195
14. Front-thigh injuries   205
15. Groin and hip region injuries   211
16. Back problems   225
17. Running risks and safety factors   237

Recommended reading   241
Index   251

Acknowledgements

Firstly, I must thank all the runners I have treated, whether Olympic medallists, marathoners, fun-runners or joggers. You have taught me a lot. My interest in running injuries owes a great deal to Andrew Etchells and Sylvester Stein, who gave me the chance for ten years to write for the British *Running* magazine (now incorporated in *Runner's World*). I have been greatly helped by John Holt, former Secretary General of the International Amateur Athletics Federation, and Derek Johnson, Olympic medallist. For their co-operation in different parts of this book, I have to thank Melinda Cambridge, Penny Webster, Gareth Jones and Peter Gardiner.

My gratitude for their help also goes to Basil Helal, consultant orthopaedic surgeon; Peter Norman, podiatrist; Michael Bartlett, artist of vision and humour; and Roger Hudson, ever-patient editor. I thank my publishers, especially John Murray himself, Grant McIntyre and Gail Pirkis, for their forbearance in the face of the inevitable delays in delivery of the manuscript.

Most of all, I have to thank my dear husband Andrew for his kindness, support, help and love during the difficult times in which this book was written.

Vivian Grisogono
London, September 1993

Thirty thoughts from dedicated runners

* Running is good for you.
* I hate missing my daily fix of running.
* Running is the best form of fitness training.
* To get fitter, you have to run more.
* To run better, you have to run more.
* Time spent on training other than running is time wasted.
* Cycling and swimming are bad for runners.
* Weight training slows you down.
* Stretching exercises can injure you.
* Jog before you stretch, to stretch better.
* If you are stiff after a run, run more to loosen up.
* When I miss some training, I train more and harder to make up for it.
* Training has to hurt to do you good.
* I train like the top runners to improve my performance.
* You have to start young to be a successful competitor.
* I race on the roads, therefore I train by road running.
* Track athletes need only or mostly track training.
* I have trained the same way for years, so it must be all right.

* Warming-up means jogging around chatting for a while before running properly.

* Who needs to warm-down?

* You have to be thin to run well.

* I never eat or drink before a run, and I never feel hungry after running.

* Running helps you get over a cold.

* Proper running shoes prevent injuries.

* Injuries only happen to other runners.

* Injuries are an inevitable part of running.

* Run through pain: you can 'run off' running injuries.

* Children's injuries are nothing to worry about.

* If I get injured, I always ask coaches and other runners for advice, as they understand running problems.

* My doctor knows nothing about injuries, so I just go to practitioners recommended by other runners.

If you accept any of these ideas as correct or true, you need this book.

Training, diet and injuries: time for a re-think

The aim of this book is to help you to understand how to run better and more safely.

One word of warning: if you are injured, and are being treated or advised by a qualified practitioner, follow the practitioner's advice rather than the book's, if they are in contradiction. You have the right to question your practitioner, if you do not understand why you are being treated in a certain way, or advised to do certain things. But you should never try to carry out conflicting programmes, especially by mixing other people's advice with that of the practitioner treating you.

Running is a relatively simple sport: anyone who is capable of walking can also run. But its very simplicity can tempt runners to do too much, and can mask the sport's built-in potential hazards.

Like any other sport, running requires fitness: you have to have enough strength, mobility, speed and stamina for your event. You also have to be fit for running in order to use running as fitness training for other sports. Running, in itself, is not complete fitness training exercise.

Running injuries are fairly clearly defined and classified, because they happen in such large numbers to so many runners. Injuries can destroy a runner's capacity for performance. Even at top levels, a runner is only a star when he or she is injury-free. Injury prevention depends on good body conditioning. Whether you are a top athlete or a health-conscious jogger, you should only be training at a level appropriate to your needs and to your capabilities at any given time.

Runners are all too often trapped in set habits, either of

their own devising, or instilled into them by others. Previous generations of runners and athletics coaches have passed down lore, preconceived ideas and received wisdom. Many of these are still accepted unquestioningly by present-day coaches, parents, mature and youthful competitors, and fun-runners.

Questioning beliefs and analysing possible weaknesses in them is a vital way of working out how to do things better. How long is it since you questioned your ideas about running and what you are trying to achieve through it? Whether you are a jogger, fun-runner, élite performer, coach or teacher, how rational is your running programme? Can you improve your performance and reduce your risks of injury? If you are a coach, can you achieve these aims for the runners in your care?

The 'Thirty thoughts from dedicated runners' are ideas I have often heard runners express, and sometimes I read them in magazines and books about running. Examining them a little more closely might help to clarify how runners of all kinds can develop a more open-minded approach to their sport. The next sections of the book give details of what can go wrong for runners, what runners should do when things do go wrong, and, most importantly, how they can try to prevent problems.

RUNNING IS GOOD FOR YOU

Yes, in the main. Running, like brisk walking, is healthy exercise, mainly because it makes your heart and lungs work harder, and by doing so trains them to work better. It has been said that you need to run no more than eight miles per week in order to improve your heart and lung (cardio-respiratory) function, in terms of general fitness.

Beyond this level of healthy exercise, the effects of running can be less than beneficial, sometimes positively dangerous. There can be a big difference between training for ultimate physical fitness and exercising for good health.

Running does not suit everybody. I have treated people who, through heredity, have had such poorly developed leg strength that they were unable to run for even five minutes on any surface without developing injury pains. While this situation is often correctable through careful and painstaking

Healthy exercise can be fun: Hash runners still smiling after 15km across country, inspired by congenial surroundings, clean air and warm weather.

training of the leg muscles, it means that running is not a suitable sport or fitness activity for that person, until correction is achieved.

Although training can alter your body composition up to a point, runners who want to compete in specific events need to assess whether the event they have chosen is suitable for their physiological capacities. For instance, if you have more fast than slow muscle, you should logically aim at sprints or perhaps middle-distance, whereas the longer distances on track or road might suit you better if the converse is true. Physiological testing can identify your capabilities to a great extent, although for practical reasons most runners have to work out their 'ideal' event by trial and error.

Biomechanically, running does not train the body's muscles equally. It only trains certain leg muscle groups for strength; it does not train the upper body equally with the legs; it reduces flexibility and mobility rather than increasing them. Running does not create good body balance and over-all muscular condition. Different events influence different muscles. Marathoners gain strength and muscle endurance (stamina) in their hip flexors, front-thigh, hamstrings and calf muscles, so their muscles usually have a 'wiry', well-defined but slim appearance. Sprinters develop power, so that their muscles are typically well-defined and bulky.

Running creates an imbalance between your legs and your upper body from your trunk to your shoulders and arms. Your arms are a vital element for forward propulsion in running, and efficient arm motion helps to prevent back strain. But your arms do not work against any resistance when you run, by contrast with your legs, which carry the load of your bodyweight. Strength gains from running are therefore much greater in the legs than the arms.

Overall physical fitness requires other types of training apart from running. This applies whether you are using running for its fitness benefits, or competing in running as a sport.

Running can be harmful if you run too much, at the wrong time or in the wrong place. It does nothing for your body's ability to use oxygen as energy fuel (aerobic capacity) if you run alongside busy roads inhaling carbon monoxide and other noxious fumes. Running in cold, damp or polluted conditions can contribute to exercise-induced asthma. Running before you have recovered fully from illness can put you at risk of damaging your heart. Running too far and/or too often is a major cause of injuries.

Only up to a point, and in the right conditions, is running good for you.

I HATE MISSING MY DAILY FIX OF RUNNING

Frustrated runner: do those around you have to suffer too?

This reflects a potentially unhealthy state of mind. Runners who feel like this are often no longer in control. Running may have become an addictive habit, perhaps an obsession. This happens because running can give an exaggerated sense of wellbeing, by exerting a specific effect on some of your brain chemicals, called endorphins. This is commonly known as the runner's 'high'. It can make the pleasure of running as addictive as any hallucinogenic drug. An obsession with running can also form part of the 'slimmer's disease', anorexia, because it is a repetitive, mainly aerobic, activity which can burn up the calories, while at the same time it is more socially acceptable than visible self-starvation.

Once running has become an obsession, for whatever reason, your sense of perspective can become undermined. You may be incapable of judging when you should *not* be running. Your aims are probably confused, and you may have forgotten why you took up running in the first place.

Was it as fitness exercise, to fight the flab, or because you are talented and want to succeed in competitions? How much running do you really need to do to keep fit, keep slim or race more successfully?

Typically, runners who feel like this tend to train alone, because this gives them more flexibility in terms of training time and place. In this situation, your running can interfere with your social or family life. Do you plan your daily activities round your running sessions? Do you take it for granted that you will be irritable or frustrated if you miss one or more sessions? Do you expect people around you to understand and sympathize?

Top-level competitors have to be single-minded and to a degree self-centred about their training and racing schedules in order to succeed. But for runners who are not competing at the highest levels, it is harder to justify a single-minded determination to keep running as a daily priority. If you are simply aiming to improve on a moderate level of achievement, as a competitive or personal aim, do you ever wonder whether it is reasonable for a mature person to be so attached to one activity that it dominates and takes precedence over every other aspect of his or her life?

If you recognize obsession or addiction as underlying your enthusiasm for running, it is time to reassess your priorities in life, and perhaps try out different forms of exercise as a way of creating more balance.

RUNNING IS THE BEST FORM OF FITNESS TRAINING

Running is certainly excellent for your heart and lungs, and you can use it for both aerobic and anaerobic training.

You do aerobic training to improve your body's capacity to produce energy using the systems which need oxygen as their energy source. Aerobic training usually consists of steady-state running at moderate to brisk speeds, so that you feel the effort, but are not completely puffed out. Anaerobic training improves the energy systems which work without oxygen. It is usually done as short intervals of intensive work (sprints or shuttle runs), with a recovery phase between each burst. For flat-out speed training, you can sprint at full tilt for 10-second intervals, giving yourself a 50-second recovery phase in order to avoid a build-up of lactic acid in your leg muscles.

Runners who train at the right intensity are very rarely overweight, so running can be said to carry the advantage of eliminating any excess fat or flab. Over-training, however, can lead to excessive weight loss, which is especially danger-ous if the runner is anorexic or tending that way.

Running can improve leg strength, but not arm strength, unless you run with weights on your wrists or in your hands. It does not help your overall flexibility or mobility.

As background training, running is not necessarily appro-priate for all sports. Canoeists need endurance and strength in their arms and trunk muscles, so it is not really relevant for them to train up their leg muscles by doing running as aerobic exercise. Some sports players are not efficient as run-ners. For instance, rowers tend to have relatively long Achilles tendons from the way their feet and legs are fixed in the boat. Many rowers therefore run flat-footedly, which limits or reduces their speed. Cycling may well be a better form of aerobic training for rowers than running.

Players of racket games or field hockey use their arms and legs differently from running athletes. If they use running as training, they have to be careful not to do so much track or road running that it alters their running style for their main sport. Shuttle runs, perhaps combined with simulated stroke play, are a relevant form of background training.

Running is a good form of fitness training, but not necessarily the best for all purposes, and certainly not the only one.

TO GET FITTER, YOU HAVE TO RUN MORE

This is true, up to a point. Every training programme, whether for general health or for racing performance, has to be progressive. You can only improve if you are gradually doing more within the overall schedule.

Long-distance runners, especially, have to acclimatize to extended periods of running, so they inevitably have to build up their training mileage, to a certain extent, as they prepare for an event. Track runners build up speed and stamina by doing repetitions over short or medium distances at a certain pace. They also have to practise specific skills, such as running round bends, and sprint starts.

An aerobic training programme, for instance, might start with just five minutes of running once a week, if you have never trained before. You then gradually build up until you are running for at least twenty minutes, perhaps up to three times a week. A marathon runner might run for one or two hours at a time, building up the weekly mileage in preparation for a race. Some marathoners train once or twice a day, six days a week, doing up to 100 or even 120 miles weekly.

Similarly, anaerobic training has to be progressive, so you might build up from six to twelve bursts of interval work, and then increase the work time, perhaps going from 30 to 45 seconds in five-second increments. The progression extends over several weeks.

'Overload' training is another way in which you can make your running programme progressive. There are several ways of making your muscles work harder, in order to train them to cope with extra work. You can run on difficult terrain such as sand; you can run up and down hills, sand dunes or steps; you can carry a weighted pack on your back, or drag a load, such as a car tyre, strapped to your waist. You can use wrist or hand weights to help improve your arm strength for running. To increase the workload, you gradually increase the distances you run, or the number of times you do a set distance, or increase the weight-loading.

However much you love running, and might want to be doing more of it, you may be limited by time constraints. After all, there are only so many hours in a day! More importantly, even though ultra-distance runners achieve great feats of endurance, there is a limit to the amount you can increase running training.

There is a threshold beyond which injuries happen. As you build up your running training, especially if you run on consecutive days, you are increasing the repetitive jarring stresses that your body is subjected to, and this can cause a gradual breakdown in your bones, muscles, tendons or joint structures, anywhere in your legs and up to your pelvis and lower back. The damage might be minor at first, but once it has happened it can only get worse if you continue to train in the same way. Some people can sustain more running than others, but all too often the injury threshold is discovered too late.

Jarring stresses through running can cause aches and pains up into your lower back.

To get round these problems, you need to assess carefully what you want to gain from your running. If you want to be fit and healthy, you do not need to run very much or very often: remember, the estimate is that you only need to run eight miles per week for a significant reduction in your risk of heart disease. Even if you are training for a marathon, you do not need to be constantly pounding the streets. Some successful marathoners do as little as thirty miles per week – combined with other forms of fitness training apart from running.

A running schedule, like any other fitness training programme, has to be based on various elements. It should be planned as a complete programme extending over six weeks at least, or preferably twelve weeks, as this is the theoretical time span needed for muscles to adapt to physical training.

TO RUN BETTER, YOU HAVE TO RUN MORE

Most runners think that running better means running faster, and that in order to do this, you need to run greater distances and do more running sessions. In fact, to run better and faster, you have to improve your fitness, and also to learn to move more efficiently, so you have to improve your running technique or style. Running more does not necessarily achieve either of these aims.

Technically, your running style and efficiency may improve with practice, especially if you have a good coach to correct any faults in your movements. However, bad habits can become entrenched through constant repetition, so you have to concentrate on good technique at all times. If you overtrain, especially if you run alone, you will probably not be able to identify and correct technique faults.

Remember, too, that running does not train your whole body equally. Your legs carry your whole bodyweight, so they effectively do 'loaded' training each time you run, but your arms do not work against any load or resistance, making them undertrained compared to your legs. If you do not do other forms of exercise to correct this, your body imbalance becomes more pronounced the more you run, and your running efficiency is increasingly undermined.

A regular training programme can lead to staleness, and failure to improve fitness and performance. This happens most often to runners who follow a set pattern of running training, without any variety, and to runners who persist with training, despite the warning signs of fatigue.

TIME SPENT ON TRAINING OTHER THAN RUNNING IS TIME WASTED

This is a very old-fashioned concept. Most other sports based on repetitive movements (for instance rowing and swimming) have long since abandoned the notion of combining fitness training and skills improvement simply by doing the sport in itself. Background training involving varied exercise is vital both for improving performance and for preventing injuries.

You have to bear in mind the limitations of running as fitness training when you are planning a training or fitness programme.

Runners need flexibility, strength and cardiorespiratory training. You need to use other types of exercise to improve your body balance, so you need to work especially on your trunk, shoulders and arms – the parts running does not reach effectively. You also have to consider the leg muscles which are tightened or left relatively weak because of the limited range of movement involved in running.

Train your arms, to run better, but don't push through the pain barrier.

Apart from injury prevention, another reason for doing background training is as a policy for the occasions when you might be injured. If you are familiar with alternative training methods, you can still maintain a reasonable degree of fitness, even while you cannot run. You cannot train as efficiently if you have to learn new training techniques from scratch in this situation. This is equally important whether you are a competitive athlete or a runner for fitness alone.

The runner who has only trained by running is also likely to have difficulty with performing remedial exercises, and is probably more vulnerable to re-injury when he or she resumes running.

Many runners have turned to the triathlon (running, cycling and swimming) in order to vary their sporting experience. This has helped to make the concept of 'cross-training' for runners more fashionable and acceptable. In my experience, triathletes suffer far fewer overuse injuries than runners, even though their training intensity and quantity might be no less. In fact, many triathletes train harder than runners, but incur less overuse (misuse) injuries.

As you can see, there are many reasons why you should vary your training if running is your only form of active exercise.

Triathlon (running, swimming, cycling) is a healthy combination.

CYCLING AND SWIMMING ARE BAD FOR RUNNERS

On the contrary, cycling and swimming can be very good for runners. Neither sport helps running training specifically, but either or both can be excellent background aerobic training. Cycling has a good training effect on the legs, especially the hamstring muscles, while swimming provides extra work for your shoulders and arms. Whether you use a static exercise bike or a road cycle, just remember to have your saddle as high as possible, and to cycle out of the saddle, standing up on the pedals, whenever you go up a hill on a road cycle.

Cycling and swimming may be suitable as alternative training, if an injury has put you out of running. Even if you are not a good swimmer, you may still be able to exercise in the pool, using floats for your arms and legs, or a buoyancy ring around your waist. A 'wet-vest' can help you to do running-related training, as it supports you in the water so that you can simulate running movements.

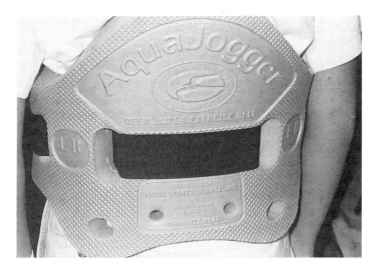

A support belt for pool running and exercises.

WEIGHT TRAINING SLOWS YOU DOWN

An old wives' tale. Top-class sprinters use weight-lifting to build up the power in their muscles, not only in their legs, but also in their arms. Using very heavy weights and doing just a few repetitions, or sometimes only one repetition at the heaviest possible load, they gain power which is then translated into speed out of the blocks and down the track. While it is true that the athlete may be too fatigued after heavy weight-lifting to run very fast at that moment, the overall longer-term effect of power training is to increase running speed, not reduce it.

Weight training with lighter weights and more repetitions is appropriate for other types of runner, as a means of building up speed and endurance, and protecting against injury by providing good muscle balance throughout the body. A varied range of exercises done as a circuit at speed can be invaluable general conditioning work, making you fitter and healthier, both for everyday life and in relation to running. Modern fixed-weights machines provide the safe means for doing circuit training using weights, because they comprise safe starting positions, full support for the spine and a good range of movement on every exercise.

Properly structured, supervised weight-training programmes should form part of every runner's background training, both in fitness and in injury.

Training the parts that running does not reach, using Norsk Sequence-training Equipment. Weight training using a varied circuit of exercises is invaluable background work for runners.

STRETCHING EXERCISES CAN INJURE YOU

Definitely not – if they are properly done. Stretching exercises should be done gently and passively: you get into the required position to stretch the muscle group without any discomfort, hold the stretched position for a count of about six, then relax. Do not bounce. Do not try to stretch further once you are already in the stretched position. Do not try to go to the furthest possible limit every time you stretch. Be guided by the state of your muscles at any given time. Sometimes they will feel tighter than at other times, for instance first thing in the morning, in cold conditions, or for some days after specially hard training sessions.

Stretching exercises are self-limiting if you do them accurately, so they cannot cause injury.

JOG BEFORE YOU STRETCH, TO STRETCH BETTER

You can usually stretch further, if you have activated your body systems, especially your circulation, by jogging around first. However, this can make it difficult for you to be aware of localized areas of tightness, and you risk over-stretching as a result.

Because stretching exercises are self-limiting, it is perfectly safe to stretch your muscles, however cold they are. Just accept that you cannot stretch as far when your muscles are cold and tight. If you feel that some muscles are especially tight, you should keep repeating the stretching exercises for them until they loosen out. If they don't relax despite careful stretching, you should probably avoid training on that day, if training is likely to stress the tight area, to avoid the risk of turning the stiffness into an injury.

Stretching is not an end in itself: it is not a competition to see how far you can go, or how much better you can stretch than the next person. You need flexibility for efficient muscle work and, to a certain extent, for injury prevention. Your overall flexibility will be improved if you do careful stretching when your muscles are cold as well as when they are warmed up.

IF YOU ARE STIFF AFTER A RUN, RUN MORE TO LOOSEN UP

Quite often more of the same helps runners to recover from hard sessions or events, so it is common practice, for instance, for marathoners to recover from a race by going out jogging each day for the next few days.

The problem is that this can create further stiffness, if any part of the body has been over-strained by the previous effort. So instead of loosening up, the stiffness can lead straight into an injury. It is far better to do stretching and gentle alternative training when you are recovering from a particularly hard run.

WHEN I MISS SOME TRAINING, I TRAIN MORE AND HARDER TO MAKE UP FOR IT

A terrible mistake. Any sudden change in your training schedule puts you at risk of injury. A sudden increase after a lay-off for any reason is inviting trouble. On the contrary, you should re-start training very lightly, allowing recovery days, and building up in easy stages.

This is especially true if you have been off training because of an injury or illness. In the first case, you have to spend time on your remedial exercises, to make sure that you have recovered full co-ordination. Otherwise you will compensate by using stronger muscles around the injured area, and you may finish up with a secondary injury which puts you out of action again. Following an illness, you are likely to be weak for some time, so you need to allow time for your body's defences to recover to the full, before subjecting yourself to tiring and rigorous physical exercise.

Impatience to 'catch up' following a lay-off too often causes further lost time through recurrence of the illness or injury which put you out, or secondary problems.

TRAINING HAS TO HURT TO DO YOU GOOD

Definitely not. Not in a real physical sense, anyway. It is true that top competitors in any sport have to push themselves to the limit, doing punishing regimes beyond their comfort limits. This pressure is important as much for its mental as for its physical effects, simply because in a hard race it gives a competitor psychological confidence to know that he or she has trained to the utmost limits. Much the same principle applies in the training of recruits for the armed forces, where this confidence is supposed to serve them well in times of danger and war.

There is a difference between psychological and physical pain barriers. It is always dangerous to push through physical pain. At the least, you might get injured; at worst, you could even kill yourself by ignoring the warning signs that your heart is not up to that amount of stress.

I TRAIN LIKE THE TOP RUNNERS TO IMPROVE MY PERFORMANCE

There are several reasons why this is unwise. Firstly, no élite athlete or coach ever quite gives away the secrets of his or her success. Not until years later, anyway, by which time new training methods may be applicable for top-level performances. Most often, published training schedules for top athletes are incomplete, leaving out some vital ingredient, so that potential rivals cannot benefit fully from the revelations.

One factor which is likely to be omitted is the use of performance-enhancing drugs for top-level training and performance. Each year, several top performers are caught, having taken such drugs. Despite supposedly stringent drug-testing, the fact that more sophisticated tests constantly have to be introduced is an indication that many athletes are still using banned substances. The dangers of many of these drugs are well documented, and include impotence, increased aggressiveness, liver damage and heart failure. Moral and ethical issues aside, there is no doubt that the possible short-term benefits of performance-enhancing drugs are far outweighed by the long-term risks to the athlete's health.

It is also true that someone else's training schedule can only be relevant to you if you have the same physical build as that person, the same movement patterns, and similar physiological and psychological capacities. Unless you are sure that all these conditions apply, the schedule is unlikely to help you improve your performance.

Trying to train like the top runners can be wasted effort.

YOU HAVE TO START YOUNG TO BE A SUCCESSFUL COMPETITOR

This is partly true, and the same can be said for all sports. If a child learns the techniques of a sport at an early age, say under ten, he or she will probably remember them for life. However, that is as far as it goes. Showing an aptitude for a sport when young is no guarantee of success later on. Many very successful competitors in many sports, including running, have started their careers relatively late, perhaps in the late teens or early twenties.

Children's achievements can be deceptive. It is well documented that pre-teenagers can run full marathon races in relatively quick times. However, it is not clear whether this has any bearing on the ability to race at top level as an adult. To date, the indications are that no successful child marathoner has come through to adult success.

The only certainties are that young competitors should not be pressurized to specialize too early (if at all) and that they should not be put through adult training schedules for any given sport. Otherwise, in sporting terms, they are likely to suffer mental and physical 'burn-out'.

Training too hard too often can lead to staleness and 'burn-out'.

I RACE ON THE ROADS, THEREFORE I TRAIN BY ROAD RUNNING

Running on hard surfaces automatically carries the risk of damage from the repetitive jarring stresses on your bones and joints. That said, if you allow your body to adapt to those stresses, and avoid making any sudden changes in your training regime, or any rapid increases in mileage, you may well be able to train exclusively on the roads without problems. Your protection from injury depends on how much background training you do alongside your running, so it is important that road running is not your only form of fitness work.

TRACK ATHLETES NEED ONLY OR MOSTLY TRACK TRAINING

Whereas running tracks used to be either grass or cinder, both very forgiving surfaces, most modern tracks are made of synthetic materials. As there are now so many different surfaces, athletes at top level need to train on as many different types as they can, in order to adjust when they race at meetings around the world.

On the track, you can do various types of running relevant to track racing, according to the event you compete in. You can do speed work in short, flat-out sprints, or longer, slower intervals, or steady-state distance running, or technique practice such as starting from blocks or running round the bends. It is obviously important to practise the skills needed for track events. However, on the fitness side, as we have seen, running is not enough in itself, so track techniques should be combined with other types of training for overall conditioning.

Track running also has certain disadvantages. In stadiums where international events take place, the track surface is often constructed in order to enhance the athletes' speed – basically to help world records to happen, as world records help sponsorship and box office receipts. Many modern tracks are too resilient or too hard to be safe for constant training, and injuries have been directly associated with some of the surfaces. Sometimes one can see vibration in the racing athletes' faces, reflecting fierce pressures underfoot.

In terms of movement patterns, constantly running in the same direction round a track is likely to produce injury through the repetitive distortion of the athlete's body, especially on the bends: running the 'wrong' way (i.e. clockwise) can help prevent this, but it is not always practical if many athletes are using the track at the same time.

Track training has to be varied as much as possible, and balanced with other fitness work.

I HAVE TRAINED THE SAME WAY FOR YEARS, SO IT MUST BE ALL RIGHT

This probably means you are stuck in a rut. It may not be a problem, if you are simply aiming to do a moderate amount of fitness training for the sake of your health. However, it is always preferable to try to vary your routine, at least at intervals, in order to maintain or improve your fitness. If you do not vary your exercise programme, you are likely to become stale, in the sense that you stop improving. In terms of physical fitness and wellbeing, this might mean that you retrogress.

At different phases of your life, your fitness needs alter. You may still be a competitive athlete as you get older, but you will not be able to train to the same intensity as you pass through the age categories. As your muscles and joints age, they too need different exercise patterns to protect them from harm, and to keep them working to their best ability. An appropriate fitness schedule for a child is unlikely to be suitable for a teenager. Further adjustments are needed as you pass from youthful maturity into middle age and then into older age.

Your normal pattern of exercise should change, in accordance with your body's needs.

WARMING-UP MEANS JOGGING AROUND CHATTING FOR A WHILE BEFORE RUNNING PROPERLY

There should be more to it than that. Your warm-up is essential preparation for any kind of exercise session. If you start with stretching exercises, you can tell whether any

Plan every part of your training programme with care, paying attention to possible risks.

muscle groups are especially stiff: if they are, you can stretch them until they loosen, but if they won't stretch properly, then you know you should not be running for the moment. So the warm-up can warn you of potential problems.

Apart from helping to prevent certain injuries, the warm-up 'tunes up' all your body systems, especially your heart and lungs, so that they are ready for greater physical effort. Part of the warm-up should be energetic, so that you break sweat. You certainly should not have spare breath for chatting as you do this.

The warm-up should be systematic, consisting of several parts, each with a distinct purpose. Without a good warm-up, the first part of your exercise session is likely to be wasted as you ease yourself in. If you over-exert yourself before you are ready, you can leave yourself too tired to complete your session efficiently.

WHO NEEDS TO WARM-DOWN?

Everyone. The warm-down can help to prevent muscle stiffness following a hard session, and this in turn can prevent strains. The warm-down need not be as extensive as the warm-up. The most important element in the warm-down is stretching.

YOU HAVE TO BE THIN TO RUN WELL

People who run a lot tend to be thin, as running, probably more than most other sports, reduces your body fat. Very few successful athletes are overweight. All too often, athletes associate successful performances with weight loss, not realizing that the important factor is more likely to be a successful fitness training programme which has incidentally led to weight loss.

Associating thinness with success can be very dangerous for runners. Firstly, thinking about losing weight may encourage you to restrict your diet, just when you most need good energy sources to match your energy output. Secondly, there is a danger threshold beyond which losing weight becomes an end in itself. Anorexia, an obsession with being thin that makes the patient fast compulsively, is a fairly

The anorexic runner is obsessed with being fat, even when he or she is obviously under-nourished.

common problem among runners. It mainly affects females, although it can also happen to males. Running is an ideal tool in the anorexic patient's armoury of devices for getting thinner and thinner. Coaches, teachers and parents should be wary of encouraging thinness in young runners. If you notice the signs of unwillingness to eat and drink regularly, combined with abnormal weight loss, you should encourage the runner and his or her parents to seek help through the family doctor. When anorexia is diagnosed, it should be treated in a specialist clinic as a matter of urgency, as very many anorexic patients eventually starve themselves to death.

I NEVER EAT OR DRINK BEFORE A RUN, AND I NEVER FEEL HUNGRY AFTER RUNNING

Many runners feel bloated if they eat or drink before going out. You often feel that you can run much better on an empty stomach, 'raring to go' with boundless energy. However, this is deceptive, as it is more accurate psychologically than physiologically. For any physical effort you need an energy supply, and this is normally obtained through food and drink.

It is true that eating too much, or eating the wrong foods can cause 'stitch' while you are running, but it is also true that a stitch in the side can happen to runners who have eaten little or nothing prior to running. It is not clear what causes the stitch, which is a painful spasm in the abdominal region, usually on the right side. Sometimes the stitch fades away if you ignore it and continue running. If it persists and hinders you, one cure for it is to stop running for a while, and gently stretch the area by standing upright and leaning gently sideways towards the opposite side from the pain. Stitch usually happens to novice runners or to runners resuming training after a lay-off. It may stop happening as you get fitter, especially if you do background training exercises to strengthen up and stretch your abdominal muscles.

Energy depletion due to inadequate food intake is not always easy to recognize. You work less efficiently if you are constantly using up your energy reserves: how long can you expect a car to run on an empty fuel tank? You need to eat at

regular intervals, especially energy-producing carbohydrates:
ultra-distance athletes and many triathletes 'eat on the run',
so runners should not develop phobias about being sick
through eating in relation to running. It is only a question of
finding out which foods suit you. You may get away with
running on an empty stomach without any ill-effects over a
long period (unfortunately), but sooner or later problems are
likely to arise.

Dehydration is a major problem. This can cause muscle
cramps, or at a more serious level can lead to collapse. To
avoid this, you should drink plenty of plain water throughout
the day, from first thing in the morning. Remember that
when you are thirsty, you are already dehydrating, so drink
before you think you need to. If you train over very long
distances, carry a small water supply with you, or set up your
run so that you reach a drinking fountain at intervals. If you
run marathons, take in water from the earliest drinks
stations.

Diarrhoea can cause dehydration as well as energy depletion. Many runners suffer from diarrhoea simply as a result
of running, especially if you eat too much fibre-based food,
although diarrhoea can also happen if you run on an empty
stomach. Diarrhoea can also be caused by infections, espe-

Eating and drinking adequately are vital elements in any running or fitness
programme.

cially through eating contaminated foods. It must never be ignored: check out the cause with your doctor, alter your diet or take medicines as necessary. Never try to run when you have recently been suffering from diarrhoea.

Immediately after a hard or long run is the time you most need to replace the energy you have used, so it is the best time to eat at least a healthy snack, even though you may not feel hungry. Probably the worst possible routine for a runner is to exercise first thing in the morning before breakfast, and then to take only light snacks during the day, waiting until the evening to take in a full meal. Your metabolism requires regular, balanced meals, and your diet is a vital part of your overall fitness programme.

If you are in doubt about what foods to eat, or how to organize your mealtimes in relation to your training, you should seek the help of a professional dietician.

RUNNING HELPS YOU GET OVER A COLD

Probably not, but this is debatable. In the very final stages of a cold, running can help to clear your airways, giving you the feeling that the last traces of congestion have gone and the cold has cleared up.

However, you have to be very careful. If you run while the cold is still developing, you are likely to make it worse. If you run in cold damp conditions you can turn a simple head-cold into a chest infection, and this in turn might lead to asthma later on. By exercising, you might also undermine your immune system, that is you reduce your body's capacity to fight off the infection.

You have to be very sure that the infection you have is simply a cold, in order to feel confident that exercise is safe. Innumerable viruses can affect humans. Many of them carry the side-effect of interfering with, or even damaging, the heart. Taking exercise while you are ill, even if you only feel a little run down rather than badly under the weather, puts you at risk of causing pericarditis, or inflammation around the heart. At worst, running despite the effects of a virus can cause death.

If you take any medicines, especially antibiotics, for any kind of infection, you should avoid training until you have had at least a few clear days of feeling well following the end of the course, without suffering a relapse. You should *never* take antibiotics and carry on training regardless. This applies not only when you are ill, but also when you have more trivial problems like an infected cut or an abscess on a tooth.

The safest course is to avoid taking exercise when you are even slightly unwell. If in doubt, check your temperature and your pulse rate. A raised temperature, for whatever reason, is an absolute bar to physical exercise. Your pulse rate first thing in the morning, known as your basal pulse, is a more sensitive indicator. If you routinely check your pulse on first waking up you can establish your normal average, allowing for variations caused by factors like alcohol or coffee the previous evening, excitement or worry. If you are slightly unwell, and your basal pulse is raised by ten beats or more per minute from the normal rate, it is wise to avoid exercising that day, even if your temperature is normal. This is a valuable guideline to use if you are recovering from debilitating long-term illnesses like glandular fever or myalgic encephalomyelitis.

Vitamins, especially vitamin C, are important to boost your immune system and help protect against illnesses. Your doctor may recommend extra vitamin C when you have an infection or illness. It is probably a wise precaution to take vitamin supplements in the recommended standard doses as an everyday routine. If in doubt, you should ask your doctor's advice.

PROPER RUNNING SHOES PREVENT INJURIES

If only... It would be nice to think that 'proper' running shoes existed, shaped to the individual foot, made out of the finest and most appropriate materials, designed to allow the foot to move in the best possible way... but I fear they don't.

It is anyway unlikely that even the best-made shoes would prevent injuries, as runners' problems are much more often related to training errors than to biomechanical defects or jarring pressures. So don't expect too much of your shoes, and be aware of the real causes of injuries, so that you can realistically try to prevent them.

INJURIES ONLY HAPPEN TO OTHER RUNNERS

Another piece of wishful thinking. Very few runners escape injury at one time or another. That is why every runner should be aware of how injuries happen, how to prevent them, and how to deal with them when they do happen.

Runners ignore injury risks at their peril.

INJURIES ARE AN INEVITABLE PART OF RUNNING

This is only true if you ignore the preventive measures you could take, particularly in relation to limiting your running training, and doing appropriate background training for fitness and injury prevention. Running certainly does carry inherent risks of injury, but these are predictable and avoidable.

RUN THROUGH PAIN: YOU CAN 'RUN OFF' RUNNING INJURIES

Definitely not. An injury directly related to running can only get worse if you persist with running regardless. What is worse, the injury will probably change your running style slightly, perhaps even making you limp, so you will throw stresses on to other parts of your body. You could then finish up with aggravation to the original injury, plus one or more secondary injuries. There might even be further, indirectly related injuries at a later stage, after you think you have recovered.

The overall time you are likely to lose in trying to sort out this unpleasant chain of events will inevitably be far greater than if you had simply taken time off in the first place, had appropriate treatment, followed through your rehabilitation regime, and then re-started your training in easy stages.

CHILDREN'S INJURIES ARE NOTHING TO WORRY ABOUT

Oh yes they are. The theory that children recover immediately from aches and pains is potentially dangerous. If a child complains of pain, or develops a limp, the problem must be taken seriously. Never assume that a child's pain will disappear spontaneously, and never think that the child is inventing an injury. The problem must be checked, through the child's doctor, and sport should be discontinued until it is absolutely certain that there is nothing wrong.

Ignoring a child's complaint or symptoms carries two dangers: firstly that there might be some very serious problem (such as a tumour or illness) which might be missed; and secondly that even a relatively simple sports injury might have longer-term effects, especially if muscular imbalance is allowed to develop around a joint, or if the growth area of a bone has been damaged. Sometimes injuries suffered during the teen years, which may not have been properly managed, lead to problems when the athlete has matured physically ten to fifteen years later.

IF I GET INJURED, I ALWAYS ASK COACHES AND OTHER RUNNERS FOR ADVICE

By experience, many runners and coaches learn a great deal about running injuries. But this does not necessarily qualify them to advise you on yours. As the saying goes, a little learning is a dangerous thing. It can be very misleading to assume that your problem is identical to one suffered by another runner, and will be solved by the same treatment, exercises or self-care measures. Some coaches and athletes even go so far as to do treatments, such as spinal manipulations and ultrasound or laser therapy. This is certainly both dangerous and irresponsible. Without full professional training, unqualified people have no way of knowing the full range of problems they might be dealing with, and they are often blissfully unaware of the dangers of applying invasive physical treatments.

Ideally, you should be treated by a medical or paramedical practitioner with an interest in, and understanding of, running and its problems. Be warned: too much involvement in the sport can be a disadvantage. I would have no confidence in advice given by a running doctor whose running career has been chequered by injuries and operations, but who continues to advise runners to run through injuries, in defiance of basic common sense. *Quis custodiet ipsos custodes?* It goes to show that no runner is immune to injury, and that even a doctor can be led by his obsession to keep running, rather than by sound clinical sense.

The practitioner helping you should be able to identify your injury, apply appropriate treatments as necessary, set out remedial exercises, self-care advice and alternative fitness training suggestions, and advise you on when you can resume running and how you should grade your return.

MY DOCTOR KNOWS NOTHING ABOUT INJURIES, SO I JUST GO TO PRACTITIONERS RECOMMENDED BY OTHER RUNNERS

It can be helpful to go to practitioners on the recommendation of other athletes, because they are likely to be sports-orientated. However, your family doctor (general practitioner) should have a central role when you are seeking treatment. In the first instance, he or she needs to be informed of your problem. It may turn out not to be a sports injury, but perhaps a medical problem needing investigations or specialist care. Or an injury might be more serious than you

The general practitioner has a
central role in the professional team
dealing with runners' injuries.

suspect, so that your doctor may have to refer you to an
orthopaedic specialist.

If you need to see more than one practitioner, whether
sports doctor, chartered physiotherapist, podiatrist, chiro-
practor, osteopath or dietician, your doctor should keep a
record of whom you have seen and what the result has been.
Most ethical practitioners inform your family doctor once
they have treated you. If you are seeing practitioners pri-
vately, insurance companies normally only provide cover if
you go through your doctor. But even if you are paying for
yourself, or seeing practitioners independently, the system of
informing the general practitioner is for your protection. If
you do not follow it, but consult various practitioners
without reference to each other or to your doctor, you can
get seriously confused by conflicting treatments and advice.

Many family doctors do now take an interest in sport-
related injuries, and are sympathetic to them, so your doctor
may be able to offer you more help than you think.

Don't look for shortcuts in dealing with your injury. Once
you have consulted a practitioner, follow the treatment
regime through to the end. If you feel you are not making
satisfactory progress, you should ask your practitioner why.
If you lose confidence in that practitioner, you should seek a
second opinion through your doctor. Try not to keep con-
sulting different specialists, looking for the instant magic
cure. You will certainly waste far more time on this than necessary.

Once you have been given a rational treatment programme, combined with alternative fitness training, it is in
your best interests to be a patient patient.

Look after yourself: fitness monitoring, warming-up and training

FITNESS MONITORING

Fitness tests can be a useful measure of how fit or unfit you are, whether your training programme is working as it should, and what areas of fitness you need to improve most.

Fitness testing can be very elaborate, when done under laboratory conditions using sophisticated machines. Aerobic tests tell you how efficiently your heart and lungs supply oxygen to your working muscles. You can run on a treadmill or pedal on an exercise cycle wired up to machinery which analyses the air you breathe out. There are also simpler tests of aerobic fitness, such as the Step-Test, and the multistage 20-metre shuttle run test (20-MST). To determine the exact composition of your muscles in terms of whether they are primarily fast-twitch or slow-twitch, you have to have muscle biopsies, in which a small piece of the muscle is extracted and analysed. Computerized testing of different muscle groups can show how efficiently they work concentrically (when they contract and shorten) and eccentrically (when they contract while lengthening out).

It is certainly worth having special exercise tests, technically termed *stress tests*, to check how well your heart and lungs are working, especially as you get older, or in the aftermath of any debilitating illness. It is also useful to have muscle measurements taken, especially after knee or back injuries, to check how well the muscles are protecting the previously injured joint(s). However, the full battery of exercise tests is probably only relevant to the very top-class performer who needs scientific guidance for the finest tuning for his or her training schedule. (Even then there is no guarantee that full physiological testing will provide the complete or correct answers about what the athlete's training schedule should be.)

A basic mechanical check of your body balance and structure is relevant to everyone, including the very young and the very old. Simple exercise tests can show you whether you are relatively strong or weak, flexible or tight, and well or poorly co-ordinated. The tests can also serve as remedial and protective exercises, providing the basis for a background conditioning programme which can easily be done almost anywhere. You should always try to work especially hard on any identified weaknesses, whether in flexibility, strength or co-ordination. It is always tempting to do the things which are easy. For runners, the temptation is to think that running is the only thing that matters. But correcting biomechanical weaknesses can help to reduce your risk of attritional long-term injuries from running, so this should be a good incentive to do background exercises.

If you always train alone, you can do the tests alone too, by feeling the effects of the different movements, and perhaps looking in a mirror to see whether there is any obvious lack of symmetry or any stiffness in given areas. However, it is much easier to do the tests with a partner, or better still have a chartered physiotherapist (physical therapist) or physiologist take you through them. If you keep a training diary, you should record your results in it, or keep a separate document of them. You should try to repeat the tests at roughly six- or twelve-weekly intervals. If possible, try to repeat the tests in the same conditions as previously, especially at a similar time of day, in a similar place, and with the same practitioner or partner.

None of the test-exercises should cause any pain, beyond perhaps a feeling of tiredness: if any test is painful, leave it out. It is useful to record your pulse rate before and after the testing session. Other useful basic measurements include your height, weight and shoe size (especially in the case of a young, growing runner), your fat percentage measurements, and your grip strength as measured on a dynamometer.

A grip dynamometer.

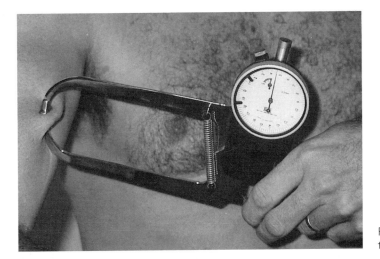

Fat callipers for measuring skinfold thicknesses.

Basic biomechanical tests and remedial exercises

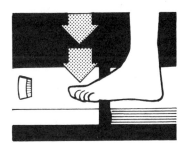

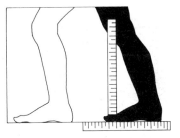

1 Barefoot, balance on one leg, timing yourself to see how long you can hold the position, keeping as still as possible. If this is easy, try it with your eyes closed. Repeat three times on each leg, recording the highest score for each.

2 Barefoot, place the toes of one foot on a weighing scale, and support the rest of the foot on a block: press your toes down into the weighing scale, and record the highest score or three tries with each leg.

3 Barefoot, with your feet a shoulder's width apart, put one leg behind the other, lean gently forwards keeping the back leg straight, and the heel flat on the floor. Drop a perpendicular from the tibial tubercle just below the knee, and measure how far in front of or behind the toes it falls. Take the best measurement (showing the most flexibility) of three on each leg.

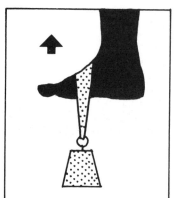

◄

5 Sitting on a high support, barefoot, with a light weight (0.5 or 1kg) resting on the top of your foot, keeping your knee still, move your foot upwards and return to horizontal, as many times as possible in thirty seconds or one minute, depending on fatigue. Record the scores for each foot.

◄

6 Standing up about a foot away from a wall, barefoot or in shoes, go up on your toes, squat down to touch the floor, then straighten up to reach with both hands as far up the wall as you can, while your partner marks the point you reach. Being timed over thirty seconds or one minute, count the number of times you can bend to touch the floor then reach up to touch the marker.

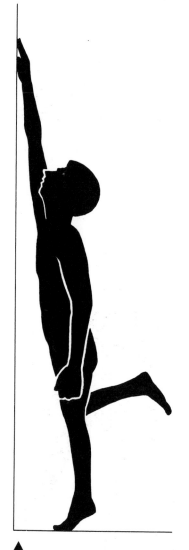

▲

4 Barefoot, stand on one leg, and go up and down on your toes, keeping your knee straight, and making sure you go up as high as possible every time (you can aim for a mark on the wall to help your accuracy). Count the number of movements you do on one leg in one minute, or thirty seconds if you find one minute too tiring, then repeat the test on the other leg.

▲

7 Lying on your stomach, barefoot, bend one knee so that your heel approaches your seat: your practitioner or partner measures the distance between the edge of your heel and your seat, or records that your heel can reach your seat, on each side.

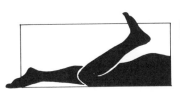

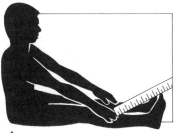

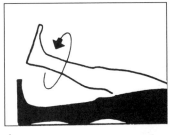

▲
8 Lying on your stomach, barefoot, kick one heel to touch your buttock, or a cushion placed over your buttocks if you cannot reach: record the number of times you touch your seat or the cushion in the space of thirty seconds or one minute, for each leg.

▲
9 Sitting on the floor with your legs straight in front of you, keeping your back straight and head up, reach gently forwards sliding your hands down your legs. Your practitioner or partner measures the distance between your middle finger and big toe on each side.

▲
10 Lying on your back on a mat, barefoot or in shoes, make circles in the air with one leg, keeping the knee locked straight. Count the number you can do on each leg over thirty seconds or one minute.

▲
11 Lying on your side, balance on your elbow, and lift your trunk upwards, so that you rest on your elbow and your foot. Count how many you can do on each side over thirty seconds or one minute.

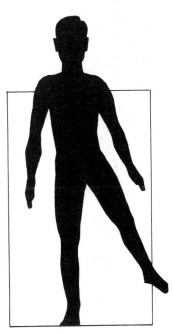

◄
12 Sitting with your knees bent and the soles of your feet together, let your knees relax outwards as far as they can go. Your practitioner or partner measures the perpendicular distance between each knee and the floor.

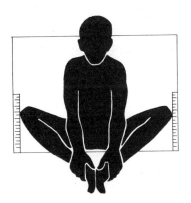

▲
13 Standing on one leg, hitch the other hip upwards towards your waist, then lift the free leg outwards, and lower it back without putting your foot to the ground. Count the number of repetitions you can do in thirty seconds or one minute, first on one leg, then the other.

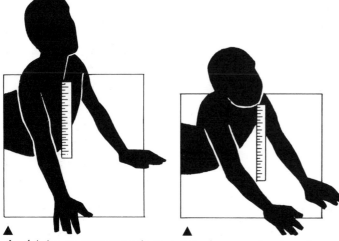

▲ 14 Lying on your stomach on a mat, place your hands under your shoulders and push your trunk upwards, keeping your hips in contact with the floor. Your practitioner or partner measures the perpendicular distance to the notch of your breast-bone and then to your chin.

▲ 15 Lying on your back with your knees bent, feet flat on the floor, sit up to touch your hands to your knees. If this is easy, cross your hands over your chest to rest on the opposite shoulders and sit up to touch your elbows to your knees. Count the number of repetitions you can do in thirty seconds or one minute.

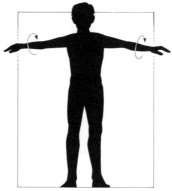

▲ 16 Lying on your back with one knee bent, the other leg straight, lift your seat and the straight leg into the air, then lower down and repeat the sequence in quick succession. Count the number of movements you can do in thirty seconds or one minute, first on one side, then the other.

▲ 17 Standing up, stretch your arms out sideways and circle them in the air, trying to keep your neck muscles relaxed. Count the number of circles you can make going backwards in thirty seconds, then going forwards for thirty seconds.

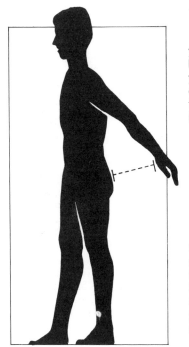

◄

18 Standing with your hands clasped together behind your back, palms towards your seat, keeping your elbows straight, lift your arms backwards as far as you can without bending your trunk forwards. The distance is measured between your palm and your seat.

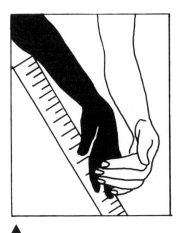

19 Standing about arm's length away from a cushion, held up by your partner or fastened to a support or wall, punch with each hand in turn to touch the cushion lightly, keeping your trunk relatively still. Count the number of punches you can do in thirty seconds or one minute.

▲

20 Standing with one arm straight in front of you, palm facing upwards, pull the fingers and wrist backwards with your other hand, to stretch the front of your forearm. The distance between your middle fingertip and the point of bone on your elbow is measured on each side in turn.

THE WARM-UP AND WARM-DOWN

Even though they are not guaranteed to protect you completely from injuries, the warm-up and warm-down can help prevent some problems, and are vital disciplines for runners of all ages. At the very least, the preliminary exercise can make you aware of potential troubles, such as muscle stiffness and perhaps infections like colds and flu. 'Tuning up' the body with a warm-up is essential preparation for more efficient muscle and joint action, and for proper co-ordination of body movement.

The warm-down (sometimes referred to as the cool-down), properly done, definitely helps to prevent muscular stiffness after running, and this in turn can help prevent muscle injuries.

The warm-up should consist of several different parts:

● *stretching exercises*, which involve holding a position absolutely still (without bouncing) for several seconds

- *mobility exercises,* which are done fairly quickly and rhythmically, so they also include some 'sweat-promotion'
- *'sweat-promotion' elements,* such as sprints, shuttle runs, a hard burst of cycling, or energetic exercises like star jumps or squat thrusts
- *mental rehearsal,* in which you visualize what you are about to do. If you are a competitive runner, you repeat to yourself (internally) the best ways of achieving perfect running style and tactics

The warm-down should also include stretching and mobility exercises, but gentle exercise such as jogging is substituted for 'sweat-promoters'.

The right order for doing a warm-up or warm-down may depend on circumstances. Runners often start their warm-up with a jog, before doing some stretching, because they feel they can then stretch 'better'. However, if a particular muscle or muscle group is tight, this can cause over-strain or a tear. Once you have loosened your joints and stimulated your circulation by jogging, you may mask the limitation in the tight muscle, and so over-stretch it without realizing this until after the damage is done.

The best sequence is to start with controlled stretching and mobilizing exercises, then do the 'sweat-promoters' and finish with some more stretching. Mental rehearsal can be done while stretching, or you can combine it with arm and leg movements similar to the running pattern. Some runners prefer to concentrate their minds while sitting and resting quietly, which is fine for a short period, provided you make sure you keep warm. The warm-up should last between fifteen and forty-five minutes, and perhaps even longer if it is very cold, or if your muscles are particularly tight. The minimum time for any kind of warm-up is five minutes, which is better than nothing – just.

For the warm-down, a logical sequence is to jog or move around fairly gently for five to ten minutes, finishing with stretching exercises. The warm-down does not have to be as extensive as the warm-up, and can even be restricted to stretching exercises alone, if you are short of time.

Warm-up and warm-down exercises are not competitive: don't worry if you are less supple than other runners. Work within your own limits, and you will gradually improve your flexibility and mobility. Many runners doing group training like to chat while warming-up and warming-down, especially during stretching. If you do this, don't forget to concentrate on what you are trying to achieve. When you are stretching, for instance, you should be looking out for tightness in any muscles, in order to do extra stretching exercises to release them. If you are doing mental rehearsal before a race, you need to be alone, so you have to isolate yourself from fellow-runners and avoid communicating with them.

Exercises within the warm-up and warm-down should not cause discomfort or pain if done correctly. If you experience pain of any kind, you should not continue your running session, whether training or racing (unless the event is crucially important to you). If the pain is still noticeable later on or the next day, you should seek advice, preferably through your doctor. If you feel run-down, queasy, unduly short of breath, or ill during or after your warm-up, check your pulse. If it is racing, keep still or move around very gently for a few minutes, and then check it again. If it is still much faster than normal in relation to the amount of exercise you have done, stop the session and, if possible, go home and rest. If you develop signs of a cold or infection during the next few days, do not try to train, but consult your doctor for appropriate treatment.

Stretching and mobilizing exercises for warm-up and warm-down

◀

1 Calf and foot stretch. Standing in front of a wall, place one foot forward to curl the toes up against the wall, and straighten the other leg behind you with the heel flat to the ground: lean gently forwards, bending the front knee and keeping the back knee straight, until you feel a slight pulling under the foot of the front leg and on the calf of the hind leg. Hold the position still for a count of six, then relax. Do three to ten on each leg.

2 Squats (knee-bends). Standing with your feet slightly apart, go up on to your toes, bend your knees, keeping your heels off the floor and your back as vertical as possible, then straighten up to lock your knees. Repeat ten to twenty times in quick succession.

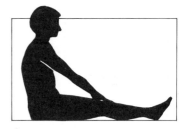

◀

3 Hamstring stretch. Place one foot on a low support in front of you; lean forward gently, sliding your hands towards your knees, keeping your back straight, head up. Hold for a count of six, then relax and stand up. Do three to ten on each leg.

▲

4 Sitting hamstring stretch. Sit on a mat with your legs straight in front of you; keeping your back straight, head up and toes pointing up to the sky, lean forward carefully until you feel the stretch on the backs of your legs. Hold for a count of six, then relax. Do three to ten.

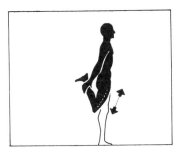

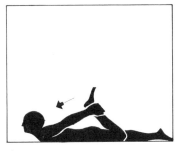

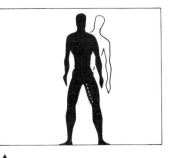

▲
5 Front-thigh stretch. Stand on one leg (using a support if necessary) and bend the other leg up behind you to hold your ankle with your hand: gently pull your ankle towards your seat, keeping your head up and your back slightly arched. Hold for a count of six, then relax. Do three to ten on each leg.

▲
6 Prone front-thigh stretch. Lying on your stomach on a mat, hold one ankle with your hand and pull your foot gently towards your seat, to bend the knee. Hold for a count of six, then relax. Do three to ten on each leg.

▲
7 Groin and inner thigh (adductor) stretch. Standing with your legs fairly wide apart, swing your weight over one hip, and lean sideways over the other leg to feel the stretch down the inner thigh of that leg. Hold still for a count of six, then relax. Do three to ten on each leg.

▲
8 Sitting inner thigh (adductor) stretch. Sitting on a mat with your legs stretched out sideways, toes turned outwards and knees straight, gently lean forward, keeping your back straight, head up. Hold for a count of six, then relax. Do three to ten.

▲
9 Hip stretch. Stand with one leg in front of you, foot flat on the floor, and the other leg stretched straight out behind you, with the ball of the hind foot on the floor, heel off the floor. Bend the forward knee, keeping the knee directly above your ankle, and holding your back and the hind leg as straight as possible: then let the hips sink downwards so that you feel a stretch on the front of the straight leg, and over the seat muscles of the bent (front) leg. Hold for six, then relax. Repeat three to ten times on each leg.

10 Hip mobilizer. Stand on one leg, with your hand on a support for balance, if necessary; bring your other knee up towards your chest, then kick backwards and downwards to straighten it behind you. Repeat the sequence five to ten times in quick succession on one leg, then repeat with the other leg.

11 Prone abdominal stretch. Lying on your stomach on a mat, bend your elbows to place your forearms on the floor, with hands palm downwards under your shoulders; gently straighten your elbows to lift your chest and shoulders off the floor, raising your head up and backwards, but keeping your hips down. Feel the stretch over the front of your trunk (but be careful to avoid any pressure on the small of your back). Hold the position for a count of six, then relax. Do three to ten.

12 Bent-knee sit-ups. Lying on your back with your knees bent, feet flat on the floor, holding your arms straight out in front of you, curl your trunk to sit up and touch your hands to your knees, then uncurl to lower back to the floor. Repeat ten to twenty times in quick succession.

13 Side-bends. Standing with your legs apart, bend down sideways to the left, sliding your left arm downwards, while at the same time bringing your right arm up sideways above your head; then reverse the movement. Do ten to twenty in quick succession.

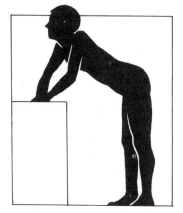

14 Forward bending. Standing with your legs slightly apart, straighten your knees by tightening your thigh muscles, and bend forwards, keeping your back flat, head up. Keep your weight forwards, and try not to let your hips move backwards. Do not try to reach your toes or the floor unless you can do so without effort. Hold the stretch for a count of six, then relax. Repeat three to six times.

15 Trunk twists. Stand with feet apart and arms up, with your elbows bent and hands at your chest, palms facing down; turn to the left, swinging your left arm straight out sideways, then turn to the right, bringing your left arm in again and taking your right arm out sideways. Repeat ten to twenty times in quick succession.

16 Arm circling. Standing with your legs apart, swing your arms up in the air close to your head, then round behind you in a big arc, keeping your elbows straight. Repeat ten to twenty times in quick succession.

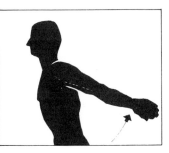

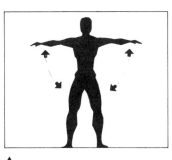

18 Arm punches. Standing straight, punch each arm in turn quickly in front of you, ten to twenty times.

19 Arm lifts. Standing straight, swing your arms out sideways and upwards as far as you can, keeping your elbows straight. Repeat ten to twenty times in quick succession.

17 Front shoulder (biceps brachii) stretch. Standing, clasp your hands together behind your back, with palms facing each other; keeping your elbows straight, lift your arms backwards until you feel a gentle stretch over your shoulders. Hold still for a count of six, then relax. Repeat five to ten times.

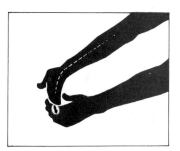

20 Forearm stretch. Place one arm in front of you, palm facing upwards, elbow straight; with your other hand, press the fingers and palm down and backwards, to feel a gentle stretch on the front of your forearm. Hold for six, then relax. Do three to ten on each arm.

'Sweat-promoters' for warm-up and warm-down

You can use just one type of exercise for this element, or a combination of several. Start gently, but then work as hard as you can: you should be sweating (at least slightly) and breathing quite fast by the end of the exercise(s), which should take between five and twenty minutes.

1 Jog fast, for five to twenty minutes.

2 Run, gradually building up speed to a sprint over the space of a minute, then rest for a quarter or half a minute. Repeat the sequence five to twelve times.

3 Do shuttle runs: sprint between two points, 30–80 metres apart, touching the ground at each end. Do one-minute intervals, with a half-minute rest, repeated three to ten times.

4 Cycle, fairly fast, for five to twenty minutes.

5 Skip, hopping from foot to foot, either continuously for five to fifteen minutes, or in five to twelve one-minute bursts, with a quarter-minute or half-minute rest in between.

6 On a mini-trampoline (boun-cer), jump or jog on the spot, either continuously for five to fifteen minutes, or in five to twelve one-minute intervals broken by quarter-minute or half-minute rest phases.

▲
7 Alternate leg thrusts: squat down to rest on your hands, kick both legs straight out behind you, then bring your knees back towards your chest with a jumping action. Do ten to thirty repetitions, in three to six sets.

▲
8 Squat thrusts: squat down to rest on your hands, kick both legs straight out behind you, then bring your knees back towards your chest with jumping action. Do ten to thirty repetitions, in three to six sets.

9 Star jumps: from standing, go down quickly into the crouch position to touch the ground with both hands, then jump up and stretch your arms upwards and outwards into the air. Do ten to thirty repetitions, two to four sets.

10 Astride jumps: from stand-ing, jump upwards and spread your arms and legs sideways so that you land with your arms outstretched and legs apart; jump again to land with your feet to-gether, arms by your sides. Do ten to thirty repetitions of the se-quence, three to six sets.

Fitness training

Before embarking on a training programme, and before each session, you should make sure you are fit enough to take exercise at all. If you have been ill, you should check with your doctor before undertaking any demanding fitness training. Check your early morning pulse and perhaps your temperature regularly, and avoid exercise if either is raised and you feel even slightly unwell. If you smoke, try to give up. At the very least, you should allow about two hours between having a cigarette and taking exercise, to allow some elasticity to return to your lungs.

There are two essential elements in any training programme: one is designed to improve the skills you need for your sport, and the second is fitness work as background for the sport. The two parts may merge or overlap, but they should not be identical. Running alone is not sufficient to provide adequate overall fitness training, whether you are a top-class athlete, aspiring competitor, fun-runner or jogger.

To set out your training programme, it is always best to be guided by a qualified coach, who can identify your individual strengths and weaknesses, and can monitor your progress, making changes to the programme as appropriate to your needs in the light of your performance and improvement or retrogression. Where injury problems have arisen, the coach, in turn, should be guided by a chartered physiotherapist (physical therapist). When dealing with health problems, including past or potential illnesses, the coach and the runner must follow the advice and instructions of the athlete's doctor. The coach, training instructor or physical education teacher has to:

- be aware of the different types of training needed for the sport
- be able to construct the programme to suit the athlete's individual capacities and needs
- be able to recognize the signs of overtraining, fatigue and staleness
- be able to modify the programme when problems arise, or if the athlete fails to improve, fitness- or performance-wise
- know whom to turn to, for more specific advice on training or injuries, if problems arise
- be aware of, and prepared to implement, the safety factors needed to prevent injury and health problems

The aims of any fitness programme are to help you improve your performance within your sport, to create efficient co-operation between your muscles, joints, heart and lungs, and to create good body balance in order to help avoid injury problems. Background fitness training should consist of stretching and mobilizing exercises, strength training, power training, speed training, anaerobic training, aerobic training and protective exercises. Warming-up and warming-down are essential elements before and after any session of running or fitness training.

The Schwinn Airdyne bicycle works the arms and legs and is excellent for warming-up as well as for aerobic workouts.

Protective exercises

Protective exercises should provide co-ordination, strength and suppleness in the parts which your sport does not reach, or which are adversely affected by your sport.

Movements designed to give the body protection from injury risks can be very simple, basic exercises, of the kind described as remedial exercises in the sections on specific injuries. A well-balanced training programme automatically includes elements of protective exercises within the overall framework. For instance, weight training or circuit training for stamina, strength and aerobic fitness should include some exercises geared towards body balance, which may not be directly related to running.

Protective exercises should, if possible, be done on a daily basis, as well as within the more formal parts of the training schedule. It is worth selecting about six to twelve exercises from the basic remedial exercises (perhaps from the injury and fitness monitoring sections of this book, for instance), working through the foot, leg, trunk, shoulders and arms, and doing about ten to twenty repetitions of each, once or twice a day (perhaps morning and evening).

Stretching and mobility exercises

These are done to improve your suppleness. You should work primarily to increase the range of movement in your arm and leg joints, and to a lesser degree the mobility of your trunk. Especially if you are an the adult, you have to be extremely careful not to over-stretch or over-mobilize the spinal joints, as this can all too easily lead to strains in the spinal ligaments. Stretching exercises are done statically, within the elastic limits of the muscle group being worked: you should never go from the stretched position into a further stretch. Always relax in between stretching movements, before stretching again. Mobilizing exercises involve gentle bouncing movements, to increase joint mobility through rhythmic compression and decompression effects. Examples of stretching and mobilizing exercises are given on pp.36–9, and stretching exercises are detailed in each section on muscle injuries. Stretching exercises should be done:

- on a daily basis, if possible, even on days when you are not training
- with special emphasis on any tight muscle or muscle group
- as the first element of a recovery programme following muscle injury
- before and after any training work

Strength training

You can improve your muscle strength for running by doing 'overload training', which means running with weights round your wrists and/or ankles, running with a resistance such as an old car-tyre attached to your waist with a cord, or a ruck-sack on your back, or running up slopes or steps. As running provides bodyload training for the legs anyway, this kind of overload training should include weights for the arms. There is a limit to the amount of weight-loading you can impose on your body during running without incurring excessive fatigue or injuries. There is also a danger that this type of training simply emphasizes your strong and weak points as a runner, without correcting them and creating proper body balance.

Strength training is best done using series of exercises either with weights, using bodyweight resistance, or using hydraulic or isokinetic training machines. With free weights, the resistance or loading is directly related to the effect of gravity. On weights machines, there are usually different kinds of pulley systems, which can cause a decrease in the resistance through certain parts of a movement: in the more sophisticated systems, such as Nautilus, there are compens-atory mechanisms such as the cam system, to make the resist-ance more constant throughout each movement. Isokinetic machines, such as the Kin Com, Lido, and Cybex, auto-matically adapt the loading through a range of movement. Plyometric training is a more recently accepted method of increasing body strength, using explosive movements which involve pre-stretch followed by full muscular contraction, and which are usually directly related to your sport.

Strength training can be both appropriate to a given sport, and protective, as you can use it to build up stability in areas which your sport does not train. A variety of different move-ments should be used to create an overall programme for the whole body. To combine good body tone with full joint movement, which is the most efficient way of protecting against injuries, you need to be doing each strengthening ex-ercise through the complete range of joint movement, so that the muscles go from full stretch to full contraction, if at all possible. This is easiest to achieve on well-designed equip-ment, such as Norsk, Nautilus, Schnell, David, and Sportesse, for instance.

Eccentric muscle work is muscle contraction to control a movement as the muscles lengthen out against the load of gravity or a resistance: this happens, for instance, in the front-thigh muscles as you go down stairs, or run down a slope. Eccentric work is essential both for sport and for injury protection (and recovery), so if you use a system which does not incorporate it, like the hydraulic resistance system Hydrafitness, you must combine these exercises with others which do involve eccentric loading. To achieve eccentric work using weights, you have to control the reverse element of any movement by slowing it down.

The correct starting position for each exercise is vital. Your back, neck and head should be properly supported when you are doing arm or leg exercises. When you use free weights, or machines without full support for the spine, try to make sure that you keep your back and neck straight, and hold your head up. Correct movements are vital for injury prevention, and to derive the full benefit from an exercise. Any leg exercise which involves bending the knee should also include the full straightening, lock-out movement, to protect the kneecap joint. Loading the back should be done with care, especially if you have already had back problems: the 'good-morning exercise', for instance, in which you bend forward standing up with a weight across your shoulders, places great pressure on the spinal joints, as does the 'military press', in which you lift the weight above your head, in a sitting or standing position.

On this Norsk leg press machine the spine and head are fully supported, and the knees must lock straight at the end of the movement.

For muscle endurance, you should be doing between ten and twenty repetitions of each exercise, and any weight-loading or resistance should be light enough to allow you to do each movement accurately through the required joint range. All strength training should be progressive: you need to increase the repetitions you do of each exercise, the number of sets of exercises, and the weight-resistance, as appropriate. The increases of work should be done in graduated, easy stages.

It takes about three months for muscles to adapt to a strength training programme, so you need to plan the strengthening work over this kind of time-frame.

Power and speed training

Power and speed training are closely linked: power is defined as a combination of speed and strength. You can increase your power in any muscle groups by doing appropriate movements with a very heavy weight, which you can only move once, up to a maximum of perhaps three times. If the loading is so heavy that you can only move it once, this is called your 'one-repetition maximum'.

Speed training involves very short bursts of high-intensity activity, such as a sprint, or hitting a punch-ball. To avoid any build-up of lactic acid in the working muscles, you might do up to ten seconds of work, followed by a 50-second pause, before repeating the effort.

As with other types of training, you aim to build up the amount of work you do over a period of time, so you start with just a few bursts of explosive speed work, and build up the number gradually. With power training using heavy weights, you should be able to increase your one-repetition maximum fractionally over a period, but when you reach your absolute maximum, you may have to choose different exercises.

Power and speed training are obviously most directly relevant to sprinters, but in fact every runner needs an element of speed. Sprinters make the most use of their arm power for propulsion, but, again, every runner needs arm impetus for forward motion, so if power and speed training are included in the programme, they must involve the arms as well as the legs.

Anaerobic training

When you do exercise at high intensity, beyond the level at which your lungs and circulatory system can supply oxygen to your working muscles, your body has to cope with the by-products of the workload, especially lactic acid. The more efficient your body is at removing the lactic acid, the better your ability to work at high intensity, and the less likely you are to suffer from sore muscles after your exercise sessions.

Interval training is one way of doing anaerobic work: you simply perform an activity or exercise very hard for a set number of seconds, then repeat the effort after the same number of seconds' rest. You can use sprints, shuttle runs, skipping, hopping or bounding for this purpose, or any exercise involving the arms as well as the legs.

A simple formula is to start with thirty seconds of work and the same period of rest, repeated six times on the first session, building up gradually to twelve exercise bursts by adding an extra one at each interval training session you do. Then you reduce the repetitions to six again, and work for thirty-five seconds, building up to twelve work-bursts over the next sessions. You can then increase the work and rest time to forty seconds through the same process, then forty-five seconds, which is probably the limit at which you can sustain a very high level of intense effort. Interval training can also be done on the basis of distance run or exercise repetitions counted, if for some reason you cannot time the bursts. For instance, the basic interval can be to sprint hard for 200 metres, then jog back. You gradually increase the sprint distance as you would the timed interval.

Anaerobic training is the type of work most likely to leave your muscles stiff and sore, so you should take care to ease out fully afterwards by doing extra passive stretching exercises.

Aerobic training

With aerobic training, you work your muscles and heart and lungs hard enough to make you feel you are exerting yourself, but not so hard that you are working flat-out. Progressively, you improve the efficiency with which your heart and lungs (cardiorespiratory system) supply oxygen to your muscles, and with which your muscles use the oxygen to release its fuel energy.

For basic aerobic fitness training, you need to do an activity at moderate intensity for a period of twenty to thirty minutes. You can use steady-state activities such as running, cyc-

The rowing ergometer provides aerobic work using the arms, legs and trunk.

ling, skipping and swimming, or you can do a continuous series of exercises over the same period of time. If you are totally untrained, you may not be able to complete the full period, and so you should start with a shorter time, perhaps even as little as five minutes, building up in very easy stages to the full period.

Planning a training programme

The elements for your programme must be related to the type of running you want to do, or your general aims for fitness and health. A competitive sprinter, for instance, places more emphasis on the explosive speed and power training. Different types of track session might be done five or six days a week, or just two to three times a week. The long distance runner or marathoner may be doing high mileage by running twice a day, six days a week, or using other training in between and restricting the running to three or four days a week. The jogger who simply wants to get fit and perhaps lose weight might simply use a basis of jogging, say two or three times a week, with alternative training twice a week for variety. Stretching and protective exercises should be a daily routine, whatever your ultimate aims.

A good combination of elements might be to do aerobic training two or three days a week; anaerobic training two or three days a week; explosive speed training, also two or three days a week; muscle strength and endurance training, two days a week; and different kinds of running training and skills practice anything from twice a week to six times a week. If you do different types of training on the same day, do speed work first, and anaerobic training last.

A well-designed circuit of exercises is an extremely economical way of combining several types of fitness training. Especially if you can use a fixed-weights system like Norsk, you can do overall body conditioning, symmetrical training to balance each side of the body plus the upper and lower halves, flexibility work, strength and muscle endurance work, anaerobic training, and aerobic training, if the circuit is done over the space of about thirty minutes with high-intensity activity at each station.

If it is an end in itself, your fitness programme should be scheduled over several weeks, up to about three months, with a gradual increase in the workload you are doing. If you simply repeat the same routine, even if you do it every day, you will not improve your fitness levels, and you may even retrogress, due to 'staleness'. After three months or so, you should make changes in the pattern you have been doing, or even take a complete break from exercising for a month or two, before starting to work out again, perhaps with a slightly different programme.

If you are a competitive athlete, your programme should be geared to your competitive season, so that you reach your peak of fitness at the right time to perform to your best possible level. This means that your major effort in training is made during the 'closed' season. For track athletes, for instance, it is particularly important to do anaerobic training through the non-racing period, rather than concentrating too much on aerobic, steady-state training for stamina, and leaving the intense training bursts until the season is due to start.

For beginner runners, and for any runner who has had an extended period off running through illness or injury, it is essential to start running with very small amounts, allowing adequate rest periods between running sessions, and building up in very easy stages. I recommend working on the basis of running once a week for one month, twice a week for the second month, and building up to three times for the next month, four times in the fourth month. Any increase beyond four running sessions a week should be made in stages about six months after starting the running programme.

At about the 23-mile mark, many marathoners tend to drop their heels as they get tired. Note the prominent knee-caps, which reflect the strain of long-distance road running on the knees.

Even if you run on the relatively soft surface of a treadmill or a mini-trampoline (bouncer), you should still be careful not too run too often, or on consecutive days. Remember that it is the repetitive movements of running that can cause injuries, as much as the jarring on hard tracks or pavements. If you run in a pool using a 'wet-vest', the muscle work is quite different from running on land, so you can safely intersperse pool running sessions with normal runs. As pool running is so much harder than ordinary running, it is wise to vary any pool sessions with swimming and perhaps arm and leg exercises in the water, to avoid the risk of muscle strains.

The amount of running you might do within each normal running session can depend on your experience. If you have never run before, I suggest that you should start with about five minutes, or perhaps running a short distance in a circuit from your home. If you are an experienced runner, you can start with about three to five miles, and gradually increase the distance week by week. It is the recovery days between runs that are your safeguard against overuse (misuse) injuries, especially stress fractures (see pp.102–9).

Running skills

Running is a relatively simple activity, and it is true to say that anyone who can walk should also be able to run. The main difference between walking and running is that one foot is always in contact with the ground when you walk, whereas when you run there is a phase when both feet are off the ground. The basic technique of running is to put one foot in front of the other, swinging the opposite arm forwards relative to the front foot. Running technique varies according to the event, and according to the individual style and physical capacities of the runner.

If you run fast, or sprint, your front leg usually lands on the ball of the foot and drives hard into the ground as your hip and knee straighten, while the knee of the hind leg is bent to a very acute angle, bringing your heel close to your seat, before it comes forward to stretch out and strike the ground in front of you. The middle-distance runner usually also lands on the toes, although some land on the heel. In general, the middle-distance runner does not bend the knees as acutely and rapidly as the sprinter, either on the knee pick-up movement in front of the body, or on the heel-kick behind. Long-distance runners and marathoners tend to use heel–toe motion when the foot strikes the ground, and may not lift the legs up as much as middle-distance runners. All runners try to minimize any sideways movement of the feet, keeping the foot motion in as straight a line as possible.

Fast marathoners maintain a high heel-lift for most of the race.

The leg, trunk or arm movements can be subject to individual variations in running. You may tend to run with a low knee pick-up and heel-kick, or a relatively high knee pick-up combined with short leg extension behind you. Your pelvis may tilt forwards, arching your back, leading to a very upright stance as you run. The pelvis may tip sideways at each step, letting your free leg drop slightly relative to the weight-bearing leg. You might bend forwards at the hips, and run in a slightly hunched position. If you swing your arms across your chest, you twist your trunk in a greater arc with each pace than if you keep your arms relatively still. If your arms do not swing forwards and backwards at all, your trunk tends to turn mainly from waist level rather than through its whole length. Some runners swing one arm only, while the other remains passive. Some drop one or both shoulders, or run with their shoulders in constant tension.

Even allowing for individual differences of style, it is always worth working on improving your running technique, especially if you or your coach can perceive obvious defects in the way you run. For the beginner runner, it is useful to be aware of some of the basic technicalities from the start, to avoid getting stuck with bad habits. People using running as background training for other sports are likely to get more out of it if they try to achieve an efficient running action. If you are a squash, tennis or field hockey player, for instance, your legs and arms will not be used to working symmetrically in an alternating pattern, nor will your legs be trained for repetitive motion in a straight line.

There are drills for improving running technique, and these are best done under the supervision of a coach. Having your running action filmed on video is an excellent way of gaining feedback as to what you are actually doing, so that you can become more aware of the strengths and weaknesses of your technique. Running drills aim to emphasize certain elements of your running action. Usually, you only run a short distance while doing the drills, so that you do not over-fatigue the area you are training, or lose concentration. You might repeat each drill a few times, with a short pause in between.

Commonly used running drills

You can work on your arm movements, exaggerating the swing forwards and backwards, while making sure that your elbows stay in, your arms keep in line with your body and you do not move your arms more than slightly across your chest. To increase the muscle work involved, you might attach light weights to your wrists.

Heel-kick drill.

Push-off drill.

Knee pick-up drill.

Stride length control drill.

To improve your push-off action, you can try to run, extending your back leg as hard as you can, and keeping your foot in contact with the ground slightly longer than normal. You can also practise exaggerating the pick-up action, bringing your knees up towards your chest in front of you, or the heel-kick behind, trying to kick your heels as close to your seat as possible. In either case, you take shorter steps than normal. To increase your stride length, you can practise driving hard off the ground while taking as long strides as you can manage. To improve your control of your stride length, one of the drills you can do is to run stretching your front leg forwards more than normal, but then pull your foot back slightly before it strikes the ground.

There are also special race techniques to practise, if you are a competitive runner. For instance, the sprinter has to practise coming out of the blocks, track runners apart from 100-metre specialists have to practise running round the bends, and hurdlers have to practise stride patterns and hurdling techniques. In most cases, you will perform these techniques in the easiest way according to your body capacities. However, for the sake of body balance and injury prevention, you should also practise the other (possibly less natural) way. The sprinter should reverse his or her foot position in the blocks for some practice repetitions; track athletes should try running round the bends the 'wrong' way, i.e. clockwise, some of the time; and the hurdler should practise taking off from each leg in turn.

Exercises for running skills

Apart from doing drills using the running action, it is also valuable to correct relative weaknesses through exercises designed to provide co-ordination and good muscle and joint balance. If the basic biomechanical monitoring tests have shown up any specific weaknesses, you should work at these, using the tests as remedial exercises (pp.29–33). There are also other useful background exercises, which you may have to do standing in parallel bars or using some support if your balance is not very good:

◀

1 Standing up, preferably in front of a mirror, lift one leg up, bending your knee towards your chest, and lift the opposite arm up, with the elbow bent to a right angle; then return to neutral, and repeat with the opposite arm and leg. Do ten movements at a time, and gradually increase your speed, taking care to keep the movement rhythmical and symmetrical.

2 Standing up, bend one knee to lift your heel behind you, and touch the foot behind your back with the opposite hand, keeping hand and foot as close to your body as possible. Return to the starting position, then repeat with the opposite foot and hand. Do ten, then repeat, gradually increasing your speed while maintaining your accuracy.

3 Standing up, take one leg back behind you with the knee straight, then bend the knee to bring your heel towards your seat; reverse the movement, then repeat with the other leg. Do ten movements, rest, then repeat, gradually increasing the speed.

▲

4 Standing, kick one leg upwards and try to touch the foot or shin with your opposite hand. Do ten movements, with control.

5 Standing, preferably in front of a mirror, swing your arms forwards and backwards rhythmically, with your elbows bent to about a right angle, and your hands relaxed. Do twenty repetitions with each arm (counting on your non-dominant arm).

6 Standing, preferably in front of a mirror, hitch one hip up sideways at the waist, bring the knee up towards the chest, then reverse the movement with control. Repeat ten times.

▲

7 Standing with your arms up in front of you, elbows at shoulder level bent to right angles, bring one knee up to touch the opposite elbow, then repeat with the other leg to the other elbow. Repeat ten to twenty times.

▲

8 Standing with your hands on your buttocks, kick one heel towards your seat, trying to touch your hand on that side, then repeat with the other leg. Do ten to twenty repetitions.

◀

9 Standing, go up on your toes on one leg, as you lift the other leg forwards, bending the knee; lower to the starting position, then repeat the other way. Do ten to twenty repetitions as quickly as possible, while maintaining a good range of movement.

10 Standing behind a marked line, hop forwards on one leg as far as you can, and mark the level you reach; then hop back, trying to reach the original line. Do three hops each way on each leg, perhaps repeating the sequence three times after a pause.

Running shoes and clothes

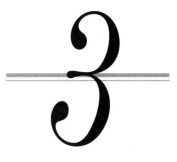

SHOES

There are different shoes for every running discipline, and shoes are constructed with features which aim to supply protection and support for different types of feet. Shoes also aim to suit different running styles. You have to choose your running shoes with care, making sure that they fit you properly, work well with your feet, and are suitable for your training or racing surface, your event, and the conditions. For instance, on a cross-country run, you may need spikes for a soft or muddy course, lightweight racing shoes for soft dry ground, or firmer, thicker training-type shoes if the surface is hard and dry.

Fell runners face similar choices, or they might need waterproof boots for very wet conditions. Track runners have to choose their spikes according to their event and according to the type of track: long spikes are suitable for cinder track running, short spikes for most modern synthetic tracks, and extra cushioning underfoot if the track is unusually hard. Road racers may use lightweight racing shoes, although for training they usually choose thicker, more cushioned trainers, like anyone else who trains on hard surfaces.

Insoles can make a lot of difference to the amount of cushioning a shoe provides, and they can also alter the way your foot moves, as the shoes themselves can, to a certain extent.

Runners who wear shoes have to be aware of what a running shoe can or cannot do, and what it should and should not do. It helps if you understand the way modern running shoes are constructed, and the reasons for particular design features.

Running shoes should be chosen with care. They can (and should) be changed long before they reach this visibly worn out state.

Shoe construction: some of the technicalities

Running shoes consist of several distinct parts, to fit in with the complex series of movements produced by the moving foot. The uppers go over the top of the foot, with a gap in the middle which is bridged by shoelaces, or sometimes by elastic or by Velcro straps. The holes for the laces may be reinforced with small metal rings, or eyelets. The lacing holes may be arranged in straight lines alongside the central gap, or they may be staggered to allow for 'variable width lacing'. The shoe's tongue acts as a cushion between the top of the foot and the lacing system with its eyelets in the uppers. In some shoes, the tongue is an integral part of the uppers, stitched in so that it encloses the top of the foot.

The whole structure covering the central region of the top of the foot is sometimes called the saddle of the shoe. The side of the central part of the shoe, which is narrowed where the front meets the rear, is often called the waist.

The front part of the shoe uppers is called the toe box, while the rear is termed the heel counter. Raised material above the heel counter at the back of the shoe is called the heel tab. It may form a single upward curve, but if it is dipped downwards in the middle it can be termed a negative heel tab, while the dip is sometimes called the Achilles notch, and the two raised edges on either side of the notch may be referred to as 'bunnies' ears'. Padding around the upper edge of a shoe where it fits under the ankle is called the collar.

The sole of the shoe is the outermost part underlying the foot, and modern running and training shoes often have a midsole built in between the outer sole and the uppers. A re-inforcing wedge of higher density material than the rest of the midsole may be inserted in the heel area of the midsole, to give extra stability under the heel: this is called a dual density midsole. Inside the shoe under the foot is the insole or insock, which may be stuck down or loose and removable.

How running shoes are made

A last is a rigid, usually wooden structure in the shape of a foot, which is used as a kind of mould when the running shoe is being put together around it. The shape of the last determines the ultimate shape of the shoe. If the sole area is shaped to be cut away under the instep, it is called a curve-lasted shoe: this is the most usual shape for track spikes, for instance. A sole which forms straighter lines under both sides of the foot is called straight-lasted or sometimes vector-lasted, and this is commonly used for heavier training shoes (although track shoes can be straight-lasted and training shoes curve-lasted).

The shoe uppers may be glued to a flexible board before the sole is attached: this is called board-lasting, and is used to provide firmer support under the foot. Shoes made without a board are slip-lasted: they have the uppers stitched together underneath, and are generally more flexible. In combination-lasting, the front of the shoe is slip-lasted and the rear board-lasted, to create more flexibility at the front of the shoe and more stability at the back.

The materials used to make running shoe uppers are very varied: leather, suede, kangaroo skin, canvas, nylon and other synthetics may be used, either forming a single construction over the foot (rare nowadays) or in different combinations. The uppers may be made of meshed materials, or ventilated with tiny holes (hopefully) to allow the shoe and the foot to 'breathe'. Reinforced areas or decorative elements may be rubber, leather or plastic. The heel counter is usually made of plastic. Padded areas are often lined with foam rubber or similar soft materials.

Insoles are usually simple soft plates inside the shoe, made of spongy foam rubber or other lightweight materials. Runners may prefer to substitute insoles with greater shock absorption, usually polymers, such as the brand names Sorbothane or Viscolas. Soft material insoles are often used over the polymer shock-absorbers. Runners who use personally fitted insoles (orthotics) either remove the existing insoles in the shoe, or, less usually, place the orthotics on top of the insoles.

Orthotics are usually provided by a podiatrist (specially trained chiropodist), who analyses the runner's feet in detail, partly by observation, and partly through video assessment of the runner in action on a treadmill. Orthotics are often supplied because of an injury problem relating to incorrect foot motion, but they may be obtained by a runner as a preventive measure, if the runner is aware of poor foot movements or 'flat feet'. Orthotics are especially important for children with foot problems. The corrective insoles can be made of hard or soft materials, or a combination of the two, according to the individual's needs. If you use orthotics, you must choose appropriate shoes whenever you change. For instance, do not try to match rigid corrective orthotics with a highly cushioned, relatively unstable shoe.

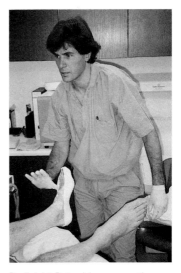

Podiatrist Peter Norman casting a patient for orthotics.
(photo A. Sceats)

Soles and midsoles are usually attached to each other and to the shoe with adhesive bonding. Midsoles are now made from various materials, often in very complicated combinations. The polymer Ethylene Vinyl Acetate (EVA) is probably still the most widely used midsole material, and it is often used as compression moulded EVA. Other midsole materials include Polyurethane, Evathane, Hytrel, Kevlar, Neo Ran, Hexalite, Phylon and Trinomic Plus. Outer soles tend to be made mainly from carbon rubber or blown rubber.

The most bewildering range of additional elements can be added to the midsole and sometimes to the outer sole. In the early 1990s, shoes were boasting contrasting methods of providing more cushioning, protection, stability, support and/or motion control underfoot, including Air Technology, Pump Technology, Anatomical Rebound Technology, Ground Reaction Inertia Devices, Evathane Plugs, Air Caps, Cantilevers, Dynamic Reaction Plates, Kinetic Wedges, Ionic Cushioning Systems, Dellinger Webs, Anatomical Cradles, not to mention ARC Cushioning Systems, Graphite Bridges under the instep, Carbon Propulsion Plates, Energy Return Systems, Gel Bubbles: an apparently endless annual list of technical innovations.

The contours of the outer sole are fashioned according to the surface the shoe is to be used on. For instance, a waffle, pimpled or studded sole is used to provide grip on soft, uneven ground, whereas road-running shoes may have a smoother undersurface.

With modern technology and materials, combined with scientific research into foot motion in relation to jarring, compression and friction forces, we can have perfect running shoes for every runner. That, at least, is the theory. But...

Caveat emptor : buyer beware

The extravagant claims manufacturers generally make for their products can confuse the unwary runner totally. Advertisements claim that modern running shoes are constantly improving on the perfection of last year's models; that scientific laboratory testing lies behind the design of each and every shoe; that 'good' shoes are essential for preventing injuries; that your performance will be enhanced by this or that fantastic innovation; or that your running will suffer if you ignore the improvements the manufacturers have slaved so hard to produce for your benefit.

Unfortunately, the advertising masks the fact that the incessant changes made to running shoes owe more to market forces than to runners' needs. Running and training shoes have become fashion items, widely used by non-runners as comfortable casual shoes – even though few models are really robust and supportive enough for constant everyday use. It has been estimated that up to 80 per cent of the sports shoes sold in Britain are bought as fashion accessories and not for exercise. Fashion has inevitably affected some of the trends in shoe design, as the leisurewear market has completely different needs from the serious running market. Many colours, trimmings and gimmicks have been added to trainers purely to appeal to the non-running public.

Every company has to vie for its market share through massive self-promotion. Shoes are sold as much on their appearance as for their quality. The need to create eye-catching shoes and to produce appealing advertising slogans are the main driving forces behind the constant search for 'improvements' in modern running shoes. The constant changes in models and styles, sadly, owe far more to the quest for profit from consumer gullibility than to the search for the perfect shoe for active runners.

Value for money?

While most companies are prepared to spend huge budgets on advertising, almost all of them are also very aware of cutting production costs in order to increase profit margins. Some models, usually sold relatively cheaply, are made by fitting several sizes to one sole which is too narrow to support the bigger sizes, so the shoe uppers hang over the edge of the sole.

Another way in which companies reduce production costs is by using small strips of material for the different parts of each shoe, rather than cutting the shoe out in larger sections. The result is that many modern shoes have numerous seams and edges which can chafe the feet, and which distort the basic shape of the shoe.

A common feature among cheaper running and training shoes is an excessively tough and rigid sole (although this is a fault shared by some expensive trainers as well).

The ideal running shoe is still a long way off.

Shoes can bite: common faults in shoe design

In some cases, the design changes to running shoes have been so far from helpful in protecting runners from injuries that

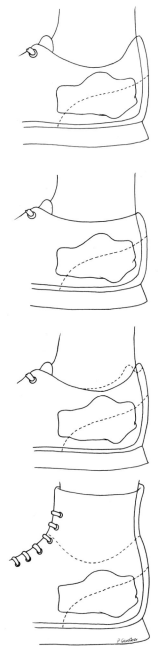

High backs: if the shoe back digs into the flesh above the ankle joint, it can damage the Achilles tendon. *(Peter Gardiner)*

they have actually caused damage. The most notorious example of this was the introduction of the heel tab on the back of most types of sports shoe in the early 1970s. Originally, it was simply a design feature for aesthetic balance which matched the height of the back of the shoe with the top of the lacing inlet – even though the human foot is not like this, and the heel-bone is lower than the top of the instep. At that time, the advertisers gave the heel tab the spurious function of 'Achilles tendon protector', although they never specified from what.

It was quickly recognized by doctors and chartered physiotherapists that the heel tab was a major cause of damage in the tendon, especially Achilles peritendinitis (see Achilles tendon friction syndrome, p.142), but those companies which had the integrity to maintain a low-backed design very quickly succumbed to market forces and began to produce high-backed shoes. Later on, many companies changed their tune, and modified the heel tabs into dipped versions and 'bunnies' ears', supposedly to help prevent friction against the Achilles tendon.

However, to date, not one company has reverted to the correct height, to match the shoe properly to the back of the ankle. Sadly, because the fashion for wearing trainers is so widespread among youngsters, and because the sports shoe market has influenced shoe design generally, high backs are now common on almost every type of shoe, and even boots have raised seams which curve against the Achilles tendon. People of all ages can suffer from the Achilles tendon friction syndrome because of badly designed shoe backs: the youngest patient I have seen with this problem was two and a half years old.

Other experiments have gone wrong too. Flared soles were introduced in running shoes many years ago, to provide extra cushioning and rear-foot stability. While the flares remained slight, they probably achieved these aims. However, when the flares spread out too widely from the shoes, they had a destabilizing effect, as the landing point on the heel was then outside the natural line for bodyweight transmission, forcing the foot to roll inwards into pronation before it could move into forward propulsion – otherwise the body's weight would be supported by the unstable edge of the sole, and not by the foot at all.

If a shoe is badly shaped relative to your foot, it can cause injuries such as broken or blackened toe-nails, blisters, metatarsalgia, 'pump bump', bruised heel, tenosynovitis, and plantar fasciitis. Inappropriate shoes can contribute to a variety of other injuries, such as shin soreness, or pain in the knee or hip. These problems are described in the sections on injuries later on in the book.

Some of the materials used for shoes, far from having 'breathing' properties, actually create extra heat within the shoe, which can cause foot swelling and excessive sweating. Sometimes it is the lining material of the shoes that creates this problem. Cases of allergy have been reported. There was a report from the University of Cape Town Medical School that a young runner had suffered a severe allergic reaction to a well-known brand of training shoes, although it could not be established whether the allergy was caused by the materials or the dye used in the shoes.

When assessing foot biomechanics in relation to your shoes, you also have to take into account the surfaces you will be running on. For instance, if your shoes are very soft and cushioned, and you run on a soft, yielding surface, there may be excessive foot movement, leading to strains in the foot joints and in the muscles and tendons of the lower leg. Rigid thick soles can reduce the ability of your feet to move freely and adapt to a hard running surface, so jarring pressures may be dangerously increased.

Poor quality control can lead to problems too. I have known runners buy pairs of shoes which were not properly size-matched. One of my patients, with touching faith in the shoe manufacturers, actually accepted the relative tightness of one shoe as a sign of a defect in his feet! I have also come across running shoes which were so poorly constructed that the heels were tipped inwards, forcing the feet into an over-pronated position. Once runners have been shown these deficiencies in their shoes in a sports clinic, it becomes easier for them to spot this type of problem and avoid repeating the mistake.

Sales assistants can add to the runner's confusion by emphasizing the technical jargon, instead of allowing the runner to assess the feel of the shoes for him or herself. One patient, ill-advised by a sales assistant, bought his normal size of shoe, without realizing that he needed a size bigger in that particular brand: after a few runs, his feet hurt enough for him to seek expert advice and find the simple solution.

All runners, including beginner joggers, should be prepared to scrutinize very critically any shoes they might buy,

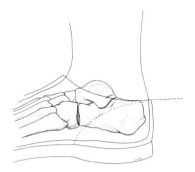

The correct height for the back of the shoe should match the back of the heel bone. (Peter Gardiner)

High shoe backs should be corrected by slitting the heel tab or cutting the excess material off. (Peter Gardiner)

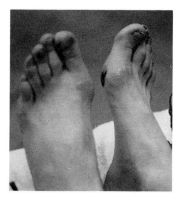

Worn feet. Poorly fitting shoes have contributed to blisters and joint distortion in this 23-year-old runner''s feet.

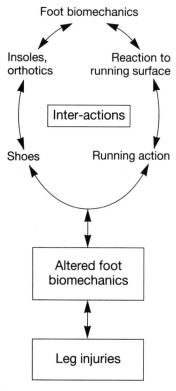

Foot biomechanics and injuries.

and should know the objective criteria they need to apply in order to make the correct choice.

Choosing the right pair

Choosing the right running shoes for your needs is not a simple matter. Price is not an accurate guide to value or suitability, so the theory that the most expensive pair you can afford will be the best for you does not apply. Even when a top-class athlete is paid to wear a particular brand of shoe, there is no guarantee that the shoe will really suit the athlete, or anyone else. The only reasonably certain way to ensure that your running shoes really fit your feet is to have them made to measure, as top runners invariably did when athletics was still an amateur sport, and not as subject to market forces as nowadays. Made-to-measure shoes are expensive, of course, but, on the other hand, they may save you many costly mistakes.

When choosing among ready-made shoes, steer clear of shoes which :

- are not foot-shaped
- do not allow your feet to spread out as you walk and jog in them
- do not support your feet fully from underneath
- are too stiff in the sole to conform to your foot movements
- have widely flared soles
- are too wide or too narrow
- pinch any of your toes
- rub at the sides of your ankles
- might chafe your skin with too many seams and decorations
- have too little or too much padding
- have a soft or badly shaped heel counter
- have heel tabs too rigid to correct easily

When you go to choose a pair of shoes, remember the following guidelines:

- if possible, go to the shop when you have been on your feet for some time (not first thing in the morning)
- do not take it for granted that a particular brand or model will suit you, just because it suited you before (it may have been changed)
- look for the simplest style of shoe you can find

- test the shoes' flexibility in your hands by bending them in every direction
- try the shoes on while wearing your usual sports socks
- insert any special insoles or orthotics that you normally use
- try a bigger or smaller size, if your own size does not feel right
- jog about in the shoes for a while, if possible
- try out as many different styles and makes as you can
- if you buy shoes by mail order, send a tracing of the outline of both feet drawn with you standing up
- choose shoes for specific purposes: if you need leisure shoes as well as running shoes, buy a separate pair for daily wear
- be prepared to exchange or discard any shoes which turn out to be wrong for you: choose a more suitable pair immediately

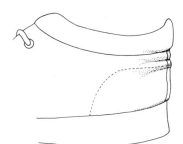

Shoddy construction: a weak heel counter quickly collapses, so the back of the foot is then totally unsupported. (Peter Gardiner)

What can your running shoes do for you?

It is important to realize that your shoes cannot run for you. Your shoes are the mitigating factor between your feet and the surface you run on. Their main function is to help your foot adapt to the running surface. Poorly designed running shoes can block the normal motion patterns of your feet and cause harm. They might correct abnormal foot movements, but only to a limited degree. They cannot prevent as many

Thirty-seven years after his Olympic triumphs, these made-to-measure leather shoes still fit double medal winner Derek Johnson. Despite the long spikes for cinder track running, they are significantly lighter than modern racing spikes in synthetic materials.

injuries as they can cause, if you choose unwisely. Improving your performance depends much more on efficient training and staying injury-free than on hoping that your shoes might act as wings for flight. Some of the world's best athletes have run barefoot on hard surfaces, sometimes over long distances, proving that shoes are not essential to high-level performances or to staying injury-free.

The best that you can ask of running shoes of any kind is that they should not alter the normal movement pattern of your feet in a detrimental way. Excessive cushioning or motion control can interfere with your natural running efficiency. Even the feeling that a pair of shoes is specially comfortable may be misleading. It is much safer if you are not aware of the shoes once they are on.

Expect no more of your shoes than that they should not impede your feet.

CLOTHES

Clothing for running need not be made in any special style or fabric. Above all, it has to be comfortable, practical and suited to the needs of the runner, the weather conditions, and the type of running being done. Many joggers and fun runners do not need to buy special clothing for running: you may be perfectly comfortable in loose-fitting leisure clothes. If you do other sports, such as a racket game like squash or tennis, you can run in the kit you normally wear for that. On the other hand, if you do serious running at any level, it is probably best to choose clothing specifically for racing and training. What is best for you is something you can only learn by experience.

Fashion dictates

Fashions change, creating new modes of dress for running. As for shoes, the dictates of clothing fashion often owe more to market forces and commercial interests than to the practical needs of runners. Increasingly, running clothing is being designed to catch the eye and look glamorous. Some of the outfits sported by elite athletes have differed dramatically from the conventional styles, often challenging the public's perception of decency. Runners seeking practical, simple clothing may discover that it is hard to find.

Traditionally, the usual style for male runners has been shorts and a singlet or vest. Females have worn knicker-like shorts plus a vest or T-shirt. Most athletes who wear shoes also wear socks, although some prefer not to. Top athletes in recent years have experimented with different types of clothing in varied fabrics, sometimes for practical reasons, and sometimes for show. Their appearance on televised top-class events sets the trend for thousands of runners of all abilities. The young, especially, like to emulate the stars, and may copy their hairstyles and mannerisms as well as their fashionable outfits.

Top-class sprinters, in particular, have been at the forefront of style changes. They have increasingly abandoned the separate shorts and singlet in favour of all-in-one, sleek, tight-fitting outfits, presumably for lower wind-resistance. They have reverted to longer-length shorts, the style of the early part of this century, apparently to keep the thighs warm. Some all-in-one suits have leggings down to the ankles, perhaps to keep the athlete cosy before and after the short burst of maximum activity involved in a sprint race. Necklines vary, some reaching quite high towards the throat, others plunging deep to reveal the maximum expanse of bristling pectorals. And that's just the men. Many top female runners have also adopted skin-tight all-in-one outfits, usually similar to swimsuits. Necklines for the ladies have, in the main, remained modest, by contrast with the daring cut-

Extravagant dress for the London Marathon, but runners like these are capable of recording surprisingly fast times for the distance.

away line at the tops of the legs and the clinging fit round the buttocks.

As if to emphasize the point that runners need not be stifled by dress convention, some top athletes even race in fancy dress on occasion, fulfilling their role as star entertainers alongside that of serious competitors. Fun runs, especially charity events, can attract a plethora of extravagant costumes. Races like the London Marathon have a 'sharp end', where the elite runners dress simply and race at world-record pace or as close to it as possible. At the 'fun end', people dressed as dragons, donkeys, fairies, waiters or cartoon characters run at a more leisurely pace, although some of these still manage to go surprisingly quickly.

Running clothes and their purposes

Whereas you may choose fancy dress for some specific reason such as fundraising or entertainment, running kit should serve practical purposes, and should be chosen with those purposes in mind:

- to cover your body decently
- to allow freedom of movement
- to preserve your body heat in cold conditions
- to keep you dry in wet conditions
- to protect your skin from the sun
- to help your sweat to 'wick out' and evaporate in hot and humid weather
- to make you visible in the dark
- to prevent body chilling after running

Whatever the conditions, you will usually need several layers of clothing for running. As you warm up, you might wear a track suit or sweat suit, perhaps with a waterproof jacket or suit on top. After you have warmed up, you should discard the layers, down to as many layers as you need for the conditions. If you are likely to slow down during a long run, or if there is a danger that weather conditions may become colder, you should carry extra layers of clothing with you in a rucksack or 'bum bag', or perhaps arrange for helpers and friends to keep them for you along your route. You should include protective rainwear if conditions are likely to become wet. Make sure you dry off thoroughly after running in the wet, and have a warm shower or bath as quickly as possible afterwards.

If you are going for a very long run, and know you will not be able to maintain a fast pace, you might choose to run the whole way in track-suit trousers and a T-shirt covered by a singlet, or even in a complete track suit. Alternatively, you might prefer to wear a sweat-shirt or jacket over your running vest or shirt, but with shorts, leaving your legs mainly uncovered. If you get too warm, you can take off your jacket or sweat-shirt and perhaps tie it round your waist or shoulders, ready for re-use if you feel chilled later on. Especially if you run on your own, it is useful to have pockets in your track suit or shorts, or to carry a small 'bum bag' for coins or a card for the telephone, and for your personal details, just in case you have an accident.

Planning your outfits for events like the London Marathon requires careful forward thinking. The race is held in spring each year, but with the vagaries of English weather, conditions could be hot, cold, wet, windy, humid or dry, and you have no sure way of knowing which it will be until the day itself. So you have to work out during the previous week the balance of probabilities, and still carry extra clothes in your kitbag in case of sudden change on the day.

If the weather is very cold, you may need to wear not only a full track suit, or even two, but also a knitted hat or a hood to prevent excess heat loss through the head. People who are specially sensitive to the cold might also need a scarf and gloves. In extreme cold, and also if you run in heavily polluted urban areas, you may have to add a face-mask to your outfit. Having adequate protection against the cold is even more important in very young (prepubertal) runners, who can overcool much more rapidly than adults.

In very hot conditions, or for very short fast runs, you might choose a lightweight outfit consisting of shorts and a singlet. If it is very sunny, you may need a sun-hat, and you should also use a filter lotion to protect your skin. Sunglasses are essential for eye protection when you run in sunshine or bright light. Child runners have relatively inefficient heat dissipation mechanisms compared to adults, so they overheat easily and must be specially protected from very hot conditions; they must also drink plenty of water.

Even if the weather is hot, it is still important to cover yourself with extra layers or a track suit after running, to avoid a sudden chill, until you wash away the accumulated sweat and cool down in the shower or bath. If you are competing in several events at a meeting, and have to wait

Andrew preparing to keep warm and dry in a bin-liner before the start of the London Marathon on a rainy day.

between races, you should try to have a shower immediately after any hard effort. If this is not possible, you should keep warm with extra layers, and change into fresh running clothes after each race if you can.

Many running events offer no showering facilities at the finish. In this case, you should change into a fresh shirt, cover yourself with extra layers of clothing even if you feel warm, and go straight home to have a shower or bath as quickly as possible.

How to choose clothes for running

Like any other clothes, running clothes can reflect the personality of the wearer. Kit which looks untidy or ill-matched can reflect an attitude which states that the wearer prefers to perform well rather than look good. On the other hand, neat, well co-ordinated clothing can reflect a discipline of mind which matches the runner's capacity for mental concentration, self-control and motivation. It is vital to choose clothes according to your own comfort, and not because of someone else's idea of what is fashionable or suitable.

If you take a pride in your appearance, you naturally want your clothes to look attractive. However, the female runner who trains alone has to be aware of how provocative certain types of running clothes can be, especially if she is running round streets among fully clothed people, or training in more isolated areas such as parklands or towpaths. Being fully clothed in a track suit does not necessarily protect the female runner from unwanted male attentions or, in the worst of cases, rape. But wearing skin-tight, cut-away bodysuits might be asking for trouble. For safety's sake, female runners should try to run with companions, or carry a personal alarm or telephone. They should never run alone while listening to a personal stereo system, as this can prevent them from hearing an attacker approach.

While it is wise for female runners to avoid eye-catching clothes, all runners should wear light-coloured clothing if they run after dark, even if they run along lighted streets. Running in unlit areas, you should have reflective strips round your wrists, waist and ankles, or, better still, wear a fully reflective jacket. It is also sensible to carry a torch if you run in dark areas where the surface might be uneven.

For all types of running clothing, even fancy dress, there are some basic principles to apply, if you are to avoid discomfort and friction injuries. Running clothes should not have heavy or raised seams, especially not in areas where rubbing is likely to occur, such as between the legs, round the shoulders or under the armpits. They should not be styled for a tight fit, and should avoid cutting into the skin, for instance round the tops of the thighs, round the buttocks and waist, across the chest and round the arms. It is particularly important that underwear worn next to the skin should not chafe. Male jockstraps and female brassières should be fully supportive, but must not be so tight as to cause constriction. Tight, chafing underwear can cause conditions such as pruritus ani, which causes itchiness and irritation round the back passage, or intertrigo, which causes reddened sore areas, especially in the groin.

Even with well-chosen clothing, you may find that you do suffer from friction on long runs, especially in hot conditions. The experienced runner guards against this by applying Vaseline to vulnerable areas such as the groin, nipples and armpits. New clothes should always be tested in short training runs, before being used for long distances or competitions.

The fabric for running clothes should be able to 'breathe', allowing for ventilation between the skin and the garment, and helping perspiration to evaporate. Mesh fabric can create a kind of airflow over the skin, so many runners prefer to wear mesh singlets. Some runners prefer natural fabrics such as cotton for their tops, shorts and socks, whereas others prefer synthetics such as nylon, or synthetic mixtures. Track suits, similarly, can be cotton or cotton mixtures, but are more often made of man-made fibres. Waterproof suits can be made of modern materials such as Gore-Tex, which allow a good level of ventilation and avoid condensation of water vapour inside the suit, while affording good protection against rain.

Layers of clothing can be the most practical for a marathon in uncertain conditions. Most 'fun end' marathoners like Andrew run for charities.

If you are in regular training, you need to keep several changes of clothing, and you need to have kit for the different weather conditions you are likely to run in. If you travel to different countries and want to run, whether competitively or for fun, you should always check first what the conditions are likely to be, and whether there are any restrictions on clothing, in case your normal sportswear might seem offensive to the people of your host country.

Looking after your running clothes
Running kit should be easy to wash, rinse and dry. Wool is rarely used for track suits now, and few runners run in

woollen sweaters, because wool can irritate the skin in sensitive people, and it requires special care when being washed.
Most running clothes are made of cotton, cotton mixtures or
easy-care synthetic fabrics, so that they can be machine
washed as an alternative to hand washing. Always follow the
manufacturers' instructions about water temperature and
suitable drying conditions. Take care not to use detergent
liquids or powders to which your skin reacts badly. If any of
your running clothes do shrink noticeably you should not
wear them for running again, as they are likely to chafe.

You should never leave used running clothes in an enclosed bag. Always wash your kit and dry it thoroughly after
running or fitness training sessions, before wearing it again.
You should try not to wear already used, unwashed kit, as
you risk getting skin infections and irritation. It is, of course,
especially important to keep your underwear clean, to help
avoid such infections as 'jockstrap itch' (technically tinea
cruris) and candidiasis.

If you have to mend frayed areas in your running clothes,
do so as neatly as possible, to avoid creating areas of friction.
Socks should be darned immediately if they show signs of
wear. However, if this creates hard patches in them, they
should be discarded.

Clothing priorities

Choosing suitable running clothes is a matter of finding
which styles and fabrics suit your needs. You must have
enough types of clothes for the different weather conditions
you might run in, and enough outfits to have clean kit on for
each running session. You must follow good hygienic
practices to avoid unnecessary and debilitating skin
problems. Running clothes do not necessarily have to look
smart or elegant, but they do have to be comfortable,
practical and clean before use.

How to cope with injuries

HOW INJURIES HAPPEN

When an injury happens suddenly and involves an accident, fall, knock or any other kind of abnormal stress, it is called a traumatic injury. Injuries which come on gradually are called overuse injuries, although misuse might be a better term. If there is an obvious cause for an injury, it is termed extrinsic, whereas intrinsic injuries happen apparently out of the blue. Every injury has an immediate phase, which is when it first starts, and a recent phase, perhaps covering the first two weeks or slightly longer. Beyond the recent phase, the injury is chronic, especially if it has lasted several weeks or months.

Runners' injuries can be traumatic. If you sprain your ankle tripping over a kerb, or if you get 'spiked', you have suffered an extrinsic traumatic injury. If your hamstring tears suddenly without apparent warning while you are sprinting, it is an intrinsic traumatic injury. However, the majority of injuries incurred by runners are overuse (misuse) injuries. Because they come on gradually, they are often allowed to develop to a chronic phase, by which time they are much harder to treat. Contrary to what many runners believe, these injuries are not an inevitable part of running. They usually happen for well-defined reasons, such as wearing inadequate shoes, poor body conditioning, incomplete recovery from previous injuries, and, above all, because of over-training.

Many traumatic and overuse injuries can be avoided, if you understand how they might happen and if you are prepared to take the necessary preventive measures.

Any of the body's structures can be damaged by running injuries. Your bones are technically your hard tissues, while your soft tissues comprise all your muscles, tendons, joint capsules, ligaments, and other mechanical structures. Your organs can also be damaged in certain injuries, especially of course your skin, which is particularly vulnerable to friction injury. Sometimes injuries are complicated by diseases or arthritic conditions, and in some cases pains are not caused by injuries at all, but by other problems, including viral infections. There are also many symptoms which runners might dismiss as simply 'running-related', but which should be checked by the general practitioner, such as headaches or dizziness after running, blood in the urine, 'stomach upsets', diarrhoea and chest pains.

FIRST AID

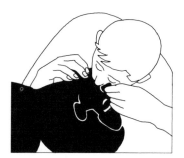

Mouth to mouth resuscitation.

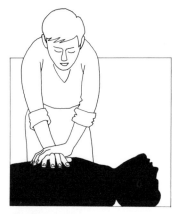

Cardiac massage.

Life-saving techniques are essential knowledge for everyone, and especially for people involved in active sports. Any major collapse which stops the heart from beating or prevents breathing can cause death. At the very least, once the oxygen supply to the brain has been cut off for a few seconds, brain cells start to die off, and this can lead to irreversible brain damage if it happens over a wide area of the brain. To prevent these disasters, you have to act quickly, that is immediately, to restore oxygen to the system.

The principles are simple.

1. Check whether the casualty is breathing and still has a heartbeat.
2. If breathing has stopped, open the casualty's mouth gently and remove any blockage.
3. Start mouth-to-mouth or mouth-to-nose resuscitation: block the nose or mouth with your hand, tilt the casualty's head back, blow into the mouth or nose, allow the air to be expelled again, and repeat a few times.
4. If you cannot feel a pulse beat in the neck after this, start cardiac massage by pressing firmly on the casualty's breast-bone, alternating about fifteen compression movements on the chest with a few breaths into the casualty's mouth or nose.
5. Continue the resuscitation techniques until medical or paramedical help arrives.

Practice makes perfect. The only way to learn effective life-saving is to attend a first-aid course, where you can practise the techniques on a dummy, and where you learn how to manage different emergency situations and all kinds of patients, young and old, male and female, disabled and able-bodied.

It is useful to carry a basic first-aid kit, once you have learned how to use it effectively. Relevant items for running accidents include airways for more hygienic mouth-to-mouth resuscitation, bandages, sterile dressings, sticking plasters, a water bottle, and chemical ice packs or a jar of ice. People who are responsible for other runners, such as teachers, coaches, club officials or race organizers, should always ensure that adequate first-aid provision is readily available.

Trained medics and paramedics must be on duty for any organized event or race. First-aiders have to anticipate problems related to the numbers of runners in an event, their ages, the degree of competitiveness involved and the conditions on the day. For instance, a supply of blankets may be needed for a long-distance event held on a cold day, as runners might suffer from over-chilling (hypothermia) at the end, especially if they have run slowly. On a muddy cross-country course, runners can suffer bad cuts, especially if they slip wearing spiked shoes, and these must be cleaned up immediately to minimize the risk of infection. Runners should always keep their anti-tetanus immunization up to date, but if you have failed to do so and you get grazed or cut, you must go to your doctor or local hospital for a tetanus jab as quickly as possible.

Dehydration can be a potentially dangerous problem. On a hot or humid day, runners can dehydrate easily, and doctors may have to use saline drips to treat victims of heat exhaustion. Dehydration can cause headaches, and the victim of heat exhaustion can become disorientated and may collapse. Runners should learn to recognize these signs in themselves and each other. Preventive measures are to take in plenty of plain water throughout every day from early morning onwards, and especially during long runs on a hot day. Club officials and race organizers should ensure that there is an abundant supply of fresh drinking water available to all runners during and after an event.

Part of the planning for any event should include contingency plans for treating any major injuries on the spot, and for transporting casualties efficiently away from any part of the course to hospital. Mobile telephones or walkie-talkie radios are essential whenever events are held over long distances, with widely spaced first-aid and drinks stations.

The major essentials for first-aid are:

- trained personnel
- a supply of clean water
- appropriate equipment
- a supply of ice
- good communications, especially with the emergency services

ACTIONS FOR INJURIES

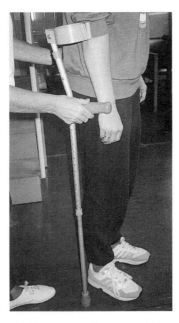

Crutches are usually measured to your wrist bone.

In the immediate and early phases of any leg injury, you may need to keep your weight off the leg when you are moving about. This usually means using crutches, which should be properly measured so that you can walk comfortably without stooping. Remember to adjust your crutches if you change your shoes and so alter your height.

If you cannot put your foot down at all, perhaps because of a ruptured Achilles or a bad ankle sprain, you take steps by placing your crutches in front of you, then hopping forwards with your sound leg, landing just in front of the crutches. If you can take some weight through your injured leg, you place the leg forwards with the crutches, then bring the sound leg through. On steps, you can use one crutch and a rail, or both crutches: going up, lead with the sound leg, then bring the crutches and injured leg up. Going down steps, lead with the crutches and injured leg, placing them on the step below, then bring the sound leg down.

If you have to use crutches over a long period, for instance after breaking a leg, check that the rubber tips (ferrules) do not get worn down, and replace them when necessary. In wet conditions, take care to keep the crutches close to you, as they skid easily if you put them too far in front of you, or try to take big steps using them. If your right leg is injured, or if you do not have an automatic-shift car, do not try to drive while you are using crutches for walking, as your insurance is automatically invalidated.

For more minor injuries, such as ankle or calf strains, you may only need the crutches for the first few days, and then you can begin to walk normally again. If you have to use the crutches over a longer term, you may need to progress on to a walking stick for support before you can take full weight through your injured leg again. If you use one stick, it must be held in the opposite hand to your injured leg.

Most running injuries do not need emergency treatment. In a way, this is a disadvantage, as there is often no clear-cut direction for the injured runner to take for relatively minor problems. You may be tempted to wait a few days and then 'try out' the injury by running again. If you are lucky, you might get away with this. However, more often than not, runners find that the pain recurs, either immediately or after a few running sessions, and it then gets progressively worse.

THE CIRCULATORY CARE PROGRAMME

Looking after your circulatory system is a vital element in preventing injury problems, and in helping healing and recovery after injury.

The fluid systems of the human body are essential to good health and efficient function. Your heart pumps blood round, carrying oxygen to all your working tissues through your arteries. Once the blood has given up its oxygen it returns to the heart through your veins, pushed back mainly by active pumping pressure from your muscles. Lymph is a watery colourless fluid, derived from blood, which bathes your tissues and plays a part in your body's immune defence system against infections. The lymph glands, such as those found in your groin or under your armpits, help to filter impurities and prevent them from entering your bloodstream. Synovial fluid is yellow-coloured, and is formed by the special membrane lining your moving joints.

Visible swelling in your body is usually caused by a build-up of excess fluid as the result of injury, or sometimes of disease. The technical name for fluid swelling is oedema. Inactivity is the enemy of your body's fluid flow. Normal movement and moderate exercise are vital to keep the fluid systems working.

Apart from injuries which disrupt the blood flow in the injured area, individuals may have specific problems related to the circulation. Varicose veins are caused by gradual failure of the valve system, leading to congestion in the veins. 'Slow' or sluggish circulation is usually evidenced by hands and feet which are always relatively cold, and it can also cause chilblains, or painful inflammation affecting mainly the hands, elbows and feet. High blood pressure is a sign that your circulatory system is working at a disadvantage, possibly because your arteries are clogged up, often by high cholesterol or fats in the blood.

Your lifestyle may not help your body's fluid systems. Travelling in aircraft can cause circulatory problems, especially foot and lower leg swelling, because of the pressure changes at high altitudes. Rich foods and excess alcohol can be damaging. A job involving standing or sitting still for most of the day undermines your circulatory flow.

Good blood flow is essential for helping an injury to heal. When an injury prevents you from moving the injured part normally, your blood flow may slow down. You have to avoid slowing the circulation down even further and, where possible, you should try to improve the blood flow with careful self-help measures of the kind suggested below. If in doubt, however, always be guided by your doctor or practitioner, especially if you already have known circulatory or blood pressure problems.

Any treatment you receive for an injury will almost certainly include elements designed to help the circulation, so that swelling is reduced, tissue congestion is avoided, any fluid that has been released into the tissues (which may be visible as bruising) is re-absorbed, and healing is promoted.

Treatments to help the circulation

Massage can be extremely effective in helping the circulation, if properly done. For some injuries, you may be able to massage yourself, although you should be guided by your practitioner as to how to do it. Usually if a physiotherapist, masseur or other practitioner does massage to help the circulation, the massage is started away from the injured area. For the foot or leg, the massage may start in the thigh or hip region, and for the hand or arm the therapist may work downwards from the upper arm, shoulder or perhaps the neck. The massage is usually gentle and may be done in straight lines and/or using circular motion.

Deep, painful massage is never done directly over a recent injury. Nor is it usual to apply heat or a heat rub, lotion or ointment when an injury has just happened. These treatments carry the risk of increasing the blood flow into the injured area, and creating congestion. Deep massage applied immediately after a muscle injury can even cause the formation of calcium or bone within the muscle, technically called myositis ossificans.

Ice applications or cold compresses, technically called cryotherapy, tend to stimulate the blood flow into and away from the injured area, after an initial constricting phase. The two main effects of cold therapy are to limit the amount of excess fluid (technically termed exudate) which might leak into the tissues surrounding torn or sprained areas, and to help promote the re-absorption of the excess fluid. Cold therapy is simple to apply: it can be done as massage with an ice cube or with ice collected into a plastic cup; you can wrap crushed ice in a damp flannel and wrap it over the injury; or you can use chemical ice packs, provided you protect your skin with oil or a damp flannel. There is no hard and fast rule about how long to apply the ice. Some people recommend just a few minutes, others half an hour or even longer. I prefer patients to apply the ice for short periods, and to repeat the treatment about every two hours. You have to watch for signs of skin breakdown. If you develop blisters or rawness, you may have over-cooled the skin, so you should stop using ice for the moment and, if necessary, seek help from your doctor.

Hot-and-cold therapy, or alternating hot and cold applications is another way of stimulating the throughput of blood, so it is often used as an alternative to ice therapy, especially in the later stages of an injury. You can dip your arm or leg into buckets of hot and icy water in turn, or apply hot and cold packs to the injury, for about two or three minutes each, up to about twenty minutes overall.

Electrotherapy modalities can also help the circulation. Low-frequency electrical currents are often used for this

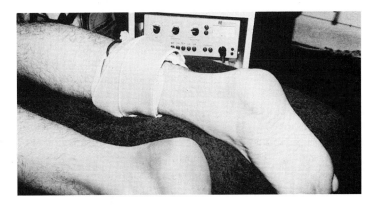

Diadynamic currents used to relieve calf soreness and swelling the day after a marathon.

purpose, such as diadynamic therapy, which is a modern version of the older galvanism or direct current; the very low-frequency alternating currents used for stimulating muscles and their motor nerves; and interferential therapy, which produces a low-frequency current 'beat' by crossing two medium-frequency currents. Pulsed high-frequency electro-magnetic energy is also used: the original form of this was Diapulse, and there are now various versions under the title of 'pulsed short-wave'. Magnetic field machines are another alternative. Most of these modalities can also achieve pain relief.

Circulatory care, bandaging and plaster casts

Whenever an injury has to be protected with a bandage or plaster-of-Paris cast, you will be warned to check at frequent intervals that the circulation is not being impeded. For a bandage or cast on your arm or leg, a simple test is to squeeze the tips of your toes or fingers. They will turn white, and then should immediately turn pink again if you are white-skinned, or darker, if you are dark-skinned, once the pressure is taken off. If the skin stays pale, or if you notice your arm or leg becoming numb or uncomfortable, the band-age or cast should be adjusted, loosened or removed immedi-ately.

You should take care to keep moving as much as possible. For instance, if your arm is in a plaster cast, you may still be able to exercise your fingers, and to keep your shoulder mov-ing by lifting your arm out sideways and above your head. If your whole hand is free you can stimulate the palm by manipulating a golf ball or Chinese iron balls. Similarly, while your leg is protected, you may be able to move your toes, exercise your hip and perhaps your knee; also take care to alter your position frequently, perhaps lying on your stomach on pillows, or lying on either side with a pillow be-tween your knees for cushioning.

Remedial exercises are usually initiated from the earliest stages of most injuries, partly to help the circulation and partly to maintain the muscles in the injured area. Alternative training is often also possible, as you may be able to do a workout using your trunk, arms and perhaps your uninjured leg. If you have a bad arm injury which is protected in a sling or plaster cast, do not be tempted to continue running, as your body will be out of balance, and you risk straining your neck and middle back.

Chinese iron balls exercise the hands and stimulate the circulation.

A plaster cast limits the amount of effort you can put into alternative training: if you work too hard, the injured area may swell inside the cast, causing congestion. Excess sweating in the cast can cause skin problems. With a removable cast, however, these problems can be avoided, because the practitioner can check on the state of the injured area, and the patient can remove the protection in order to bathe or shower after exercise. Removable casts have been used successfully to allow athletes with serious injuries such as Achilles tendon rupture to continue energetic training.

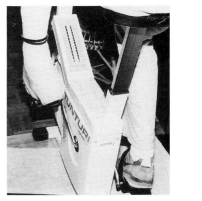

The removable cast makes hard aerobic exercise possible.

Self-help measures

For most running injuries, especially those which are not serious enough to need a plaster cast, there are various things you can and should do during your everyday life to help prevent circulatory problems.

In the case of a leg injury, if you have to sit down during the day, make sure you always use a cushioned but firm chair. If your chair is hard, place a cushion on it. Support your leg on a stool or box cushioned with a pillow. Do toe, foot and leg exercises about every ten minutes. Use a golf ball or similar round hard object to stimulate the arch of your foot by rubbing the sole of your foot over the ball for about one minute, every half-hour. If you have a foot massage machine, use it two or three times a day. Try to get up and walk around whenever possible.

Standing still when you have a leg injury can cause problems, because it is difficult to counteract the downward pressure of gravity on your circulatory system, so foot and leg swelling are almost inevitable. You have to try to keep your legs moving. Wear flexible shoes with low, but not flat, heels, and use cushioning heel pads or insoles. Wear support stockings if these have been recommended or prescribed by your doctor. Above all, try to sit or lie down with your feet up whenever you can. When you do get a chance to relax, you can lie on your back with your legs up on a soft support, or on your stomach, perhaps over a pillow, with your feet lifted on bolsters. To help your feet and legs to drain more efficiently overnight, you can lift the foot end of your bed on to blocks roughly two inches high.

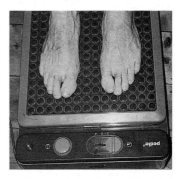

A foot massager stimulates the leg circulation.

Golden rules

● Drink plenty of plain water throughout every day,

starting in the morning.
- Never constrict the blood flow by sitting or lying with your legs or ankles crossed over each other.
- Do not wear tight shoes, socks, stockings, garters, belts or clothing.
- Do not sit or stand still for long periods.
- Never let your legs or arms rest against a hard surface.
- Try to stop, or at least to cut down, if you smoke.

Danger signs of complications

When the blood flow in one part of your body slows down significantly, the blood can actually form a clot and block its vessel. When an injury has made you inactive, this is most likely to occur in your veins, and the technical name for the clot is a deep vein thrombosis (DVT). If part of the clot breaks off, it can travel in the bloodstream to cause blockage elsewhere. A moving clot is called an embolus or embolism. It can be extremely dangerous if the clot lodges in the heart, lungs or brain.

One warning sign that your circulation is slowing down is muscular cramp. In most cases it is not dangerous, and is simply cured if you drink plenty of plain water and, if necessary, take electrolyte drinks. However, severe cramp can be a warning of a serious blockage in the blood system. In this case, you usually see a lot of swelling round the cramped muscles, the skin may look reddened and shiny, and the region may be extremely painful and tender to touch. If this happens to you, you should go to your doctor or casualty department immediately. After the necessary tests, you will probably be given drugs to control the situation.

A less serious, but still highly damaging, problem which can arise following any injury in the leg or arm is disruption to the sympathetic system which controls your blood flow, among other body functions. The injured area remains extremely painful after it should have healed. It becomes very sensitive to any sort of pressure. It is especially painful if you try to exercise it, or if it is treated directly with surgery, massage or electrotherapy, but it can also be painful when you are at rest. The skin alters, and can become very clammy or cold relative to the rest of the limb. X-rays may show that the bone underneath is losing its hardness and becoming osteoporotic. The most telling sign is the tendency for the area to change colour, becoming deep purple or bluish when its position is altered so that gravity is suddenly pushing the circulation downwards.

This problem is called Sudeck's atrophy. It is most common in the foot, but it can happen in the hand, and in other regions of the body. Once it has happened, it has to be treated with care and patience, as full recovery can take several years, in the worst of cases. Treatments are usually applied away from the affected area, and may consist of electrical muscle stimulation, perhaps in association with acupuncture, and massage. Exercise for the part has to be very carefully graded, and the patient has to fulfil the circulatory care programme constantly. As the sympathetic nerve system is greatly influenced by emotions, positive thinking is vital for recovery. Training in relaxation and positive thinking techniques are often vital elements in the treatment programme.

Self-help measures for injuries include:

- ice or cold compresses to relieve pain, swelling and inflammation
- the 'circulatory care' programme
- no running
- alternative training, providing it does not cause pain

Things to avoid:

- self-diagnosis and self-treatment
- running on regardless of pain
- heat rubs and self-massage, especially in the early stage of injury
- negative thinking

Every running injury which hinders your training should be diagnosed and treated by a properly qualified practitioner.

You need to find the appropriate practitioner to deal with your problem, who can also understand your needs as a runner, whatever your standard. This is sometimes easier said than done, but if you persevere you will find the right person or team eventually, even if not at first. In Britain, there are many courses in sports medicine for practitioners, including postgraduate diploma courses for doctors and chartered physiotherapists. There are also many clinics and individuals specializing in sports injury treatment, although it is true that few now operate within the public National Health Service.

The **general practitioner** or **family doctor** is the first person to consult. He or she may be able to advise you on your

injury, organize relevant tests and investigations, or, alternatively, may refer you to an appropriate specialist. Remember
that not all injury problems are as simple as they might
appear. If you have a known medical condition, such as diabetes, epilepsy or asthma, you should let your doctor monitor
your health at regular intervals, and you should refer to him
or her at any minor hint of trouble. The same applies to
female runners who wish to keep training during pregnancy.

For some injuries, you may need to be referred to an
orthopaedic surgeon, especially if you are likely to need an
operation, perhaps on a torn cartilage in your knee. For
certain joint problems and injuries to your muscles and bones
(musculoskeletal system), you might be referred to a **rheumatologist,** a specialist not only in injuries but also in the arthritic problems and diseases which could affect your body. In
certain situations, you might need to see other types of
specialist, such as a **chest specialist,** an **ear, nose and throat
(ENT) consultant, gynaecologist** (specialist in female problems), or a **urologist** (specialist in urinary or waterworks
problems). If you suffer from food intolerance, or if your diet
might be inadequate for your needs, the general practitioner
may refer you to a **dietician** or **nutritionist** for detailed analysis and advice.

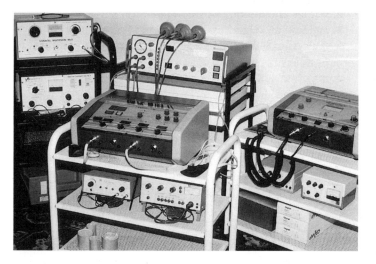

Electrotherapy machines used in the
Author's practice.

Paramedical treatment is generally needed for most running injuries, whether or not you have needed specialist investigations and treatment.

Chiropractors and **osteopaths** are trained manipulators whose expertise may help joint problems, especially in the back and neck. They often use massage and electrotherapy as well as manipulative techniques in their overall treatments. These professions were once considered to be 'fringe' medicine, but they are now becoming widely accepted as respectable treatment systems. The same might also be said about **acupuncture** (the ancient system of healing by applying needles to points in the body's meridians), **reflexology** (healing through meridian points in the foot), **shiatsu** (a system of body mobilization techniques), and **aromatherapy** (massage using healing oils).

A **chiropodist** deals specifically with foot problems, not only treating injuries and infections in the skin and toe-nails, but also making specially fitted insoles, or orthotics, to correct biomechanical defects in your foot movements. **Podiatrists** are chiropodists with advanced training, some of whom do surgical procedures (operations) for certain foot joint problems.

Chartered physiotherapists (**physical therapists**) are trained to treat injuries with massage, manipulation, electrotherapy, hydrotherapy (exercises in water) and remedial exercises. Because they are trained in biomechanics and therapeutic exercise, physiotherapists can also set out body conditioning programmes and alternative training regimes.

How to get the best from your practitioner

To help the practitioner to help you, you need to be able to describe your problem accurately and concisely. Try to work out in advance what you need to say, and what you need to take with you. Remember that your time with the practitioner may be limited, so you have no time to waste in answering the relevant questions and asking your own. If you are accompanying an injured child you should go through the necessary information beforehand, to make sure that the description of what has happened is accurate. These are guidelines to cover most situations:

- Take all your running shoes to show the practitioner, plus any other shoes that you wear a lot.

- Take your training diary, if you keep one.
- Be prepared to give the practitioner details of how your problem started, what you were doing at the time, and how the pain and any other symptoms have progressed or changed since they started.
- Do not hide the fact, if you have already consulted other people about the same problem. The practitioner needs to know what conclusions have already been reached, what treatments you have had, and what advice you have been given.
- Describe any changes in your normal running schedule.
- Describe any unusual activities you have been doing (at home, school or work).
- Give details of your normal diet, and any obvious changes if they coincided with the injury.
- Describe your general health, and whether you had any illness problems before, as, or after the injury started.
- Female runners may need to remember timings in relation to their hormonal cycle. For instance, did the injury coincide with the onset of a period, or perhaps in mid-cycle? Might you be in the early stages of pregnancy?
- Give a brief background account of any previous injuries you have suffered.
- Tell the practitioner if you have had any serious illnesses in the past, if you suffer from any medical condition such as asthma or diabetes, or if you have any known allergies.
- If you are worried that you might have some serious disease, or that your injury might have long-term consequences, do not be afraid to say so, and ask your practitioner's opinion.
- Be prepared to ask further questions if you do not understand what the practitioner tells you.
- Wear suitable clothing for a physical examination, such as shorts or modest underwear.
- Tell the practitioner if any part of the assessment, examination or treatment worries, angers or frightens you.
- If your practitioner asks you to undergo investigations such as X-rays and blood tests, make sure you ask what these are for (if you want to know). Do not be afraid to discuss the issue if you feel that any investigations or treatments might be unnecessary.

THE AIMS OF TREATMENT

The primary aim of treatment is to get you back into action: this is technically called **functional recovery**. In order to achieve functional recovery, there must be pain relief, reduction of swelling, healing of the damaged tissues, and restoration of normal movement and co-ordination to the injured area.

Pain relief can be achieved, up to a point, by pain-relieving medicines: non-steroidal anti-inflammatory drugs (NSAID) are frequently prescribed by doctors because they may also help the injured tissues to heal. In some cases, an injection may be used by a doctor or surgeon for pain relief. Pills can also be used, in certain circumstances, to reduce swelling produced by damaged tissues. Massage, manipulation, acupuncture and various forms of electrotherapy can all contribute to pain relief, and in many cases to reduction in swelling.

Helping healing is more problematical. It is debatable how much any drugs or physical treatments can actually speed up healing for damaged tissues. Simple damage heals by natural means. The healing time varies according to the tissue, so that strained ligaments, for instance, go through the first stage of healing within about ten days, whereas a light bone like the outer leg-bone (fibula) needs three weeks, and a major weight-bearing bone like the shin-bone (tibia) needs at least eight weeks. In some cases, such as a torn knee cartilage (meniscus) or cruciate ligament, the damaged tissue cannot heal through nature alone, and surgery may be needed before normal movement can return.

The important factor in the healing of an injury is how well the tissue heals functionally. Natural healing may leave the injured area weak and tight: for instance, a torn muscle might heal with a scar, so the muscle loses some of its ability to contract efficiently, as well as part of its pliability. Because of this, resting completely is rarely appropriate treatment for a running injury. The best way to prevent shortening (technically contracture) of injured tissue is to initiate gentle movement in the tissue at the earliest possible stage. You may need to rest from running, but you will probably need to be active in different ways to help your injury to heal. This is another reason why an alternative training programme is so important for an injured runner.

Active and functional healing are the aims which underlie

every treatment programme I set out for injured runners. I rarely use 'passive' treatments such as ultrasound, although it certainly can have a role in helping healing and reducing pain, as do interferential therapy and Diapulse (high-frequency electromagnetic energy). Much more often I use electrical currents such as diadynamic therapy (a kind of modified direct current which stimulates the blood flow) for pain relief, swelling reduction, and possibly to help promote healing. I use massage for the same purposes, and in order to be fully aware of the state of the injured tissues. For joint injuries, passive movements and gentle manipulation are added to the treatment programme as quickly as pain allows.

Electrical muscle stimulation is a vital part of my treatment programmes. It helps to re-educate your motor nerves, so that they activate your muscles very precisely, with full co-ordination. This type of stimulation can be used to gain isometric (static) strength around injured joints, so that you work with the current to gain stabilizing force through the joint's surrounding muscles. At a later stage, the muscle stimulation can be used to help the concentric strength of the muscles, as you actively move the joint while contracting the working muscles. The muscle stimulation can be used following muscle injuries, and can help to gain fibre activity even before it is possible for you to tense the muscle at all without pain.

Faradic units are the older version of muscle stimulators, and they are still perfectly adequate for basic muscle re-education. However, modern electrical muscle stimulators provide variable frequencies, unlike faradic units. In some injuries, electrical stimulation at a specific frequency is the primary treatment of choice, so a modern machine is vital. Where this is the case, or where a patient is very weakened with inhibited muscles, I usually recommend the patient to use an appropriate small muscle stimulator at home, more or less on a daily basis, if possible.

Electrical muscle stimulation is part of exercise therapy and helps functional recovery.

REMEDIAL EXERCISES AND HOW TO DO THEM

Electrical muscle stimulation is used in order to help you to exercise at an early stage of your injury recovery, and to make your exercises more accurate and efficient. Active exercises have to start as quickly as possible, but without causing any pain to the injured area. Your physiotherapist will explain the details of what you should be doing, and what you should feel.

Recovering good sensation, awareness and balance mechanisms (technically proprioception) in the injured tissues is an in-built part of the exercise programme. The remedial exercises should not feel difficult, especially in the early stages following an injury. They should not make you strain to do them, and you should not expect to be making any massive physical effort for them. This may seem boring, and you may feel you are not achieving much, but it is important to be very precise about the way you do the exercises. Any physical effort should be reserved for the alternative fitness training programme set out for you to do alongside your remedial exercise programme.

Isometric exercises are the first stage for an injured bone or joint: you tense the muscle group, hold the contraction for a count of about three, then relax completely. You have to allow a few seconds before repeating the contraction, to avoid muscle fatigue or the risk of raising your blood pressure. Isometric exercises provide stability to an area, and they may have to be continued indefinitely, especially after knee injuries.

Gentle stretching exercises, in which you lengthen the muscle group without strain and hold the stretch for a count of about six, are used for muscle injuries, and for later-stage joint problems. You should always relax completely before repeating the stretch. Never go into a stretch position and then try to stretch further, as you may tear the muscles by going through their elastic limits. Always be guided by the way the muscles feel at any given time. If they are especially tight or sore, reduce the range in which you stretch, so that you never feel more than a very mild stretching sensation, and you never get a pain reaction after you have stretched.

Strengthening exercises using joint movement generally form the second phase of the rehabilitation programme: these are usually done with light weights, which you gradually increase as you get stronger. Eccentric strengthening action is essential. When you lift or push a weight or resistance, especially against the effect of gravity, the muscle work is concentric, which means the muscles shorten as they exert their effort. On the reverse movement, if it is done in a slow controlled fashion, the muscles work eccentrically, and pay

Always be guided by the feeling in your muscles when stretching. Don't try to reach your toes, for instance, if your hamstrings are tight - you might injure your back.

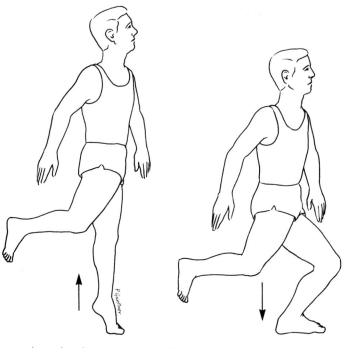

Concentric work: going up on your toes against gravity. *(Peter Gardiner)*   Eccentric work: bending your knee in the direction of gravity. *(Peter Gardiner)*

out or lengthen. This is a very important part of the remedial process, as eccentric action is vital to joint protection and to many sports activities. Poor eccentric control can even be a primary cause of problems such as 'runner's knee' (see pp.185–94).

The remedial exercise programme gradually develops, combining increased movement and improved strength in and around the injury. The final stage involves co-ordination work, using the injured area in conjunction with its surrounding parts, to regain proper interaction between them. Fitness testing, although useful as a confidence-booster, should be unnecessary. If you have followed the rehabilitation programme through to its proper conclusion, the final stage will be your safe return to sport.

The treatment regimes consist of a constant process of assessment, reassessment and progression, both in the treatments administered and in the self-help regimes prescribed.

WHAT SHOULD YOU DO IF TREATMENT DOES NOT SEEM TO BE WORKING?

Recovery should be progressive, and this means you should be aware of an improvement in your condition over a space of time. If this does not happen, you have to ask your practitioner why, and what changes can be made to rectify the situation. Treatment should not be static: if you are being treated in a certain way, or with the same modalities at each session, and you are not improving, your case is not being assessed on an individual basis. Sometimes both surgeons and athletes regard surgery as a cure in itself. This is incorrect. After surgery, because the surgeon's knife has interfered with the tissues and therefore the nerve systems, there is the same need for an accurate remedial programme as after any injury. Even the best-performed operation can fail to put the athlete back in action, if the detailed process necessary for functional recovery has not been followed.

The factors that can go wrong in treatment programmes include the following:

- the diagnosis was inaccurate
- secondary problems have arisen, or were present but not obvious when treatment started
- the treatment methods are inappropriate
- the remedial exercise regime is inadequate

Problems with treatment may even be your fault if:

- you do not attend for treatment regularly and punctually, as asked
- you fail to follow your practitioner's remedial exercise programme to the letter
- you try to do other activities which the practitioner has not recommended
- you expect the treatment to cure your problem without any effort on your part
- you consult several practitioners at the same time, and try to follow conflicting advice
- you develop a negative attitude to the problem, instead of working positively to get yourself active again

If treatment does not seem to be working, your practitioner should refer you back to your doctor, perhaps for further investigations in case an element of the diagnosis has been missed, or for referral to another practitioner for different or more specialized treatment. For instance, a chartered physiotherapist might feel that, as treatments have not brought you to full recovery, your problem might need surgery. Usually the physiotherapist writes a report for your general practitioner, so that he or she can consider this possibility and decide whether the referral should be made. On the other hand, if you have already had an operation, but it does not seem to have worked, your surgeon might refer you to a colleague with greater specialization in your type of problem.

The patient–practitioner relationship can only succeed if there is mutual trust, and if both sides do their best. As patient, you always have the right to seek alternative treatment if you are not satisfied. But do be careful not to fall into the trap of seeking shortcuts to a cure. You are much more likely to prolong your problem. The longer you carry an injury, the harder it is to rehabilitate. Functional recovery requires time and your fullest co-operation in the remedial exercise programme. Recovery is quickest if you receive appropriate treatment and follow your treatment programme strictly, from as soon as possible after the injury has happened.

Food intolerance and injuries

A balanced, varied diet is essential both to good health and to good running performance. However, foods and drinks, including some which are supposedly healthy, can also cause unwanted reactions. These usually take people by surprise, because very often the reactions happen in relation to foods and drinks which are a long-standing part of one's normal diet.

FOOD INTOLERANCE: THE EXPERIENCE

Whereas a few years ago food intolerance reactions were dismissed by many doctors as 'fringe medicine' and nonsense, they are now widely recognized as a factor in physical problems, and the subject has been researched and written about by respected nutritionists and dieticians. Even so, the influence of food and drink reactions in physical pain is sometimes missed by practitioners. In some cases, a supposed injury may have no physical cause at all, but may be due only to food intolerance. In other cases, unexplained flare-ups in an injured joint, or the failure of an injury to recover, can be due to food intolerance.

In my practice, I have seen food intolerance reactions in a variety of different situations. I have seen specific joint problems caused by different triggering agents, including orange juice and home-made white wine. Among my Asian patients, recovery from knee injuries or operations has very often depended upon their ability to reduce the amount of curry they eat. The most severe food intolerance reactions that I have seen have happened to patients who have been extremely frightened by the experience of injury and operations, in many cases on top of other stresses in their working and personal lives. Reducing their stress, monitoring their food intake, and encouraging positive attitudes have been major factors in eliminating the food intolerance and in promoting their physical recovery from their injuries. The youngest patient I have seen suffering from a food intolerance reaction was two years old at the time: he developed an acutely tender, painfully swollen foot after eating lots of clementines in the space of a few days. His father was aware that he too suffered occasional reactions to citrus fruits. After a few days without fruit, the little boy was able to walk normally again.

WHAT IS FOOD INTOLERANCE?

Food intolerance is similar to allergy, in that you suffer reactions after you have taken in the particular item or combination of items to which you are intolerant. It differs from allergy, in that the reactions are not constant. When you are allergic to something, you usually learn from an early age that that substance will cause a reaction, so you also learn to avoid it. With food intolerance, on the other hand, you might be able to eat or drink particular things without any reaction for long periods, and then you can suddenly go through a phase where they 'disagree' with you.

WHAT HAPPENS IN FOOD INTOLERANCE?

Different types of reaction can be associated with food intolerance. You may notice skin blemishes, nausea, vomiting or headaches. Your joints may suffer, giving you acute pain, swelling, stiffness and a burning sensation. Sometimes the joints also look reddened. Knees, toes, fingers, wrists and elbows seem to be specially vulnerable, but almost any part of the body can be affected. The reaction may only happen in one joint, or several joints may be affected at the same time.

The characteristic of a food intolerance reaction is the intensity or violence of the symptoms. You may start to notice the reaction within an hour or so of eating or drinking the 'provocative' substance. The symptoms get worse over the next few hours. They might then subside to a certain extent, but they usually remain with you over the next few days, even if you change your diet to eliminate the irritant. The symptoms can last for up to two or three weeks, or for as long as you continue to eat or drink whatever has caused the reaction. Typically, the symptoms disappear as if by magic, once the episode has passed.

Because the symptoms of food intolerance fluctuate, you will not necessarily react to the same things all the time, or for ever. Most often, the food intolerance affects you only during a certain phase, or perhaps when you eat or drink certain combinations. So, although you might need to identify the pattern which proves why the symptoms are occurring, it is rarely necessary to leave out all the possible trigger substances all the time.

WHY DO FOOD INTOLERANCE REACTIONS HAPPEN?

We do not know for certain what causes food intolerance reactions. The reasons are difficult to identify, because so often the foods or drinks involved are things you normally eat and drink, and are used to. It is not clear whether changes in food production methods (in terms of pesticides, fertilizers and animal feeds) might have a part in making certain people increasingly sensitive.

Irregular eating, especially if you go for long periods without food, or eat only a limited number of different foodstuffs each day, can definitely make you more susceptible to food intolerance reactions. It seems likely that relative dehydration, caused by failure to drink enough water, might contribute.

It is also known that emotional stress has a definite effect in making people vulnerable to food intolerance. This can be a factor when food intolerance complicates a running injury. It is quite common for an injured joint, especially the knee, to become sensitive and suffer food intolerance reactions, even though it may never have had any such problems before the injury. This can delay recovery from the injury or from surgery following the injury. It happens most often to patients who are worrying unduly, perhaps fearing that the injury will never heal, or that they have some terrible disease which they have not been told about.

It is possible that certain viral infections might also make you more vulnerable to food intolerance reactions, although it is not clear whether this is the direct effect of the virus, or an indirect effect of the stress and fatigue associated with being ill.

Food intolerance.

CAUSES

Irritant foods:
> ... eaten too much
> ... eaten too often

Increased sensitivity:

due to ...
diet change
lack of variety in diet
physical stress
mental stress
fear
tiredness
environment change

EFFECTS

Within an hour or two of eating or drinking an irritant, any of these symptoms can appear:

... headaches

... joint pain

... joint stiffness

... joint swelling

... burning

... skin redness

In some cases, the reactions occur because you are suddenly eating a lot more of some potentially triggering substances, such as tomatoes or oranges, perhaps because they are in season and available in large quantities.

WHICH FOODS AND DRINKS ARE ASSOCIATED WITH FOOD INTOLERANCE?

There is no hard and fast rule about which foods and drinks might trigger reactions, but certain substances are known to be especially likely to do so, including chocolates, cheese, eggs, cereals (especially wheat), tomatoes, citrus fruits (especially oranges), shellfish, pork, bacon, spicy foods, cow's milk, coffee, tea, fizzy drinks, fruit juices, most alcoholic drinks, preservatives and colouring. Some people react after eating beef or veal.

DEALING WITH FOOD INTOLERANCE

You need to keep a diary of your food and drink intake in relation to any symptoms, such as headaches, joint swelling or pain. Sometimes it is easy to establish a link between them, but it can be a lengthy process. The diary might provide proof that your problem is not related to food or drink, in which case you may need to ask your doctor whether you need further tests to establish what is causing your problems. If you habitually eat or drink any of the known potential trigger-substances, you should eliminate those for the time being, to see if that changes your symptoms. Alongside checking whether there are items obviously causing reactions, you should also try to make changes in your normal diet, introducing greater variety, if possible.

To identify food intolerance scientifically, a specialist doctor or nutritionist can have a detailed analysis done in a medical laboratory. This analysis can uncover the finest details of your reactions to various substances in your dietary intake, and at the same time can pinpoint any deficiencies you might be suffering from, for instance in vitamins and minerals. It is, however, extremely expensive, so most patients would only undergo this assessment if food intolerance seemed extremely likely to be the problem, yet could not be identified through the simpler methods of keeping a diary and altering the normal diet.

If you realize that you do suffer from food intolerance, you will be able to recognize the symptoms, whenever the reactions happen. This makes it easier to overcome problems as they arise. In practical terms, it means that you can eat or drink things you like, even though you know you might react to them. If a reaction happens, you simply have to go on a very bland, varied diet for a few days, until the reaction subsides.

SELF-HELP GUIDELINES FOR OVERCOMING FOOD INTOLERANCE

- Eliminate suspect foods or drinks.
- Avoid spicy foods.
- Avoid convenience foods.
- Cut down or cut out tea, coffee and alcohol.
- Do not drink fruit juices or fizzy drinks.
- Eat regular, well-balanced meals.
- Vary your diet as much as possible.
- Include plenty of fresh green vegetables in your meals.
- Drink plenty of plain water throughout the day.
- Rest, or practise relaxation techniques, for part of each day.
- Try to reduce any known stresses: think optimistically and positively.
- Gradually re-introduce the suspect foods and drinks, monitoring carefully to see if you do have any adverse reactions.

Bone problems

6

The bones which form your skeleton are the hard tissues of your body, and they support your entire structure. They act as levers for movement, activated by muscles or their tendons at the joints where two or more bones meet. They form protective enclosures for vital parts such as your heart and lungs, the organs in your abdomen, your brain and your spinal cord. Your marrow bones form and store blood.

BONE DAMAGE

Different types of damage can happen to the various parts of each bone and the various types of bone. Bone damage also varies according to the age of the patient, as the immature bones of a child are very different from the bones of a young adult, which are different again from those of an old person.

It usually takes great pressure or a large force to injure a bone: any major break in a bone or dislocation of a joint can only happen as a result of accidents such as a bad fall, or being crushed under a heavy load. However, bones can also suffer from attritional damage, which is less dramatic and often more difficult to diagnose, and therefore to treat. Running carries the risk of attritional injuries to the bones. Runners who have suffered traumatic injuries, whether major or minor, should be aware of the consequences of those injuries in relation to running.

When a bone breaks, there may be only one area of damage, in which case it is called a simple fracture. If the bone has shattered in more than one place, it is a com-

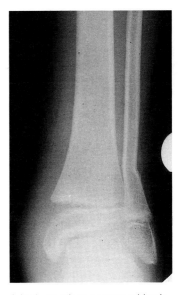

A bad wrench to a young athlete's ankle region has broken the outer leg-bone (fibula) and caused separation of the tibial epiphysis (growth line of the shin-bone).

minuted fracture. A bone break which is not accompanied by skin damage is called a closed fracture, whereas with a skin wound it is termed an open or compound fracture. When other important structures such as nerves and blood vessels are also damaged with the bone, the injury is called a *complicated fracture*. In an osteochondral fracture, the hard covering of cartilage over the bone surface within a joint is damaged as well as the bone's main substance.

Especially in children, damage to the bone cartilage in a joint can cause fragments of bone to break away. This is called osteochondritis dissecans, and is especially common at the lower end of the thigh-bone within the knee joint. Children's bones are more pliable than in adulthood, so when they break a bone it does not necessarily break right through, but may simply be bent and distorted: this is called a greenstick fracture. If the fracture happens to the growth area of a bone (technically the epiphyseal plate, growth plate or growth cartilage), it is an epiphyseal fracture. An apophysis is the area of any bone which forms the attachment point for a tendon. It is often no more than a knob or bump. In early childhood the apophyses are generally separate from the main bones, and they gradually grow together and fuse, or bond, on to their main bone as it matures. During the growth and fusing phase, the apophysis is especially vulnerable to attritional or traumatic injury. If the apophysis is strained, the injury is called apophysitis, and it causes pain or aching whenever the area is put under pressure. The most vulnerable points in young runners are the heel (Sever's 'disease'), just below the knee (Osgood-Schlatter's 'disease'),

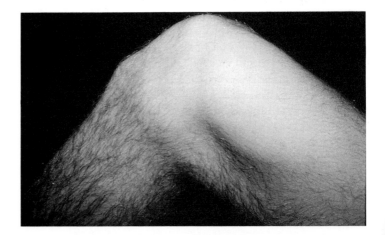

Osgood-Schlatter's 'disease' has caused a prominent lump below the knee in a 16-year-old athlete.

and along the ridge of the hip-bone under the waist, technically known as the iliac crest. If the knob of bone is pulled away completely by a sudden violent force, it is an apophyseal avulsion fracture.

Children can also suffer bone diseases, or sometimes unexplained disturbance to growth points in a bone. In the foot, common sites for this are the second metatarsal head (Freiberg's disease), and the navicular bone (Kohler's disease), where osteochondritis can cause overgrowth of the bone. Failure of the head of the thigh-bone to grow properly within the hip joint is called Legg-Calvé-Perthes disease, or simply Perthes disease for short.

Like children, adults can suffer from avulsion fractures, in which a tendon pulls away its attachment point on a bone. This is especially common in the seat-bone (ischial tuberosity) where the hamstring tendon is attached, and it can also happen below the knee where the patellar tendon is attached to the tibial tubercle. If the bone is sheared away completely there is severe pain and deformity, but a more minor avulsion fracture may cause only a small fragment of the bone to break away, so that the runner only feels a localized tender spot and general aching as a result.

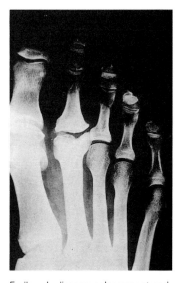

Freiberg's disease: enlargement and deformity in the second metatarsal head.

Where a tendon or ligament exerts pressure against a bone, small outgrowths of bone may be formed as a result of the continual use. These are called bony spurs, or exostoses. In runners they are especially common under the heel, at the attachment point of the plantar ligament or the plantar fascia. They do not necessarily cause pain, unless there is inflammation in the area, perhaps caused by overuse or by direct jarring through badly cushioned shoes.

Bone fragments can also form as loose bodies within muscles or tendons. This can happen if an injured muscle (especially the front-thigh quadriceps group) is treated with over-vigorous massage too soon after the injury. The bone particles are called myositis ossificans, and they cause progressive tightness and pain in the affected muscles. Repetitive stress from running, bounding or hurdling can cause tiny bone particles to form in the patellar tendon where it joins on to the lower tip of the kneecap: this is called Sinding-Larsen-Johansson syndrome or 'disease', more commonly known as 'jumper's knee'. Similar bone particles are sometimes formed in the medial ligament of the knee (Pellegrini-Stieda's 'disease'), following a strain or part-tear in the ligament.

TREATMENT FOR BONE PROBLEMS

A ny severe or significant bone injury is usually treated by an orthopaedic specialist, who decides whether surgery is needed, perhaps to stabilize a bone or joint, or to remove any bony debris from a joint, ligament or muscle. In some cases, surgery is avoided, if at all possible. For instance, it is unusual for the bone fragments in myositis ossificans to be removed surgically, mainly because they tend to re-form if this is done. On the other hand, surgery may be the treatment of choice: this is certainly true of Sinding-Larsen-Johansson syndrome, where the problem tends to be intractable unless the fragments are removed and the patellar tendon freed and perhaps reinforced with stitching.

If the patient is a child, the child's doctor will refer him or her to a paediatric orthopaedic specialist, who deals mainly or exclusively with children's problems, and who will probably monitor the child's progress over several years, if the bone growth points might have been harmed.

Diagnosis has to be accurate in order to exclude any more serious conditions, such as bone tumour or other types of bone disease. You may undergo several different types of test, so that the specialist can be sure of what is wrong, and from that conclude what treatment will be best.

During any healing or inflammatory phase, treatment might be with drugs, or perhaps injections, and the injured area is probably rested. In many cases, physiotherapy techniques may be used for pain relief. For children, however, electrotherapy modalities such as ultrasound are generally not used near any bone growth areas, because there are fears that they could be harmful.

As soon as healing has taken place, or any inflammation has died down, with or without surgery or other forms of intervention, the functional recovery programme has to start, so progressive exercises are set out by the chartered physiotherapist (physical therapist). There are no shortcuts to returning to running. If you re-start running before you have recovered fully, you risk re-injury or secondary injury. In the case of bone problems, this can put you out of running for a very long time overall, so it is worth being patient in the first instance. The principle of full functional recovery is vital for every patient, of any age.

OSTEOARTHRITIS

Osteoarthritis (also often called osteoarthrosis) is wear-and-tear degeneration affecting a bone and its cartilage covering inside a joint. It is distinct from the inflammatory condition, rheumatoid arthritis, which is a progressive, debilitating disease. Osteoarthritis can be hereditary, but is often the result of continual attritional pressure on the joint. It usually comes on in late middle age or old age, but in certain circumstances a joint can become osteoarthritic as early as the late twenties.

If you suffer pain from an arthritic joint, you might feel it during the night when the joint is perhaps too warm, during or after exercise, after the joint has been held still for a length of time, or perhaps if the weather changes to become damp or cold. There may be visible swelling in the osteoarthritic joint, and it may feel warm or burning. It may gradually become more stiff, so that eventually it appears deformed.

Painful osteoarthritis is more likely to affect a joint if:

- the joint has been subjected to continual weight-bearing pressure, as in running, without being properly supported by strong and pliable muscles
- it has suffered from previous injuries, especially if functional recovery afterwards was incomplete
- its range of movement has become limited, because of your habitual activities
- there was bone disease or disturbance to growth points in childhood
- the joint has become stiff through misuse or inactivity
- you suffer from food intolerance (see pp.91–6) and do not pay due attention to your diet

Osteoarthritis need not necessarily cause pain. A joint can look very heavily damaged on X-rays, and even badly deformed in shape, without being painful. It is more likely to remain painless if you keep yourself generally fit, and keep the muscles around the affected joint in the best possible condition. You should also try to keep your diet under control, avoiding any foods or drinks which you have found by experience to be irritant to the joint.

Treatment in the early stages might be hydrotherapy (exercises in a warm pool) or different forms of physiotherapy for pain relief. Remedial exercises are essential, and I also use electrical muscle stimulation to help regain or maintain adequate nerve-muscle efficiency. Supports might be needed to protect the joint and reduce the pressure on it, and you should probably use shock-absorbing insoles (such as Sorbothane or Viscolas) in your shoes. You should try to wear comfortable, sensible shoes each day, avoiding shoes with hard, stiff soles, or high heels for women.

Weight-bearing activities such as running might have to be limited, but generalized exercise such as cycling, swimming and gymnasium workouts may be recommended. In the worst of cases, if the joint has become too painful and deformed to be bearable, surgery may be used. In the case of the ankle, this might involve fusing the joint to limit its movements and so reduce pain. For the hip or knee, the last resort is to replace the joint completely. Although it is possible to return to running following this type of surgery, you have to be very careful to limit yourself to short sessions, and to take every care to help preserve the new joint by using good shock-absorbing insoles in all your shoes, and maintaining a daily routine of protective exercises.

STRESS FRACTURES

Stress fractures are probably the most serious type of injury which is specific to running. Far too many runners suffer from them, yet they are totally avoidable, if you train correctly. Once you have had one, you should learn from the experience, so that, in principle, you should never suffer a repeat.

Stress fractures are sometimes called 'fatigue fractures'. By definition, stress fractures happen in the normal bones of healthy people, without any obvious accident or injury to explain the crack or break in the bone. A stress fracture is very different in type from a broken bone caused by a direct accident such as a skiing fall. In the traumatic fracture, the bone is broken by an abnormal force applied to it. The stress fracture is a gradual, insidious process, in which the blood supply and crystal structure of the bone are undermined by repetitive stresses.

Running is by nature a sport involving repetitive movements, so it automatically places repetitive stresses on your bones, through the combination of pressure as your feet land on the ground, and the muscle exertion involved in the shock absorption and push-off phases. If these repetitive stresses are greater than the capacity of your bones to absorb them, the bones may crack under the pressure. This is usually only a slight break at first, but it may develop into a complete fracture of the bone if you ignore the warning signs and carry on running.

Why do stress fractures happen?

Stress fractures can happen no matter what surface you normally run on, or what shoes you wear. They do not happen simply through jarring, because you run on hard surfaces, or because your shoes are not cushioned enough.

The primary cause of runners' stress fractures is excessive running. However, there is no set mileage at which stress fractures are likely or bound to happen. Some runners do very high mileages of 100 miles a week and more without suffering, whereas others might get one or more stress fractures through running very short distances, perhaps totalling less than five miles a week. It all depends on the vulnerability of your bones, and this is influenced by various factors, including the normal training levels your body is used to, diet, hormonal changes (in females), growth spurts in young runners, and previous injuries.

Your bones might be relatively weak simply because they have not adapted to the amount of running you are trying to do. This is a special danger for novice runners, and for those building up mileage as part of seasonal training or in preparation for a marathon. It is also a risk for runners resuming training after a lay-off for illness or holidays. A bone may be specifically weakened following a traumatic fracture which has been treated by immobilization in a plaster cast, so the early recovery period when you are re-starting running after the injury is a particularly dangerous time for causing stress fractures. Even after you have recovered fully from the traumatic fracture, perhaps years later, you might still be vulnerable to stress fractures around the area where the traumatic fracture has healed. Following any injury, but especially injury to a bone, it is important to rebuild muscle strength and flexibility in the region fully, before getting back to normal training.

Your bone strength can be undermined if your diet is inadequate, causing a deficiency in the minerals needed to keep your bones really healthy. This is, of course, likely to be a major problem in a runner who is suffering from anorexia. Teenagers going through growth spurts may be at risk if they are doing a lot of running training during the phases when their bone growth has overtaken their muscle strength and pliability. Female runners might suffer from relative weakening of the bones and loss of bone density during and after the menopause, especially if there is a history of osteoporosis (the technical name for bone weakening) in the family. Sometimes female runners become vulnerable through hormonal changes relating to the menstrual cycle. Occasionally, very poor circulation of blood in the legs, perhaps associated with varicose veins, can contribute to stress fractures.

The stress which causes the fracture or crack is directly related to the way your muscles and tendons pull repetitively against your bones as you run. The problem may simply be the continual pressure from overuse between the muscles and bones, but it is aggravated by running despite muscle tightness, and by failure to do adequate background training to keep your muscles strong and flexible. Biomechanical factors such as over-pronation of the foot can also have an effect, by causing inefficiency in the way your leg muscles work.

Defining precisely how much running is too much, in relation to bone strength, is difficult, if not impossible. In my experience, the most important causative factor for stress fractures is running without allowing sufficient recovery days between sessions. The mileage in each session is less important than the number of days per week that you are running. Recovery days allow the muscles and bones to adapt to the repetitive stresses involved. Running on consecutive days increases your risk of stress fractures during any phase when your body has not adapted to the repetition. Running twice a day on a daily basis, of course, adds further danger.

Which parts of the body can suffer from stress fractures?

Any bone in the body can be damaged by repetitive stress. In tennis players, for instance, stress fractures can happen in the arm or rib bones, while rowers, baseball pitchers and cricketers can get them in the spinal bones. Runners usually suffer in the legs, and this can mean anywhere from the feet to the pelvic joints. The most common areas are the foot, shin-bone (tibia), and the outer leg-bone (fibula), but stress fractures in runners are also well documented in the kneecap (patella), thigh-bone (femur), and the groin region (especially in the fine bone called the pubic ramus).

What do you feel when a stress fracture happens?

The pain of a stress fracture is usually quite minor at first. You may notice an ache over the affected bone only *after* running. There may be some soreness at night. The pain gradually gets worse if you carry on running, and you then start to notice the pain as you run. Typically, with a few days' rest, the symptoms disappear, but they return very quickly if you re-start running too soon. You may notice slight swelling and/or bruising, and tenderness if you press directly on the injured part.

Although most stress fractures heal properly with the correct treatment and care, one complication which can arise is chronic non-healing, with the pain symptoms recurring over an indefinite period of time. In the worst of cases, if the problem is allowed to develop to its final stage, the bone gives way altogether in a complete fracture, causing all the pain and distortion you would expect from a broken bone.

How is a stress fracture diagnosed?

In the first instance, you might consult a doctor, chartered physiotherapist or other paramedical practitioner. The history of how your pain started and progressed is vital to the diagnosis. If you keep an accurate training diary, the details are easier to set out. You need to state precisely:

- What you were doing when you first felt the pain: was it after or during a run, or perhaps not related to running at all?
- The pattern of pain from the start. Try to identify times when it has subsided, and episodes when it has become more noticeable.
- Your running background: how long have you been running, and what is your normal training schedule?
- Your running programme in the month leading up to the first symptoms.
- Any changes in your normal training pattern, including increased mileage, more frequent running sessions, different running surfaces, new shoes, new or altered orthotics, changes in the type of running (for instance road running or cross country after the track season),

or the introduction of repetitive routines such as hopping or bounding.

● Any previous injuries to your legs or back.

The practitioner then examines you. You may have to do various movements standing up, perhaps even including jogging on the spot and running. When you sit or lie on the couch, the practitioner presses over the area of pain, to see if there is localized tenderness or warmth. At the same time, note is taken of any visible bruising or swelling.

X-rays may be ordered, in case there is a definite break in the affected bone. However, a clear X-ray showing no damage does not rule out the possibility of a stress fracture. Very often, the stress fracture does not show up on X-ray until the bone is healing. While the bone is still painful it may not have begun to mend, or it may still be in the earliest stages of healing. If there is any doubt about the diagnosis, you may be referred to a specialist for more detailed investigations. Even in the very early stages a stress fracture usually shows up on a bone scan as an area of increased activity. If necessary, the doctor or specialist may order further checks such as blood tests, to exclude the possibility of bone disease.

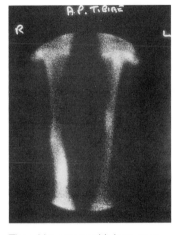

The white area on this bone scan shows a stress fracture in the right shin-bone (tibia) which was not visible on X-ray.

How is a stress fracture treated?

A stress fracture is usually treated by rest from any pain-causing activities combined with limited exercise to stimulate the circulation and the bone-healing processes. The circulatory care programme (see pp.75–8) is vital. Even with a stress fracture in the foot or leg, you may be able to play games such as tennis (on forgiving surfaces such as grass, clay, shale or carpet), squash, badminton, racquetball or basketball. In some cases, pneumatic leg braces have been used to provide some protection and support for stress fractures in the shinbone or outer leg-bone. If it is not possible to do any running movements at all without pain, you are limited to swimming, perhaps running in shallow water or in a deep pool using a wet-vest, cycling, exercising with weights, and exercises standing still, sitting or lying down. What you cannot do is any form of straightforward running on any surface (including a treadmill), skipping, hopping or jumping. If walking is painful, you may be supplied with crutches so that you do not take your full weight on your injured leg.

To help the recovery process, physiotherapy treatment might consist of massage, electrical muscle stimulation, and

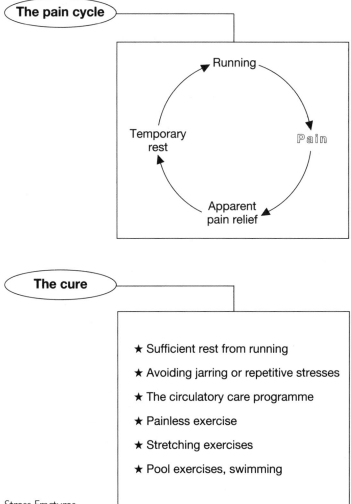

The pain cycle

Running

Pain

Apparent
pain relief

Temporary
rest

The cure

★ Sufficient rest from running

★ Avoiding jarring or repetitive stresses

★ The circulatory care programme

★ Painless exercise

★ Stretching exercises

★ Pool exercises, swimming

Stress Fractures.

possibly other electrotherapy modalities including low-frequency alternating electrical currents, diadynamic currents, interferential therapy, or high-frequency electromagnetic energy.

It is rare for the injured area to be immobilized in a plaster cast, because total immobilization carries the risk of weakening the bone even more, preventing it from healing. However, in certain circumstances the doctor or surgeon may decide that a cast is necessary. In this case, it is especially important for the patient to follow the circulatory care programme, and to do as much painless exercise as possible to stimulate the bone to heal.

If possible contributory factors such as biomechanical imbalance, hormonal or circulatory problems, or mineral deficiency have been identified, they must be treated. You may then be referred to a podiatrist for custom-made orthotics, to a dietician for specific advice on nutrition, or to the appropriate specialist in relation to the hormonal or circulatory problems.

In normal circumstances, healing takes place within about three weeks in the case of the finer bones such as the metatarsals in the foot and the outer leg-bone (fibula). The shin-bone and thigh-bone need protection from pain for at least eight to twelve weeks, sometimes longer. To check on healing, your doctor may order repeat X-rays or bone scans.

As a last resort, surgery may be needed, in which case your doctor will refer you to an orthopaedic surgeon. If the stress fracture has developed into a complete break, and the bone has shattered, it may have to be stabilized. This is usually done with metal: either a pin is inserted down through the centre of the bone, in the case of the shin-bone or thigh-bone, or sometimes the parts are fixed together with screws and perhaps a plate. The metal is usually removed when the bone has healed completely. If a stress fracture has failed to heal despite adequate treatment and care over a long enough period, the surgeon may drill small holes in the injured bone to stimulate the healing processes.

Self-help measures for stress fractures

- Use ice or cold compresses around the injured area.
- Follow the circulatory care programme (see pp.75–8).
- Do any kind of alternative exercise which does not cause pain, and which your practitioner recommends.
- Do not 'try out' the leg before your practitioner gives you permission to run, or before you have had an adequate period off running and the leg is completely painless.
- When you are allowed to re-start running, follow your practitioner's advice to the letter. You should start with a very short distance, perhaps under a mile, and stop immediately if you feel any pain. Do not try to run again until the pain has completely subsided, and then only when your practitioner allows.

- Do not run on consecutive days. For the first month, you may only be running once a week, increasing to twice a week for the second month, three times in the third month, then four. Only then, if all is well, are you likely to be allowed to increase to five sessions per week.
- Increase your running distance in easy stages. Never make any sudden big changes.
- During running sessions, try varying direction by running sideways and backwards now and then.
- Try to alternate steady-pace sessions of gradually increasing distance running with sessions of shorter-interval sprinting.
- Do background fitness training or other sports on the days you do not run.
- Be disciplined about warming up and cooling down on every exercise session.
- Stop running and refer back to your practitioner if you feel any hint of pain over the previously injured bone after or during a running session.
- If you have to stop running for a time, for any reason, re-start at the beginning of the recovery programme. Do not try to pick up where you left off. On no account should you try to do more running to make up for lost time.

Returning to running has to be done in graduated, easy stages, to minimize the risk of the stress fracture returning, or occurring in another bone. Running training should be strictly limited, and you should try to maintain a varied training programme indefinitely, even after full recovery. Always remember that any change in your normal running routine is a danger time for your bones. Especially if you are building up mileage, do not simply add on more miles per session according to some theoretical formula, but increase your training in progressive stages, allowing plenty of recovery time between runs so that your bones can adapt to the increased repetitive stresses.

TRAUMATIC FRACTURES

The type of noticeable break in a bone which follows some accident is usually treated by an orthopaedic specialist. According to circumstances, the broken bone may be immobilized in a plaster cast to allow it to heal; fixed surgically with internal rods, or tacked together with a plate and screws; fixed externally with a type of metal brace screwed in through the skin; supported externally with a pneumatic or removable cast; or simply left to heal according to nature.

You have to be unlucky to incur a traumatic fracture through running, but accidents do happen. If you do break your ankle, thigh or arm, perhaps in a bad fall or by getting hit by a car, you will be treated as an emergency in the nearest casualty department. Once you are under treatment for this type of injury, you must be guided by the surgeon or your doctor as to whether or when you can run, how much you can do, and what type of exercise you can do at any stage apart from running. In most cases, you should be referred to a chartered physiotherapist (physical therapist) for detailed guidance on remedial exercises for the injury, plus alternative fitness exercise to maintain your general condition.

Following a leg fracture, you may not be able to take weight through the leg for some considerable time, so you will start by moving about on crutches keeping your foot off the floor, then gradually putting the foot down and increasing the amount of weight you allow to go through it as your strength increases and your pain decreases. The circulatory care programme (pp.75–8) is vital at every stage of recovery. You also have to be aware of the warning signs of circulatory problems or infections: if the leg feels unusually hot, swollen or uncomfortable within the cast, for instance, you should refer immediately to your doctor or casualty department for help. From the earliest stage, remedial exercises are normally set out, to keep your circulation and muscle strength at as good a level as possible.

The worst mistake is to think that the leg will heal itself with time, and then you can go back to normal running. You have to keep improving your muscle strength with specific (probably boring) remedial exercises. You have to work patiently on the co-ordination of the leg, building up its ability to take your bodyweight in very careful easy stages. This is especially important if the fracture is close to a joint, as the disruption to the joint's nerve mechanisms (proprioception) can be very damaging to your co-ordinated leg movements. Swimming and exercising in a pool are valuable methods of improving your overall fitness and the state of your leg, once any wounds have healed sufficiently to go into the water.

Running too much too soon, even if it only seems like a

small amount to you in the context of your normal schedule, is risking the possibility of a re-fracture or a stress fracture. Even though they heal solidly, and in some ways become stronger than before, the major leg bones remain vulnerable to re-fracture for at least a year after a traumatic fracture. For this reason, you have to maintain a balanced programme, including alternative fitness training (cross-training), protective remedial exercises, and controlled amounts of running, for at least one year if not longer after the accident.

The other factor to consider in returning to running after a leg fracture is the importance of not limping as you run. To avoid any relative weakness in the injured leg, you have to work particularly hard at the progressive strengthening programme for all the muscles around the fractured area, and then the leg muscles in general. If you launch into running without paying attention to regaining full strength and co-ordination in the injured leg, you are likely to cause unwanted stresses in other parts of the leg, or in the other leg, and this can lead to secondary injuries elsewhere. If you remember that it takes about three months for muscles to adapt to a specific training programme, you will realize that your recovery programme has to be followed patiently and meticulously.

Arm fractures can also limit your running. If you cannot swing your arms freely, you place stress on your neck and middle back (thoracic spine), and you limit your overall propulsion efficiency. There is no question of running properly with your arm in a sling, as you would completely distort your running mechanics. So you have to avoid running until you can move your arm properly again, and you also have to take care to re-strengthen your arm muscles, and regain proper co-ordination in your arm and shoulder, before re-starting running training. As with all other recovery programmes, the specific arm exercises should be continued long after you feel the injury itself has fully recovered, in terms of healing.

CONCLUSION: COPING WITH BONE INJURIES

Any bone injury or damage affects your basic mechanical structure and interferes with your normal pattern of movements. Prompt and accurate diagnosis and treatment

are crucial to sound healing. Progressive exercise rehabilitation then brings you back to full fitness. Bone injuries could
carry long-term risks of later bone damage or osteoarthritis,
so you must take care to recover completely, to follow your
remedial exercise programme through, and to refer back to
your doctor immediately if there is any hint of pain over the
previously injured bone or its surrounding tissues.

Foot injuries

7

How the foot is formed

The normal foot has twenty-six bones, linked together by ligaments and capsules where they form joints, and moved by the muscles and tendons attached to them and acting on them. Technically, the toes are called phalanges, the big toe is the hallux, the long bones in the centre of the foot are metatarsals, and the short, squat bones in the midfoot and rearfoot are the tarsals. The heel-bone is the calcaneus. Two tiny 'extra' bones called sesamoids lie under the ball of the big toe.

The most important ligaments in the foot are the 'spring' ligament, which links the heel-bone to the navicular and supports the inner (medial longitudinal) arch, and the long plantar ligament, which stretches under the sole of the foot and links the heel-bone to the cuboid and the near ends of the middle three metatarsals. The plantar fascia is a strong fibrous band which extends from the heel to the toes, separating the skin from the muscles along most of the sole of the foot.

There are four layers of little muscles under the foot, and one layer over the top (dorsum), which create movements between the bones of the foot. The small foot muscles are called intrinsics. Longer muscles extending downwards from the calf also act to move the foot and toes.

How the foot works

The nerve systems in the foot control all the foot's reactions, and are vital to the foot's ability to respond instantly to different situations. As the body's base of support, the foot is responsible for your balance mechanisms when you are standing up or moving about. The muscles and their tendons have to react all the time to different signals, to keep you upright, moving efficiently and accurately, and to help prevent falls. The bone arrangement in the foot allows for both pliability and rigidity, according to need.

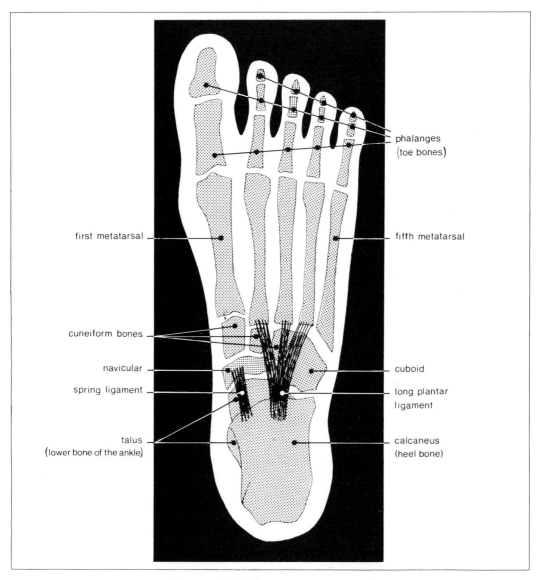

Left foot, seen from under the sole. Bones and major ligaments.

The normal movement of running consists of two phases: the contact (or stance) phase, when the foot is on the ground, and the swing phase, when the leg moves through the air. The moment when the foot lands on the ground is called foot strike. During the phases of walking or running, the foot spreads out when it is on the ground supporting your body-weight. The foot is relatively rigid as it lands on the ground at the moment of foot strike; it becomes more pliable as the foot rolls forward in the contact or stance phase, and it then becomes more rigid again when the weight reaches the ball of the foot and forefoot ready for the push-off (take-off or propulsion) phase. The surface affects the way your foot has to react. When you walk or run over uneven surfaces the foot becomes more pliable to adapt to the surface. It is relatively pliable when you run on a treadmill or grass, but more rigid on firm or hard ground. Many synthetic track surfaces offer a combination of hardness and resilience, creating complex foot reactions biomechanically.

The inner (medial) arch is the inside half of the foot, form-ed by the line of bones from the heel to the ends of the meta-tarsals, where they join the first (big), second and third toes. 'Fallen arches' or flat feet are the terms used to describe relatively flattened medial arches (pes planus), while a high arch is technically called pes cavus. From the ball of the big toe across the heads of the metatarsals to the little toe, the bones form a kind of strut or pillar, which is often called the transverse arch. The outer, or lateral, border of the foot, which consists of the heel-bone, cuboid and outer two metatarsals, is sometimes called the lateral arch, but it is neither as curved nor as pliable as the medial arch, and it lies relatively flat to the ground.

The toes can bend to bring the tips of the toes towards the ground. Where the toes meet the metatarsals, at the meta-tarsophalangeal joints, they can bend upwards and to a cer-tain extent downwards. Usually, the big toe is bigger and longer than the other toes, and it transmits bodyweight from the ball of the foot forwards during the push-off phase. Some people have a second toe which is longer than the big toe, and the main weight-bearing area in the forefoot may be under the second metatarsophalangeal joint instead of the first. This is called Morton's foot.

In the midfoot and under the ankle at the subtalar joint, the sole of the foot can turn inwards, technically into in-version, to lift the medial arch upwards, and outwards, into

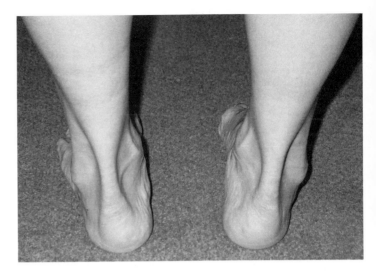

Slightly over-supinating feet.

eversion, lifting the outer border up relative to the inner side of the foot. When the foot is on the ground and taking weight, it can twist inwards to bring the medial arch and forefoot closer to the ground: this is called pronation. The opposite twisting motion, which lifts the medial arch away from the ground, is called supination. The forefoot has to pronate and supinate relative to the rear bones, the calcaneus and talus, when you walk and run, in order to distribute your weight evenly.

THE RUNNING FOOT

Runners often think of pronation as a problem in itself, and one which must be corrected by orthotics or foot inserts. In fact, pronation is only a problem if it is excessive, and especially if it occurs too early, at the heel-bone. Slow runners and joggers are probably more likely to over-pronate. In some cases, over-pronation is encouraged by shoes with very flared soles. Over-pronation at the heel can also be the result of pressures from other parts of the leg. It can be the direct result of stiffness or poor mechanics in the ankle, knee or hip. It can start following any leg injury as the result of altered mechanics, if you run before you have recovered fully.

Most runners land on the heel (heel strike), but sprinters and racket games players often land on the ball of the foot (forefoot strike). From heel strike, the foot rolls forwards and twists into pronation, to bring the weight over the ball of the foot ready for the push-off (take-off or propulsive) phase. Forefoot strikers might land on the outer side of the foot and then pronate quickly to push off the ball of the foot and the big toe. The foot remains much more rigid throughout the contact phase in forefoot strikers than heel strikers.

Running style is very individual. The supposed ideal pattern for the runner is to land on the outer edge of the heel at foot strike, then to transmit weight forwards first along the outer border of the foot and then inwards to the ball of the foot, with push-off from the ball of the foot and the big toe. In practice, many runners deviate from this norm, often without any adverse effects. The foot is very adaptable. If it were not, barefoot runners would be unable to go far or fast, whereas in many countries in the world they do both, usually out of practical necessity, but sometimes as international competitors. Very many runners tend to over-pronate at the heel, while some over-supinate. I once saw a runner in training who actually landed at every step on the outer sides of his feet rather than the soles – apparently without harm!

You can judge for yourself what kind of footfall pattern you have with a few simple checks. The skin under your feet has hardened areas where you take most weight. This might be on the outer edge of your heel, along the outer border and on to the ball of the foot and the big toe. Hard skin patches may reveal weight-bearing areas on the outer side of the forefoot. If you have Morton's foot, there may be hard skin under the head of the second toe. You may have more hard skin under your forefoot than your heel, or vice versa, indicating that you run on your forefoot or that you are a heavy heel-striker.

Your shoes will show areas of wear where they take most load, once you have used them for a reasonable amount of training. You may notice the normal pattern of wear at the outer edge of the heel, curving round to the ball of the foot, or there may be wear across the heel on to the inner edge, indicating over-pronation. At the forefoot, the wear may be under the outer side, instead of under the ball of the foot. If you run heavily, the shoes will wear down relatively quickly, perhaps after a couple of months, whereas a lighter runner might use one pair of shoes for a year or more without significant signs of wear. The wear pattern may be different on each shoe, reflecting an imbalance in the way your feet strike the ground and react with it.

You can also check your foot motion by running a few paces with wet feet (carefully) over a smooth floor surface such as linoleum. The wet imprint shows you how much of your foot makes contact with the ground, so you can see if you are noticeably flat-footed, with most of the sole in contact, or if you land mainly on the forefoot, with little heel contact, or if you over-supinate, with most of the contact along the outer edge of the foot. You can do a similar test by running in a sandpit with wet feet, without shoes. You can see the main points of contact outlined in the sand, and you can reproduce the imprints by running for a few steps on absorbent paper, so that the sand sticks to it.

A full biomechanical check is usually carried out by a podiatrist, who assesses your feet when you are standing still, and also when they are not bearing your weight. Your feet will be examined in different positions, for instance from in front and behind, and with you sitting up on the couch, then lying face down on it. The most important part of the assessment is to judge your running motion, and this is often done by making a video of you running on the ground or on a treadmill. If the full biomechanical check is not needed, the practitioner makes the assessment more simply, by eye.

FOOT PROBLEMS

Foot pain can be caused by inflammatory joint problems, including gout. It can also be referred from the hip or back. The condition ankylosing spondylitis (see p.228), which primarily affects the spinal joints, can also cause plantar fasciitis, giving pain under the sole of the foot.

Injuries can happen through trauma, friction or overuse (misuse), and can affect any part of the foot structure, including the toe-nails, skin, bones, joint structures, muscles and tendons.

Toe-nail problems

Toe-nails can be damaged by careless trimming, pressure from tight shoes, irritation from seams in the shoes, or by a direct blow.

You should cut your toe-nails straight across, leaving them very slightly longer than the toe. This is especially important in the big toe, where ingrowing toe-nails are very common if you cut the nails back too hard and in a curve. The nail tends

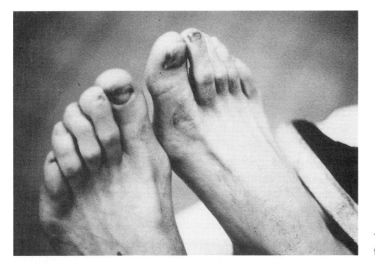

Toe-nails badly damaged by ill-fitting shoes.

to drive into the flesh at the side of the toe, which can become very painful. Unless you can control the problem by carefully easing the nail from the skin, allowing it to grow, and shaping it correctly with an emery board, the ingrown toe-nail is best treated by a chiropodist or podiatrist who can cut the painful area of nail away under local anaesthetic.

Pressure or irritation on one or more toe-nails can cause blackness in the nail, indicating bruising under the nail. This can also happen through trauma, for instance if you drop a heavy object on the toe(s). If you feel pressure under the toe-nail, you may be able to relieve it by boring gently through the nail with a sterilized needle to release some of the bruising. If in doubt, consult your doctor, chiropodist or podiatrist.

It is important to avoid any risk of infection in the feet, to prevent the danger of more generalized blood poisoning. Always make sure you use sterile procedures if you try self-help measures such as boring through the nail. Keep any cuts round the nails very clean and covered with sterile dressings. Signs of infection in a nail include a change of colour, in which the nail becomes very pale or yellowish, and a bad odour. Nail infections should always be treated by a qualified practitioner.

Skin problems

Areas of hard skin, or calluses, are normal in the parts of the foot which are most active in transmitting your bodyweight, such as your heel and the ball of the foot. The hard skin is protective, but it should not be allowed to become too thick. If it seems to be spreading, you can control it with skin-softening and removing lotions, and by paring it down gently with a pumice-stone. Areas which are specially vulnerable to friction, such as the outer side of the little toe, can form localized hard spots called corns, and these can become painful. Sometimes the hard skin conceals infections such as verrucae, which are warts caused by a virus. If you notice that the calluses on your feet are becoming excessive, painful or brittle, or if you think there might be infections under them, you should consult your doctor or chiropodist/ podiatrist.

Fungal infections such as tinea pedis, or so-called 'athlete's foot', should also be treated by a professional practitioner. They are very contagious, and can spread very quickly between runners in communal shower areas. Fungal infections can cause blistering, oozing, itchiness, burning and crusty scaly skin. Once acquired, they can spread quickly from between the toes on to the sole of the foot, and then on to the other foot. To avoid fungal infections, you should always wear shower slippers in communal washing and changing facilities, and keep your feet and socks scrupulously clean. Dry your feet thoroughly after washing them. You can use a medicated powder if necessary, especially if your feet tend to sweat a lot. Always allow your running shoes to dry out after use, and never store them in a bag for long periods.

Blisters are caused by friction, usually between the foot and the shoe. They are more likely to happen in hot conditions, when your foot swells more than usual inside the shoe.

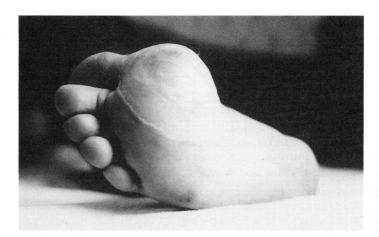

Huge blister caused by a ten-mile run in new shoes.

Your shoes might be too narrow, or they may have stitching, seams or reinforcements which press against your foot. When the skin is irritated by rubbing, fluid forms between the skin layers, which is either clear or, in the case of a blood blister, deep red. A large painful blister may have to be drained, and this must be done under sterile conditions. After draining, the skin may be treated with an antibiotic powder if necessary, covered with a special gel-filled type of dressing, or hardened with an appropriate spirit. It may then be taped, to prevent pain while walking and running.

To prevent blisters, long-distance runners often spread Vaseline over vulnerable areas. Some runners avoid wearing socks, while others use two pairs. You must make sure that your shoes fit you well, with space for normal foot expansion, but no seams or edges which might rub against your feet. If your feet are particularly soft, you may need to encourage calluses, in order to protect your feet from blisters; a chiropodist or podiatrist may use special hardening lotion for this purpose.

Bone injuries

Stress fractures (see pp.102–9) can happen in any of the foot bones, although they are relatively unusual in the first metatarsal. The most common stress fracture in runners happens in the second metatarsal, and it is called a 'march fracture' because it was first described in army recruits who were doing unaccustomed long marches and running drills. The 'march fracture' is especially common in runners who have Morton's foot, or a relatively long second toe, as they tend to weight-bear under the second metatarsal head instead of under the ball of the foot. Runners who over-supinate might suffer from a stress fracture in the fourth or fifth metatarsal head, while runners who land heavily on their heels at each step may fracture the calcaneus. The navicular bone can be damaged in runners who over-pronate heavily, although navicular stress fractures are most common in high-jumpers and hurdlers. Stress fractures usually do not show up on X-rays until they are healing, although bone scans can confirm the damage. In the foot, the diagnosis is often simply made on the basis of the history of the pain process, and the tenderness when pressing directly on to the suspect bone.

Stress fractures are caused by over-training in relation to what you were doing before. There is usually only slight pain over the damaged bone, which gradually gets worse until you

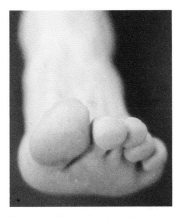

Slight swelling under the 4th metatarsal head, where the athlete had a small fracture following intensive hopping and bounding sessions.

have to stop running because of the pain. If you try to keep running, you risk shattering the bone completely. To cure the problem you have to rest from running for at least six weeks, do alternative painless exercise, and then gradually re-start running training, on the basis of one or two sessions only per week at first.

Apophysitis is an injury very similar to a stress fracture, which only happens to immature, growing bone. The apophysis at the back of the heel-bone (calcaneus) has the end of the Achilles tendon attached to it. During the growth phase when the apophysis is fusing on to the main body of the heel-bone, it becomes vulnerable to pressure from the Achilles tendon and to repetitive jarring, both of which can happen as a result of excessive running or jumping. It is a problem which happens between the ages of about ten and fifteen, and is called Sever's 'disease', although it is not caused by illness but is simply a mechanical injury. The disruption to the apophysis usually shows up on X-ray.

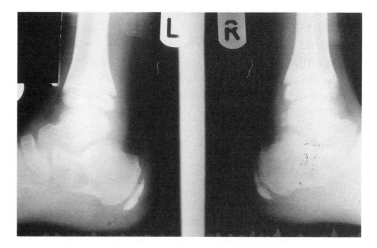

Slight left Sever's 'disease' in a ten-year-old athlete.

Once the pain starts, the young runner has to avoid any painful activities. Heel cushions may help reduce any discomfort when walking. Treatments are usually restricted to ice or contrast baths, and possibly gentle massage around the edge of the heel and the lower end of the Achilles tendon, which can also be done as self-help routines. Electrotherapy modalities such as ultrasound are not generally used over bone growth areas, for fear that they might cause harm, and because there is no evidence that they can help overuse bone problems.

Osteochondritis is damage to a bone and its covering cartilage, and it is another problem which can affect young runners, usually in their teens. In the forefoot, it is most common in the second and third metatarsal heads, where it is called Freiberg's disease, and it also happens in the navicular bone, where it is called Kohler's disease. It usually follows some trauma, such as a direct blow or harsh twist, which causes inflammation over the bone. Sometimes, however, the cause remains a mystery. The young runner feels pain on exercise, and tenderness on direct pressure over the injured area. X-rays will show the damage, and the treatment is rest from painful activities, and alternative exercise, for between six and twelve weeks, or as long as necessary for the pain to subside. In the worst of cases, surgery may be needed to remove any damaged fragments of the bone.

Big toe stiffness

Technically called hallux rigidus, stiffness in the big toe joint usually comes on gradually, often as the late result of a traumatic injury which might have happened years earlier. The metatarsophalangeal joint can be damaged by a blow on the big toe, or a bad jarring stress, perhaps caused by stubbing the big toe hard. Injuries like this which have happened during a growth phase in childhood or adolescence are especially likely to lead to later hallux rigidus.

The stiffness causes pain when the toe is bent either way, and you may feel the pain on the top of the foot, under the ball of the big toe, or both. It is very noticeable on pushing-off in running, especially in sprinting and hopping, and worst of all on coming out of blocks for a sprint start. Badly fitting, high-heeled, thin-soled or stiff-soled shoes can all contribute to the pain. Conversely, shoes with good flexible support underfoot, and properly fitted medial arch inserts, can help to alleviate the pain. Acute pain in the big toe joint usually eases if you rest from painful activities and do remedial foot exercises for both strength and mobility. Physiotherapy can help this process with electrical muscle stimulation and gentle manipulative techniques. If the problem persists, giving a lot of pain, your doctor may refer you to an orthopaedic specialist for an operation to correct the joint and relieve the pain.

Sesamoiditis

Pain under the ball of the foot, on either side of the big toe joint, can be caused by inflammation involving one or both of the tiny sesamoid bones. One or both sesamoids can be broken by a sudden jarring force, especially with the toes pushed back (upwards) into extension, as might happen if you land heavily on your forefeet from a height. Bruising and inflammation in one or both sesamoids can be caused by repetitive strain. This can happen simply through long-distance running, but it is usually associated with some change in biomechanics caused by worn or new shoes, or running on an uneven or sloping surface. A long session of practising sprint starts out of blocks can irritate the sesamoids.

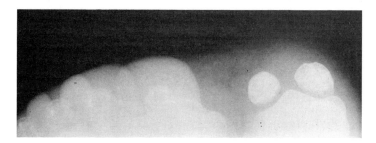

Damaged sesamoid bone (on far right of picture).

Padding under the sole of the foot can relieve direct pressure on the sesamoids. Treatment is usually aimed at restoring efficient muscle function to help hold the sesamoids in the right place: electrical muscle stimulation combined with remedial exercises is vital. In the worst of cases, a very badly damaged sesamoid might be removed surgically.

Bunion

The technical name for a bunion is hallux valgus. The condition is usually hereditary, but it can be aggravated or even caused by activities involving heavy wear on the toes, such as gymnastics and ballet, and by tight shoes with pointed toes. The head of the first metatarsal bone becomes thickened, while the big toe is pulled towards or even across the second toe, creating a protrusion at the inner side of the forefoot. A fluid-filled bursa (natural cyst) may form over the bump. Because the muscles have to work at an abnormal angle, the bunion tends to get worse once it has started.

To relieve discomfort and prevent friction from shoes, pads can be placed over the protruding bone. Corrective arch supports or custom-made orthotics may be prescribed to help the foot to function more normally. Muscle re-education, especially using electrical stimulation for more efficient contractions, is vital. If all else fails, and the toe becomes extremely painful, your doctor will refer you to an orthopaedic surgeon for corrective surgery.

Hammer toes

Tight tendons on top of the foot can pull the toes so that their middle (interphalangeal) joints are bent upwards, while the toe tips claw towards the ground. This deformity can be associated with a tight, high arch, or it may be caused or aggravated by tight shoes. If hammer toes are painless they may not need treatment, although you probably have to protect the protruding parts from friction by choosing your shoes carefully, and perhaps arranging padding made of chiropodist's felt as cushioning against friction. You may also need an arch support to relieve pressure on the ball of the foot. Foot exercises can help prevent the deformity from getting worse. If the hammer toes cause severe pain, or become so pronounced that you have difficulty wearing shoes, it may be necessary to have surgery to correct them.

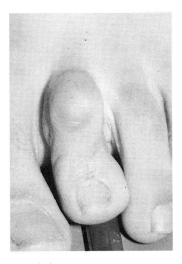

A single hammer toe.

Metatarsalgia

Pain in the joints of the forefoot between the heads of the metatarsal joints is often caused by tight shoes which have not allowed your feet to spread out during running. The injury causes pain on twisting movements involving the forefoot, especially if you run on rough ground in the shoes which have caused the problem. Squeezing the sides of the foot together usually reproduces the pain. Treatment may include remedial exercises, electrotherapy, and perhaps an injection from your doctor into the painful area. Above all, your shoes have to be checked and probably replaced. You may need corrective insoles or orthotics in all your shoes to relieve pressure on the metatarsal heads while the injury recovers.

If a nerve becomes swollen and inflamed as the result of pressure between two metatarsal heads, it causes very localized, sharp pain whenever the two bones are pressed together during certain foot movements. The pain is usually relieved instantly if you take your shoe off and rub your foot. The inflamed nerve is technically called a neuroma, and this condition is called 'Morton's metatarsalgia' or interdigital neuroma. Sometimes the neuroma is big enough to feel by squeezing the top and sole of the foot gently at the affected area. In this case, it is likely to need surgery to remove the swollen nerve. More often, the pressure on the nerve can be relieved by placing a small pad of chiropodist's felt under and just behind the metatarsal heads, doing remedial exercises, and perhaps using slightly bigger or less rigid running shoes.

Plantar fasciitis

The plantar fascia, often together with the long plantar ligament, can become strained if the sole of the foot is over-stretched. The most common cause of this is rigid shoes, although it can also happen if the shoe's arch support is inadequate. Tightness in the calf and Achilles tendon can be a contributory factor. Once the fascia is strained it causes pain when you stretch it, whether by running, especially sprinting, going up and down on your toes, or pulling your toes back towards your body with your hands. It can also ache if you sit or stand still for long periods, or when you stand up after sitting still. The sole of your foot feels tender on pressure, and there may be one acutely sensitive spot, usually just in front of the heel-bone.

The problem may be treated with physiotherapy modalities, such as massage, electrical muscle stimulation for the intrinsic muscles in the sole of the foot, and perhaps Diadyne or ultrasound. You also have to do exercises to stretch your calf. Your doctor may inject the painful area. You may need different running shoes, and perhaps corrective insoles or orthotics. Running and painful activities have to be avoided until the pain and tenderness have subsided completely, which can take several weeks.

'Spring' ligament strain

The so-called 'spring' ligament supports the medial arch of the foot. When it is strained, the injury is similar to the pain of plantar fasciitis, although the pain is located under the inner side of the foot. Apart from supporting the arch with inserts or orthotics and allowing the ligament to heal, it is vital to regain full efficiency in all the muscles supporting the medial arch, to prevent any tendency for the foot to over-pronate as a secondary result of the injury.

Heel bruise and bursitis

Repeated trauma from running, especially if you land heavily on your heels, and if your shoes are not cushioned enough, can cause deep bruising and inflammation, usually in the protective fat pad or the bursa (fluid-filled cyst), both of which provide natural cushioning under the heel-bone. This is sometimes called 'policeman's heel'.

Once it has happened, it tends to last for several weeks, sometimes months. It is usually treated with physiotherapy modalities such as massage, electrical stimulation for the intrinsic muscles of the sole, and remedial exercises. Your doctor may inject the painful area. Most importantly, the heel has to be protected from direct pressure with shock-absorbing heel cushions, and perhaps with pads cut in a ring shape to remove pressure from the centre of the heel.

Bursitis can also happen at the back of the heel, under the attachment of the Achilles tendon. A localized focus of pain is felt when you push off your toes, and there may be a visible swelling. This usually happens because of friction from the shoe-back, and is a particular danger if the heel counter is too soft or badly shaped. The injury is often called 'pump-bump'. If it does not respond to conservative (non-surgical) treatment, such as physiotherapy, it may need an operation to 'clean up' the area, followed by remedial therapy not only for the foot and heel, but including exercises for the Achilles tendon. Recovery from surgery can take several weeks, so it is not a quick cure.

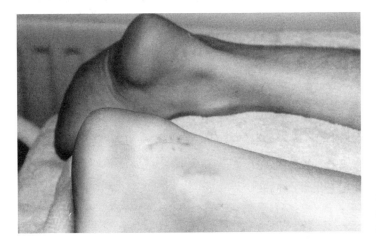

'Pump-bump' after surgery, showing the remains of the lump caused by shoe friction.

Heel spur

A small outgrowth of extra bone can arise if any tissue suffers repetitive trauma at its attachment to a bone. In runners, this is especially common where the plantar fascia and long plantar ligament are attached to the heel-bone. Quite

The common site for heel spur.

Tenosynovitis usually happens over the top of the foot.

often, the extended sliver of bone can exist without causing pain. It is often found on X-rays incidentally, without being associated with problems. Sometimes, however, it is painful, causing a localized pain spot when the sole of the foot is stretched. The pain may be relieved by foot supports and pressure-reducing padding, but if the bony spur causes continuing problems it may need to be removed surgically.

Tenosynovitis

Inflammation in the fluid-filled covering sheath of a tendon causes pain and a 'grating' sensation over the affected area when it is moved. The tendons over the top of the foot are particularly vulnerable to tenosynovitis, which is often caused by friction from tight shoelaces or irritation from a badly designed shoe tongue. Tenosynovitis can also be caused by running too much, or it can follow a direct blow to the top of the foot.

Once it has happened, you have to protect the foot from friction and you will probably have to stop running for at least two weeks, depending on how painful the foot is. The tenosynovitis can be cured by rest, or it may be treated, perhaps by an injection from your doctor or by various forms of physiotherapy. You must check your shoes for tightness over the uppers, and make sure that the tongue is wide enough to cover the top of your foot, and is properly padded. You may need to line the shoe tongue with padding, perhaps made of chiropodist's felt, to provide extra cushioning, especially if the lacing eyelets are reinforced with hard rings. You have to avoid any painful activities, especially movements involving stretching the foot and toes downwards, until the pain and grating have disappeared.

FOOT EXERCISES

R emedial exercises for the foot aim to restore and improve co-ordination, strength and mobility, with special emphasis on the small intrinsic muscles, which are always inhibited when the foot has been painful, and which may have been weakened anyway if you habitually wear tight, rigid or high-heeled shoes. It is useful to do the exercises with both feet, but one at a time, so that you can concentrate on specially weak muscles. It is always best to do foot exercises barefoot, but you should also try to activate your foot muscles every day, even when you are wearing shoes and perhaps sitting or standing still.

Strengthening exercises for the intrinsics

1 Sitting or standing, with your foot flat on the floor, press your toes flat into the floor, keeping your ankle still and your toes straight (not allowing your toes to curl). Hold the pressure for a count of two, then relax completely. Repeat five to ten times.

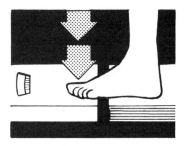

2 Sitting with your toes on the edge of a weighing-scale and the rest of your foot supported at the same height, press your toes downwards on to the scale, keeping the toes flat. Hold for a count of two, to see how much pressure you can generate. Repeat five to ten times.

3 Repeat (2), pressing with the big toe only.

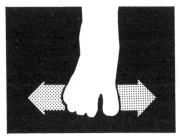

4 Sitting with your feet flat on the floor, spread your toes outwards, then bring them together again, keeping them in contact with the floor. Repeat five to ten times.

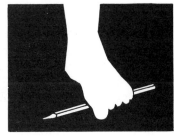

5 Clench a pencil under your toes, lift the pencil up, hold for a count of three, then put your foot and the pencil down again. Repeat five to ten times.

6 Place a card between two toes, then move your ankle up and down ten times, keeping the toe grip on the card. Repeat between each pair of toes in turn.

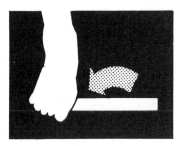

◄

7 Place your forefoot over a nar-row strip of cloth on the floor, so that your foot is at one end, while the other extends sideways away from your toes. Keeping your heel in contact with the floor, twist your forefoot so that the cloth is moved along under your foot, then reverse the movement to bring the strip back to the starting position. Repeat five to ten times.

8 Standing or sitting, with your feet flat on the floor, roll your feet slightly outwards to lift the inner arch while keeping the fore-foot and heel in contact with the floor. Repeat three to five times.

Stretching exercises

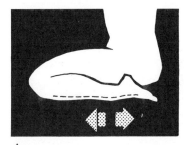

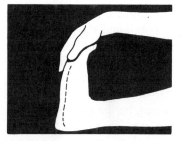

1 Kneel down on a soft surface, with your toes bent, the ball of the foot in contact with the floor, heel off the floor. Sit back on your heels, to feel the stretch on the sole of the foot. Hold for a count of six, then relax. Repeat three to six times.

▲

2 Kneel down on a soft surface with the top of your foot in contact with the surface. Gently sit back to feel the stretch over the top of the foot. If you cannot feel the stretch, place a small support under the toes to lift them. Hold for a count of six, then relax. Repeat three to six times.

▲

3 Sitting with your leg straight or slightly bent, pull the top of your foot towards you, bending the toes, to feel the stretch under the foot. Hold for a count of six, then relax. Repeat three to six times.

4 Standing with your toes pressed against a low upright surface or block, keeping your heel flat on the floor, bend your knee to feel the stretch under the foot and on the lower calf. Hold for a count of six, then relax. Repeat three to six times.

Ankle injuries

THE FORMATION OF THE ANKLE

The ankle is a very stable joint. It is formed between the lower ends of the shin-bone (tibia) and outer leg-bone (fibula), and the bones fit very closely together. On the inner side of the ankle you can feel the protruding end of the shin-bone, which is called the medial malleolus, while the more prominent edge of the outer leg-bone on the other side is called the lateral malleolus. The medial ligament forms a strong binding on the inner side of the ankle, while the lateral ligament on the outer side is slightly less strong. The front of the ankle is the least protected part, in terms of ligaments.

Just above the ankle, the shin-bone and outer leg-bone are bound together by the very strong lower (inferior) tibiofibular

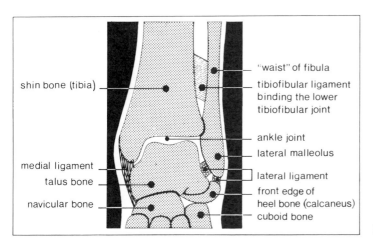

shin bone (tibia)

medial ligament
talus bone

navicular bone

"waist" of fibula
tibiofibular ligament binding the lower tibiofibular joint

ankle joint
lateral malleolus

lateral ligament
front edge of heel bone (calcaneus)
cuboid bone

Left ankle, front view.

ligament. Very little movement happens in this joint, which is technically called a syndesmosis, although the two bones separate slightly as your foot is moved upwards at the ankle. The inferior tibiofibular joint is closely connected to the ankle functionally, so it can be injured together with the ankle.

The ankle is a pure hinge joint, and can only move backwards and forwards. Its forward movement points the foot downwards, technically into plantarflexion, and this action is performed by the calf muscles on the back of the lower leg. The opposite movement, technically dorsiflexion, brings the foot up towards the shin, and happens through the action of the muscles on the front of the shin, the anterior tibial muscles. When the foot twists inwards and outwards, the movement happens below the ankle, in the subtalar joint and the midfoot. The muscles which perform these actions lie on either side of the lower leg, and pass down the sides of the ankle into the foot.

The ankle is the link between the versatile lever of the foot and the rigid lever formed by your lower leg bones. It therefore has a role in propulsion and shock absorption when you walk, run and jump. It has a very rich nerve supply, which provides your brain with feedback as to the position of the joint. This in-built awareness system, technically known as proprioception, is vital to the balance mechanisms which help you to keep upright, to steady yourself if you stumble or overbalance, and to prevent yourself from falling.

ANKLE PROBLEMS

Ankle pain and swelling can be caused by inflammatory arthritis, infections, gout, circulatory problems, or pain referred from the hip or back.

ANKLE INJURIES

The ankle is most often injured by awkward twisting, which can happen if you catch your foot on a kerb, tread on a stone or piece of wood, or miss your footing on a step. Your shoes can contribute to ankle injuries, especially if they have excessively flared or rigid soles, or if the sides are too high and pressurize the ankle. Ankle injuries can be associated

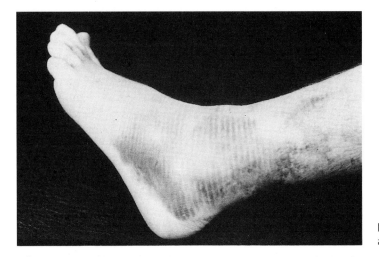

Most ankle injuries cause bruising and swelling.

with biomechanical defects such as over-pronation, over-supination, stiffness in the knee or hip, or previous leg injuries which have caused compensation.

THE DAMAGE

The ligaments are usually the first structures to be damaged, but ankle injuries can also involve the joint capsule, tendons close to the joint, and the bones themselves. In every ankle injury, the nerve system is disrupted: this affects the joint's proprioception and therefore your balance mechanisms.

If the ankle is injured with the foot turning inwards, in an inversion strain, the outer ligaments are strained or torn. In a severe injury, the lateral malleolus might break off in an avulsion fracture, and perhaps the tip of the medial malleolus too. In an eversion injury, the medial ligament is damaged or torn, which might cause a break in the medial malleolus, together with an impact fracture in the lateral malleolus. If the foot is forced downwards, the capsule at the front of the joint may be torn, and there may be a crack in the bones at the back of the ankle. Injury with the foot forced upwards against the lower leg can cause a fracture at the front of the ankle, and it can also disrupt the lower tibiofibular ligament, making the tibiofibular joint unstable.

In a major injury, you probably cannot put weight on the foot, and it may be obvious that bones are broken. After first aid, you should be treated in the local casualty department as quickly as possible.

Most ankle injuries are more minor. There may be acute, severe pain at first, but you may then be able to put your foot to the floor and take weight gently, without pain. If so, you should try to keep walking on the foot, rather than letting it stiffen up by keeping it still. If you sit down, try to keep the foot moving, avoiding any movements which cause pain. Ice or cold compresses should be used to relieve pain and limit swelling. Any support bandage for the ankle should be soft, and should extend from the toes to just below the knee. You can use cotton-wool wadding covered by a crêpe bandage, or one or two layers of tubular bandage. You should not encase the ankle in non-stretch taping (strapping), as this would cause constriction if the joint continued to swell inside the support.

Immediately following an ankle injury it may not be obvious what has been damaged, and how much damage has been done. Minor fractures are often missed, especially if the ankle alone is X-rayed, without taking account of the possibility of a spiral fracture higher up the leg on the outer leg-bone. The clue to such spiral fractures is bruising and swelling extending up the leg. In fact, if the bone is still held together, these cracks heal as quickly as any torn ligaments, so they usually do not require special treatment. You may notice a feeling of heaviness, rather like tiredness, in the bone as it heals over the four to six weeks following the injury, but otherwise you will probably not have any special sensation of bone damage.

TREATMENT FOR THE INJURED ANKLE

If there has been major damage to the ankle, surgery may be needed to stabilize loose fragments of bone, for instance if one or both malleoli have been fractured, or if a ligament is completely broken. With or without surgery, the ankle may have to be protected in a plaster cast, and you may need to keep your weight off the foot for a period of time.

For the more minor sprains, treatment usually consists of massage and electrotherapy modalities to control the pain and swelling; ultrasound is very widely used in the immediate and early stages. I use massage and diadynamic currents for the swelling and bruising at any stage following the ankle

sprain, plus electrical muscle stimulation, especially to improve efficiency in the muscles and tendons controlling the
movements over the damaged region of the ankle. Damaged
ligaments are usually healing by ten days after the injury, and
the sprained ankle should be fully recovered within six to
twelve weeks, depending on the severity of the sprain.

If the ankle does not respond to treatment, it may need
further assessment by an orthopaedic specialist. Further
checks may be done, such as X-rays or bone scans, or the
surgeon may look inside the joint through the arthroscope, in
so-called keyhole surgery. There might be bone fragments in
the joint from an impact injury: this is called an osteochondral fracture, and is most likely to happen over the front
of the joint, on the top (dome) of the talus. The presence of
the fragments may only become obvious after the main
symptoms have died away, when a small localized area of
pain and swelling persists just over the front of the ankle.
Surgery may be needed to remove the pieces and clean out
the joint.

Disruption in the lower tibiofibular joint can make the
ankle unstable under pressure when the joint is moved into
extreme plantarflexion and especially dorsiflexion. An X-ray,
called a stress view, taken with the foot pressed by hand into
its extreme ranges, usually confirms the abnormal freedom
between the shin-bone and the outer leg-bone. If the injury is
causing continuing pain, swelling and disability in the injured
leg when you try to run, surgery may be needed to tighten up
the tibiofibular joint again.

In the worst of cases, if severe damage has been done to
the joint surfaces in the ankle, making even walking painful,
the surgeon may decide to fuse the joint, limiting its
movement in order to lessen the pain. After this, it is probably unlikely that you could do any serious running,
although walking and sports like golf are perfectly possible,
besides any other activities which do not involve weight-
bearing through the foot.

PROTECTING THE ANKLE

It is always a mistake to tape a joint up in order to do
activities which would otherwise be too painful. So do not
be tempted to wrap an injured ankle in non-stretch taping in
order to keep running through the injury. You risk creating

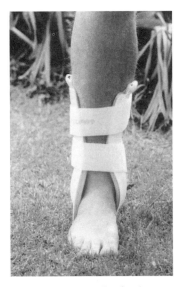

An Aircast stirrup splint for the ankle.

further damage to the joint surfaces, and you will also prevent the vital nerve mechanisms from recovering. Although (preventive) prophylactic ankle taping is widely used in the United States, I do not recommend it, but prefer athletes to strengthen their ankles for natural protection against injury.

On the other hand, while you are getting over an ankle injury the joint may need some support to prevent it from being jolted by unexpected twists from rough pavements or soft ground. A support may also give you extra confidence in the joint when you first start running again. The best way to provide adequate support without limiting the whole joint and interfering with the nerve mechanisms is to use stirrup taping (strapping) on either side of the ankle, or a stirrup splint.

To control swelling, which may continue to gather in the ankle by the end of each day for months after the injury, you can use a tubular or crêpe bandage, or some other soft wrap-around support, but you should avoid wearing these throughout the whole day. If the swelling does persist, you must use the circulatory care programme (see pp.75–8) for as long as it takes to eliminate it. Painless swelling is only a problem in that it can limit the joint movement. If the swelling is accompanied by pain, you should check with your doctor or practitioner in case there is unhealed or secondary damage in the joint.

If your shoes have contributed to your ankle problem, you must choose a more adequate pair, in a style which does not interfere with your normal ankle movements. You may feel more confident in high-sided shoes, like some cross-trainers or basketball boots, but you should remember that, like taping, your shoes cannot totally prevent unwanted stresses on the ankle, so there is no substitute for the programme of protective remedial exercises.

ANKLE EXERCISES

Ankle exercises are best done barefoot, to help the nerve mechanisms recover maximum sensitivity and accuracy, but they can also be done in shoes. The thicker the shoe soles, the less valuable the exercises are for training the nerve-muscle co-ordination.

Wobble and rocker boards are invaluable for re-training the balance mechanisms. The wobble board is a flat disc of

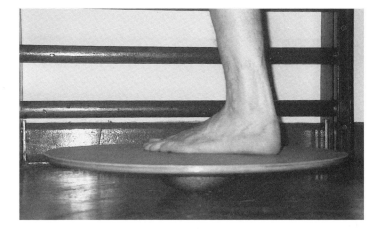

Wobble board.

wood attached to a rounded rocker. You stand with one leg in the centre of the wobble board, trying to hold your balance. When this becomes easy, try doing arm exercises, or throwing a ball in the air, against a wall, or to a partner. A rocker board consists of a flat square of wood attached to a wooden cylinder: this can be made fairly easily from a board screwed or glued to a rolling pin. You use the board in two ways: firstly balancing on it with the cylinder at right angles to the line of your foot, and secondly with the cylinder in line with your foot.

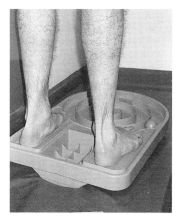

The Wobbler for dynamic balance exercises.

The wobble and rocker boards used in this way train your static balance mechanisms, or your ability to hold your balance standing still. You also need to train your dynamic balance mechanisms. You can do this by doing leg movements such as knee-bending while balancing on the boards. Or you can use equipment such as the Wobbler (which was originally designed as a children's toy, but provides excellent leg work for adults too).

There is highly sophisticated equipment for measuring and exercising balance mechanisms, but static and dynamic balance training exercises can also be done without any special balancing equipment.

Ankle exercises

1 Sitting with your feet off the floor, place the sole of your uninjured foot on top of the injured one. Press the injured foot upwards, resisting the movement with the uninjured foot. Hold the contraction for a count of three, then relax completely. Repeat five times.

2 Stand on one leg, holding your balance and keeping absolutely still. Try not to use your hands to steady yourself if you overbalance. Hold the position for as long as possible, and try to increase your balancing time progressively. Do three on the injured leg to one on the unaffected leg, and repeat three times.

3 Stand on one leg with your eyes closed, holding your balance. Repeat as for (2).

4 Stand balanced on one leg, and do arm-circling movements. Repeat as for (2).

5 Stand balanced on one leg, and throw and catch a light ball, either by yourself or with a partner. Repeat as for (2).

6 Standing, go up and down on your toes slowly, rising as high as you can every time. Repeat ten to twenty times.

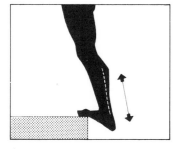

7 Stand with your toes and fore-feet on the edge of a step, drop your heels downwards, then go up on your toes slowly. Repeat ten times.

8 Repeat (6), one leg at a time. Start with three movements, building up to ten, on each leg in turn.

9 Stand on one leg, bend your knee, then rise up on to your toes. Repeat the cycle without a pause. Start with three consecutive movements, and build up to ten, on each leg in turn.

10 Walk on your heels for twenty paces, then on your toes, and then on the outer edges of your feet, forwards, backwards and sideways.

11 Hop forwards, backwards and sideways for twenty paces in each direction, on each leg in turn.

12 Skip using a jump-rope (skipping-rope), starting with both feet jumping together, and progressing to alternate foot movements. Build up to several minutes of skipping. Do not skip on consecutive days, and try to use a soft surface.

Achilles tendon and calf muscle injuries

9

THE STRUCTURE AND ACTIONS OF THE CALF

The Achilles tendon (technically known as the tendo calcaneus or calcanean tendon) is the longest and strongest tendon in the body, and it forms a strong band at the back of the lower leg. It links the back of the heel-bone with the calf muscles, gastrocnemius and soleus. Unlike many other tendons, the Achilles tendon is not lined by a sheath lubricated with synovial fluid, but it has a special covering called a paratenon.

Soleus is the underlying muscle which supports your lower leg: it feeds into the Achilles tendon at its lower end, and its upper part is attached to the back of the leg-bones. Soleus is basically a slow-twitch postural muscle, which is always active to some degree when you are standing up, as it helps to hold you upright against the pressure of gravity. Soleus acts to move the ankle joint, helping to point the foot downwards into plantarflexion (p.132). If soleus is specially weak for any reason, you will find it very difficult to go up and down on your toes on that leg keeping your knee straight.

Gastrocnemius is the bulky muscle at the upper end of the calf. It also joins on to the Achilles tendon, and at its upper end it has two tendons which are attached to the back of the thigh-bone, just above the knee. It is mainly a fast-twitch muscle, which acts as you push off your toes when you walk, sprint, jump or hop. Because it is a two-joint muscle, acting on the ankle and the knee, it not only helps to pull the foot downwards into plantarflexion, but also helps the hamstrings

to bend the knee, for instance when you do knee curl movements against a very heavy resistance.

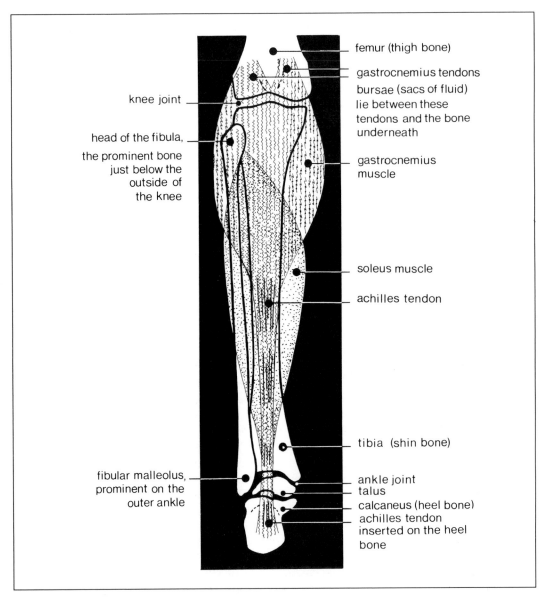

femur (thigh bone)

gastrocnemius tendons

bursae (sacs of fluid)
lie between these
tendons and the bone
underneath

knee joint

head of the fibula,

the prominent bone
just below the
outside of
the knee

gastrocnemius
muscle

soleus muscle

achilles tendon

tibia (shin bone)

fibular malleolus,
prominent on the
outer ankle

ankle joint
talus
calcaneus (heel bone)
achilles tendon
inserted on the heel
bone

Calf structure, left leg

ACHILLES TENDON AND CALF MUSCLE INJURIES

Traumatic accidents can cause tears in the calf muscles and the Achilles tendon, for instance if you trip, or if you catch your leg against a rigid bar. The Achilles tendon itself can tear unexpectedly, as an intrinsic traumatic injury, if it has been weakened previously. Complete tears of the Achilles tendon are more common in sports involving sprinting and changing direction, such as squash, badminton, hockey and football, but they can also happen to runners.

Any tear in the muscle or tendon causes the feeling of an 'explosion' in the leg. If the Achilles tendon is completely torn or ruptured, you may feel that someone has actually hit you in the back of the leg, even though no direct blow has happened. When part of the calf muscle is completely torn, or the Achilles tendon is partly torn, walking is painful, especially if you try to roll your foot normally from heel to toe. You may be able to walk by turning your foot outwards and keeping your foot flat on the ground, or it may be more comfortable to walk on the ball of the foot, keeping your knee bent. If the Achilles tendon is completely torn, you can only take weight on the foot by turning your leg outwards. Your foot feels limp, and you cannot point it downwards into plantarflexion at will. You may notice bruising over the injured area, although this may only appear some days later, having tracked downwards from the injury into your leg and foot.

Overuse injuries can affect any part of the calf and Achilles structure. In the calf muscle itself the pain can feel similar to cramp, and you feel it every time you point your foot downwards, when you go up and down on your toes while standing up, when you walk or run, or when you stretch the calf by leaning forward keeping your heel flat on the ground. The gastrocnemius tendons behind the knee can also suffer from strains, perhaps through over-stretching, riding a bicycle with the saddle too low, or through running too much, especially on hills or camber. Sometimes it is the bursa underlying the gastrocnemius tendon which becomes inflamed, usually as a result of friction from slightly awkward movements. In either case, there is usually a tender spot behind the knee, and you feel pain when you bend the knee fully or against a heavy resistance, or when you straighten the knee hard.

The Achilles tendon can be strained or partially torn through over-training: this can happen in any part of the tendon, so you might feel pain anywhere from the back of the heel up to where the bulk of the gastrocnemius starts. The injured area feels tender, and hurts when you go up and down on your toes, when you run, or when you stretch the calf and Achilles.

ACHILLES TENDON SORENESS

This is a common problem among runners, and is a kind of irritation of the tendon. You might experience the soreness in one or both Achilles tendons, just above the back of the ankle. At this level, the tendon has a very poor blood supply, and is particularly vulnerable to injury. At first, the pain might only come on after running, but later on it becomes noticeable during running. The affected tendons usually feel very stiff first thing in the morning, and very painful if you have to walk down stairs. But they ease out as you get moving, especially if you walk around barefoot, or in backless slippers or sandals. If you press the painful area on an affected tendon, it is acutely tender to touch, and may also feel thickened. There may even be a visible lump around the tendon. In some cases there is swelling in the grooves just underneath the tendon behind the ankle.

In the early stages, the pain and stiffness ease off as you warm up and start running, but they return towards the end of the session or afterwards. The morning stiffness gets worse if you carry on running without treating the injury and removing its cause. If the problem is allowed to develop, walking becomes painful, and you find it difficult to go up and down on your toes.

This injury is almost invariably caused by friction from the backs of your running shoes, and for this reason I call it the Achilles tendon friction syndrome. All modern running shoes have high backs, relative to the formation of the ankle joint (see p.60). Some styles of army boots, fell-running boots, cross-training shoes and walking shoes have the particular problem that their rigid seams cause direct pressure against the lower end of the Achilles tendon.

The high shoe backs or rigid seams do not *inevitably* cause the Achilles friction syndrome, but they constitute a threat to the Achilles tendon, and unlucky runners suffer for it. Some

High shoe backs can cause Achilles tendon soreness. The height should be no more than 2 inches for the average male runner, 1¼ inches for the female.

runners suffer the problem in one tendon, some in both at the same time. Sometimes one tendon appears to recover, then the other suddenly starts to hurt. It is not clear why the pain can be so arbitrary. Given that all modern running shoes have the pernicious high backs, it is only surprising that not all runners are afflicted by the friction syndrome.

Achilles tendon soreness can come on when you change shoes, if your new pair has higher, harder or differently shaped heel tabs from your previous style. It can also happen if your shoes wear down, so that you have insufficient cushioning under your heel. The problem may be associated with other factors, such as over-pronation in the foot, hip stiffness, or a previous injury to your knee or leg muscles, but friction from your shoes remains the primary cause of the specific pain pattern associated with the friction syndrome.

The friction can cause damage. Paratendinitis or peritendinitis (peritendonitis) are the technical names for inflammation in the tendon's covering (paratenon), whereas inflammation in the Achilles tendon itself is known as tendonitis. Friction may lead to minor tears in the Achilles tendon. In the worst of cases, the central part of the tendon may degenerate: this is technically called focal core degeneration.

FACTORS WHICH CAN CONTRIBUTE TO ACHILLES TENDON AND CALF MUSCLE INJURIES

- re-starting training too soon, without fully recovering from previous injuries to the calf muscles, Achilles tendon, knee or hamstrings on either leg
- previous injection(s) into the Achilles tendon
- fatigue: both generalized weariness and localized leg tiredness
- high-backed sports shoes
- thin, flat-soled shoes without enough cushioning in the heels
- shoes with rigid soles
- worn-down shoes
- shoes inappropriate to the running surface
- over-pronation or over-supination in the feet
- calf muscle tightness or weakness in either leg

- calf cramps, due to lack of sufficient fluids or electrolytes
- varicose veins
- calf tightness or cramping related to the menstrual cycle in females
- stiffness in the hip(s) or knee(s)
- insufficient warm-up, especially before speed training
- training after sitting still
- (females) training after wearing high-heeled shoes all day
- over-training, especially using explosive sprinting routines
- over-training on hills, road camber or track bends
- racing too often, or without sufficient preparation

DIAGNOSIS AND TREATMENT OF ACHILLES TENDON AND CALF MUSCLE INJURIES

Immediate treatment for any traumatic injury to the calf or Achilles tendon is ice applications or cold compresses. You may need to be taken to the hospital casualty department, or simply taken home. You will not be able to use the injured leg for driving, so you may have to organize transport, or someone to drive your car for you, so that you can lie down on the back seat of the car. You should try not to take weight through the leg, if it is very painful.

Calf muscle problems are diagnosed on the basis of the history of the pain and how it started, and on the clinical assessment (examination) of your legs. Traumatic injuries are relatively easy to diagnose, as you are able to tell the practitioner what accident happened to your leg, or what you felt happened, to cause the pain, swelling and/or bruising. If there is a tear in a calf muscle, the area feels tender when the practitioner presses it. In the first instance, you may be given a supportive bandage and advised to rest with your leg up for the first few days. It may be necessary to protect the leg by using crutches for the first three or four days, if walking is very painful. The crutches are discarded as soon as you can put your foot to the ground and take weight through it comfortably.

Calf muscle tears are usually treated with physiotherapy. I generally use only massage for the first phase. Later I use massage plus electrical muscle stimulation combined with active exercises. (I now never use passive modalities like ultrasound on the calf muscle at any stage, as I feel, among other reasons, that they can only help healing in a limited way, if at all.) Passive stretching exercises within painless limits are started as soon as possible, once you can put the foot down. Progressive strengthening exercises are then combined with the passive stretching to restore full function. Although you may seem to make rapid progress in the first two weeks following the injury, the whole recovery process can be quite slow, taking anything up to twelve weeks or even longer.

If the Achilles tendon itself is torn completely, the practitioner usually tests it by having you lying on your stomach, supporting your foot so that it does not flop (into dorsiflexion) and then squeezing the calf muscle gently; if the foot does not react by pointing slightly into plantarflexion, the

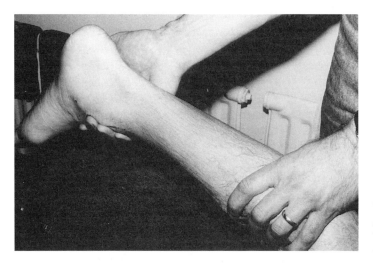

The Simmonds' (squeeze) test for Achilles tendon rupture: this tendon is completely torn just above the heel-bone

tendon is torn. Sometimes the gap in the torn tendon is obvious, and can be seen and felt. A partial tear in the Achilles tendon can be as painful as a complete tear, but the calf squeeze test (technically called Simmonds' test or Thompson's sign) produces slight movement of the foot.

A partly torn Achilles tendon may be treated in a similar way to the injured calf muscle. However, any significant tear in the tendon may need surgery to strengthen the tissues. Then the pattern of recovery follows that for the completely torn tendon.

For a totally ruptured Achilles tendon there are three possible types of treatment: surgery, protection in a complete plaster cast, or protection in a removable cast. If surgery is chosen, the surgeon tries to leave as small a scar as possible. If at all possible, so-called keyhole surgery is used, in which the tendon is stitched through a series of tiny holes spaced along its length: this is called the 'Ma technique' after the inventor. Following surgery, the tendon is usually protected in a plaster cast for several weeks. The exact type and size of the cast depend on the surgeon and the type of operation performed: for instance, some surgeons use a below-knee backless cast, whereas others enclose the whole lower leg and the knee as well. The cast may be changed after the initial healing period of ten to fourteen days, to alter the position of the ankle. While the leg is in plaster, you must look after the circulation (see pp.78–9), and report immediately to your doctor or surgeon if you notice any discomfort.

The option of treating the ruptured Achilles simply by immobilizing it in a plaster cast for up to twelve weeks is little used nowadays, because it weakens the whole lower leg, and therefore probably creates a greater risk of re-rupture at a later date. By contrast, protecting the tendon in a removable cast, as an alternative to surgery, is part of an active rehabilitation programme which can start from the earliest stage of the injury. The physiotherapist monitors the healing process for the tendon, does active treatments such as massage and diadynamic currents for any pain and swelling, gentle electrical muscle stimulation, and sets out careful remedial exercises to preserve the lower leg muscles which are not directly linked to the Achilles tendon. With this treatment programme, there is continual monitoring of the actual state of the leg and the torn tendon. Its greatest advantage is that it allows the patient to exercise hard, for instance for aerobic conditioning: this is because the tendon is fully protected in the cast, but the leg can be uncovered and washed in the bath or shower, so there is no risk of uncontrolled swelling or infection, as there is within a total plaster cast.

Whatever the treatment chosen for the ruptured Achilles tendon, physiotherapy and graded remedial exercises are essential for regaining full activity in the leg, and minimizing the risk of re-rupture. Full recovery from this major injury can (exceptionally) be gained within about fourteen weeks, but it is wiser to think in terms of six to twelve months.

Overuse injuries in the calf and Achilles tendon have to be carefully diagnosed by your doctor or orthopaedic specialist, in case you have problems other than an injury, or in case other factors are underlying the injury. Conditions which can cause pain in the lower leg include circulatory problems, gout, some food intolerance reactions (see pp.91–6), and pain referred from your hip or lower back. Once your injury has been diagnosed as an overuse strain, it is usually treated with physiotherapy: I use a similar regime to that for calf muscle tears. If over-pronation is a significant factor, custom-fitted orthotics may be supplied by the podiatrist. If hip stiffness has contributed, you have to do flexibility exercises for the hip region as well as lower leg exercises. In all cases, functional recovery must be complete before you re-start running, to avoid the risk of re-injury to the calf or Achilles, or of secondary injury to the knee, hamstrings or hip.

In all cases of Achilles tendon or calf injury your shoes can play a significant role, so you must be careful to choose shoes with a properly constructed heel counter and good cushioning under the heels. You must also be prepared to cut down the shoe backs, to avoid any impingement on the Achilles tendons.

DIAGNOSIS AND TREATMENT FOR THE ACHILLES TENDON FRICTION SYNDROME

Soreness caused by friction against the Achilles tendon is diagnosed on the basis of the pain pattern, including the severe stiffness first thing in the morning, the tendency for the pain to ease as you get moving, a sore tender spot in the lower Achilles, and perhaps a lump over the tendon, or swelling just around it. It may be that you have pain when you go up and down on your toes wearing your running shoes, but none if you repeat the movement barefoot.

The first priority of treatment is to eliminate the cause of the pain. High backs on your sports shoes must be cut down. The height of your heel is likely to be between one and two inches, so any extra height beyond this is too much. Extra cushioning may be needed under your heels, to relieve the pressure on your tendons and to raise your feet inside your shoes so that your ankles have room to bend unhindered. All your shoes have to be checked: if you have boots with seams which cut into or drag against the Achilles tendons, or day shoes which are a little higher than your ankles, pad them out under the heels. If heel pads cannot prevent the friction, you should discard those boots or shoes. If over-pronation is a factor in the problem, you may need corrective orthotics from a podiatrist, although these are not a substitute for correcting your shoe backs.

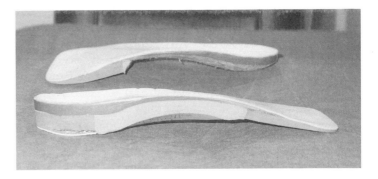

Custom-made orthotics, showing reinforcement to control excessive pronation.

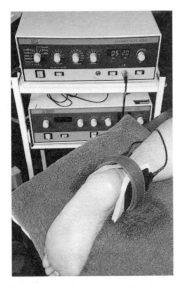

Diadynamic currents to relieve Achilles tendon soreness.

Physiotherapy treatment is aimed at the symptoms. The pain and any swelling can usually be reduced with ice, massage, diadynamic currents, and electrical muscle stimulation combined with active exercises. In the earliest phase especially, pulsed ultrasound can help. In some cases the problem of Achilles tendon soreness can be cured in one treatment session, if you make certain that none of your shoes impinge on the tendon any more.

In long-standing cases, some doctors inject the paratenon to relieve the pain: this has to be done very carefully and expertly, as injecting into the tendon itself can make it vulnerable to 'spontaneous' rupture, usually within a few weeks of the injection. If you have been suffering from Achilles tendon soreness for a long time, and there is bad damage to the tendon or its covering, surgery may be needed to clear away any debris, and perhaps to stitch the tendon if it has been slightly torn or frayed.

Surgery is not the first choice of treatment in the early stages because it inevitably causes a lot of discomfort, and recovery can take several weeks, sometimes months. Surgery is a waste of time if you do not also correct the backs of your shoes.

Sadly, it often happens that runners delude themselves into thinking their problems are over because they have had the Achilles tendon(s) operated on. For some time they can get away with wearing high-backed shoes, because the nerves are numbed by the surgical scar. However, when the pain recurs it can be both severe and demoralizing. This sequence of events has put an end to many runners' careers, even at élite level.

Once you have suffered from Achilles tendon soreness caused by shoe friction, you must remember that the problem will always recur if you wear the wrong shoes. This might happen if your running shoes wear down, if you buy new ones and forget to cut the backs down, or if you buy new day shoes which are a fraction too high. The warning signs are tenderness over the tendon(s), and especially stiffness in the tendon(s) first thing in the morning. If these occur, you must carefully check all the shoes you have been wearing the previous day, and if necessary cut them, pad them, or discard them.

Remedial exercises for the Achilles tendon and calf

1 Standing with one leg behind the other, feet slightly apart and parallel to each other, lean gently forwards, bending the front knee and keeping the back knee straight, to feel a gentle stretching sensation on the calf of the hind leg. Hold the position for a count of six, then relax. Do five to ten on each leg.

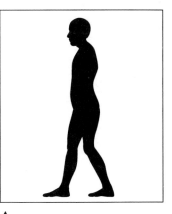

2 Standing with one leg behind the other, feet slightly apart and parallel, bend your back leg until you feel the stretch, hold for six, then relax. Do five to ten on each leg.

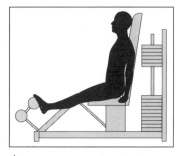

3 Standing with one leg behind the other, with the hind foot flat on the floor, and the toes of the front leg pressed upwards against a wall, bend the front knee so that you feel a stretch on the lower calf of the front leg, and along the whole calf of the hind leg. Hold for six, then relax. Do five to ten, then repeat with the leg positions reversed.

4 Sitting, barefoot, with your heel resting on a support and your forefoot on the edge of a weighing scale, press the ball of your foot downwards on to the scale, to measure how much pressure you can exert through the foot (not using your body at all). Hold for a count of three, then relax. Do five on each leg.

5 On a leg press machine, with light weights, straighten your knees out and use your feet to press the footplate downwards, controlling the reverse movement. Do five to ten repetitions.

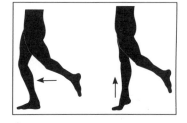

6 On a leg press machine, using one leg against a very light weight, keep your knee straight and press your foot down against the footplate, then control the reverse movement. Do five to ten on one leg, then repeat with the other.

7 Standing, preferably barefoot on a mat, with your feet slightly apart, go up on to your toes, then slowly down again, keeping your knees straight. Do ten to twenty.

8 Standing on one leg, preferably barefoot, keeping your foot flat on the floor, bend your knee as far as you can, then straighten your knee and go up on to your toes, then lower your heel and bend your knee again to repeat the cycle. Do five to ten consecutive movements on one leg, then repeat on the other leg.

9 Standing, steadying yourself with your hands on a support, place the ball of one foot on a weighing scale, with your toes held upwards off the scale. Transfer your weight on to the ball of your foot , keeping your trunk straight, and see how much pressure you can register on the scale. Do five on each leg.

10 Standing, preferably barefoot on a mat, with your toes off the floor, go up and down on the balls of your feet, keeping your toes off the floor throughout the movement. (You may need to steady yourself with your hands on a support.) Do three to six.

11 Standing on one leg, preferably barefoot, go up on your toes, then slowly down again, keeping your knee straight. Do five to ten on each leg in turn.

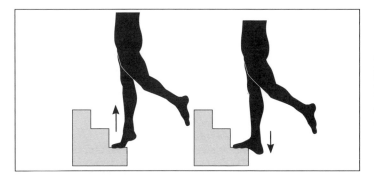

12 Standing on one leg with the ball of your foot on a step and your heel over the edge, go up on your toes, then slowly lower your heel downwards below the level of the step. Do five to ten repetitions on one leg, then repeat with the other leg.

SELF-HELP MEASURES FOR ACHILLES TENDON AND CALF MUSCLE INJURIES

- Follow the circulatory care programme on pp.75–8.
- Do not run again until you can go up and down on your toes, squat down and hop without pain.
- Cut down *all* your running and sports shoes: never run in uncorrected shoes.
- Use heel pads, arch supports and orthotics in all your shoes, as advised by your practitioner.
- Maintain good flexibility and strength in your calf.
- Always stretch your calves before and after every training session.

Shin problems

10

THE STRUCTURE AND FUNCTIONS OF THE SHIN

The shin consists of two bones, the main shin-bone (tibia) and the outer leg-bone (fibula), which are linked together by a strong fibrous structure, and surrounded by long muscles. You cannot actively move the shin bones in relation to each other, but they automatically slide slightly during certain movements at the ankle or knee. The shin-bone has no covering muscles at its front inner side, so you can feel the hard ridge of the bone with your hands.

The muscles and tendons of the shin region work the foot and ankle, but at the upper end the shin bones form the main attachment points for most of the major muscles of the thigh which activate the knee. Directly behind the shin-bones lie the muscles and tendons which point your toes and foot downwards, the calf muscles (gastrocnemius and soleus) with their Achilles tendon, and the long toe flexors. The main muscle which points your foot downwards and turns the sole of your foot inwards, the tibialis posterior, lies behind the inner edge of the shin-bone, while the peronei, which turn your foot outwards under the ankle, lie behind the outer leg-bone. The front outer half of the shin is covered by the fleshy anterior tibial muscles, which draw your foot upwards at the ankle. At the top of the shin, the patellar tendon (which anchors your quadriceps muscles) is attached to a prominent bump of bone called the tibial tubercle or tuberosity. The inner thigh muscles (adductors) are attached to the upper inner edge of the shin-bone, the hamstrings are attached

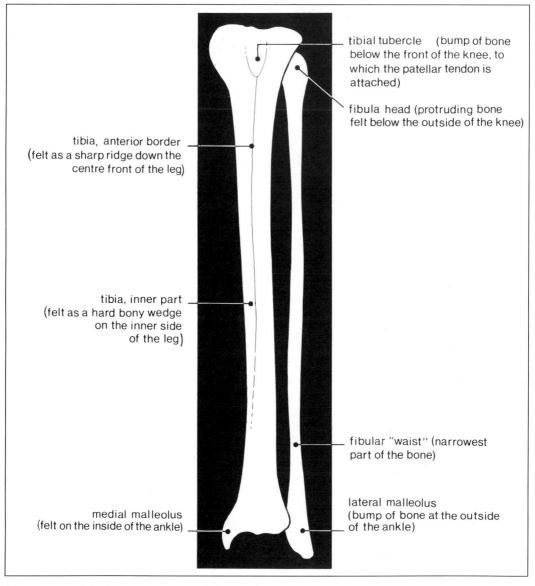

tibial tubercle   (bump of bone
below the front of the knee, to
which the patellar tendon is
attached)

fibula head (protruding bone
felt below the outside of the knee)

tibia, anterior border
(felt as a sharp ridge down the
centre front of the leg)

tibia, inner part
(felt as a hard bony wedge
on the inner side
of the leg)

fibular "waist" (narrowest
part of the bone)

medial malleolus
(felt on the inside of the ankle)

lateral malleolus
(bump of bone at the outside
of the ankle)

Shin structure, left leg from in front

behind the shin-bone and the outer leg-bone, and the ilio-tibial tract reaches the top of the outer leg-bone.

The balance of muscles in the lower leg plays an important role in the functional structure of your foot. If the anterior and posterior tibial muscles are not working efficiently and in harmony, the medial arch of the foot is not supported

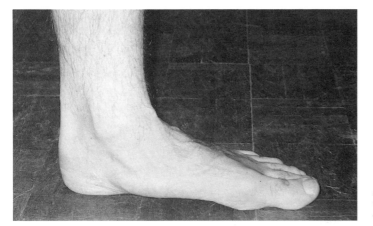

An over-pronated foot with flattened medial arch and stress on the inner shin muscles.

properly, and you tend to walk and run flat-footedly, in over-pronation. If your posterior tibial muscles (along the inner edge of the shin-bone) are tight, or the peroneal muscles are weak and over-stretched, the sole of your foot tends to turn inwards into inversion, and you over-supinate.

When you run, the shin is subjected to jarring, and to pressures from the muscles and tendons which are attached to the bones. As your foot lands on the ground, all the force of the ground reaction against your bodyweight is transmitted upwards from your foot through your main shin-bone. The outer leg-bone is not a weight-bearing bone (which means that it does not support your bodyweight when you stand, walk or run), but it is pulled inwards towards the shin-bone as your foot points downwards into plantarflexion, and pressed outwards as your foot comes up into dorsiflexion. The thigh muscles exert a pull in order to move the shin at the knee: for instance the patellar tendon pulls on the tibial tubercle at the top of the shin-bone in order to straighten the knee against gravity, whereas the hamstrings pull against the top of the back of the shin-bone and outer leg-bone to bend the knee.

There are also indirect forces acting on the shin. As your lower leg muscles, namely the long toe flexors, posterior tibials, anterior tibials (dorsiflexors) and peronei, contract to move your foot in the direction you wish to go, they also exert some pressure against the bones they lie close to, even though they do not create any direct action in those bones. If your shoes or insoles change your normal pattern of running they also alter the way the lower leg muscles and tendons interact, so the pressures absorbed and exerted by these structures are changed. (This may or may not be a good thing.)

SHIN INJURIES AND SHIN PAIN

A ny of the structures of the shin, whether skin, bone, liga-ment, tendon, tendon sheath or joint capsule, can be injured through trauma or overuse (misuse). You might fall and bark your shin, or you can be spiked by another runner during a track race. All shin injuries may be influenced by poor foot mechanics, and a few of the injuries might be directly caused by them. Therefore, if you have a shin injury, you might need to consult a podiatrist and have corrective orthotics fitted. Orthotics are not an easy cure, however.

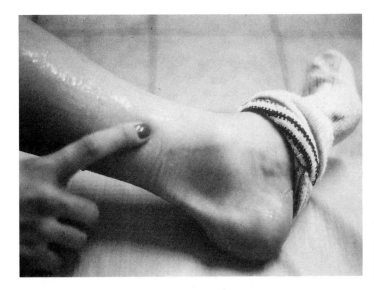

The most common site for shin soreness is the lower third of the shin-bone (tibia).

Every problem has to be properly assessed, diagnosed and, if necessary, treated. Remedial exercises are essential.

Other factors can play a major role in shin problems, such as poor circulation and varicose veins. Shin pain can be influenced by food intolerance (see pp.91–6), or caused by referred symptoms from the hip or back. Fortunately rarely, shin pain can be caused by diseases, including malignant tumours.

STRESS FRACTURES IN THE SHIN BONES

Because of the complex forces acting on them, the bones of the shin are especially prone to stress fractures in runners (see pp.102–9). The stress fracture is not caused by simple jarring forces. It is primarily the result of repetitive strain through muscle or tendon action against a bone. When a stress fracture occurs it is always due to over-training. The exact location of the stress fracture usually depends on the runner's style or patterns of movement. A stress fracture along the inner edge of the shin-bone may reflect a tendency to over-pronate, related to excessive stretch over the posterior tibial muscles, but it can equally occur if those muscles are tightened and you tend to over-supinate, turning the sole of your foot inwards into inversion. Runners who pull their feet up hard into dorsiflexion may suffer stress fractures in the area of the central ridge of the shin-bone, but this can also happen if you run with excessive inversion.

Stress fractures in the outer leg-bone (fibula) are very common and relatively easy to identify. As the bone is non-weightbearing, the fact that you have increased your running training, and that the bone is painful and tender to touch, can be sufficient to indicate that a stress fracture has happened. The most common site for a stress fracture in the outer leg-bone is just above the ankle, at the so-called 'waist' of the bone, where it takes the stress of moving inwards and outwards in relation to the shin-bone during ankle movements. Stress fractures can also occur in any part of the bone, up to its top end, so this always has to be considered when the outer leg is painful in a runner.

Special tests are usually unnecessary, as stress fractures in the outer leg-bone can be diagnosed fairly safely on the basis of the history of the pain pattern matched to the tenderness directly over the bone. The cure is about six to ten weeks' rest from running, combined with alternative painless exercise to stimulate the circulation along with the healing processes for the bone.

The inner edge of the shin-bone is possibly the most common region for stress fractures in runners. It can happen to runners of any age. Very often shin pain is classified as 'shin splints', or 'shin soreness', implying that the problem is some kind of benign bruising or muscle strain. In fact, all shin pain associated with running should be treated as a stress fracture until it has passed, or until proven otherwise. In the phase before the bone actually cracks, there may be inflammation over the covering of the bone, or periostitis. Although this is not a stress fracture in itself, it can develop into a stress fracture if it is not treated correctly. Remember that the main structure in your shin is the bone, so pain over it may well mean the bone is damaged, and ignoring the pain could mean trouble. At the very least, stress fracture problems which are not allowed to heal properly go on causing pain and limiting your running. At worst, fortunately rarely, the stress fracture can become complete, causing a major break in the bone, and landing you in hospital as an emergency.

All too often, runners treat so-called shin soreness with a few days' rest, and possibly ice. The pain apparently subsides, so they run again, and the pain recurs. And so it goes on – sometimes over several years. The pain may stay at a constant level, or it may very gradually get worse. What you should do, if you suffer from shin soreness, is to consult a sports medicine practitioner for advice. The practitioner will probably request a bone scan, to confirm or exclude the possibility of a stress fracture. If the bone scan shows a 'hot spot', and you have been over-training, this will be sufficient to confirm the diagnosis, and your practitioner will spell out the programme of rest and controlled exercise needed to cure the problem and bring you back into action. If you have not been over-training, your doctor may do other checks, including blood tests, to make sure you do not have some medical condition or bone disease.

Shin stress fractures may be treated with diadynamic currents, interferential therapy or high-frequency electromagnetic currents, all of which might help to reduce any pain and to stimulate the circulation, possibly helping the bone to heal. The main core of the rehabilitation programme is progressive exercise therapy, so the main physiotherapy treatment modality may be electrical muscle stimulation, to help the muscles and nerves work as efficiently as possible, and also to stimulate the local circulation. Massage may be used to reduce any muscle tightness and to improve the blood flow round the bone. If your circulation is very poor you may be recommended to use a foot vibrator each day, if you have to sit still for long periods. Sometimes special leg splints are fitted, to reduce the pressure on the bones as you walk or take part in sports. Ice is usually the chosen method of keeping any pain and swelling under control.

Shin-bone stress fractures take longer to heal than those in the outer leg-bone, so you have to rest from running for at least ten to twelve weeks. If you are being monitored by your doctor, you should wait until the repeat bone scan is clear. In most cases, monitoring may not be needed: you can be confident of curing the problem if you resist running for the necessary time, do alternative (painfree) training, such as cycling, swimming, gymnasium workouts or even sports like squash which use varied movements on a sprung floor. Above all, the secret of complete cure is to return to running in very easy, progressive stages.

MUSCLE AND TENDON INJURIES IN THE SHIN

Injuries to the muscles and tendons which work close to the shin bones can mimic shin soreness, so that the pain might not feel very different from that caused by a stress fracture or periostitis. However, the soft tissue injuries are identified by the pain they give rise to when the practitioner tests them against a resistance or stretches them, whereas the bone itself is not especially tender to touch. If you strain the muscles and tendons, you may be aware of having done an awkward movement, or perhaps of having done too much of one particular type of running drill during a session. You may also feel pain when you turn your foot or ankle in certain directions, whereas the stress fracture is usually painless on non-weightbearing movements.

Muscle and tendon injuries are usually treated with rest from running or any other painful activities, and physiotherapy, which may consist of ice (cryotherapy), massage, electrical muscle stimulation, or perhaps other modalities like interferential therapy, diadynamic currents, or high-frequency electromagnetic currents. In the earliest stages, ultrasound might be used.

Painless movements are begun as quickly as possible, and you gradually progress through stretching exercises and a strengthening programme for the affected muscle(s) or tendon(s). You should delay your return to running until you are sure that you do not have any pain or limitation of movement left over from the injury.

Compartment syndrome

Excess fluid swelling within the sheath which surrounds a muscle group can cause a typical pattern of pain: when the muscle group has been worked, for instance when you have run, the fluid gathers, creating tension in the region. Damaging muscle tension can also happen if the muscles are overdeveloped relative to their containing sheath. The tension leads to constriction, which creates pain. If you ice the area, the pain and swelling disappear very quickly. This situation can arise if you have injured the affected muscle group previously, causing a tear and inflammation. It can also happen if you have an imbalance between your fast and slow muscles, whether through unbalanced training or because you were born that way.

The compartment syndrome happens mainly in the anterior tibial region on the front of the shin, or, less often, in the posterior tibial region behind the inner side of the shin-bone. If you are a fast runner, and you tend to draw your foot up hard and land heavily on your heel, you may be more likely to injure the anterior tibial muscles in this way. The muscles along the inner side of the back of the shin can be injured if you tend to turn your foot inwards or outwards. It usually happens as an overuse injury, starting with only minor symptoms, but gradually causing more pain and limitation as you try to carry on training. Sometimes, however, it can happen as an acute injury, especially if you have hit your lower leg muscles very hard, causing severe bruising in them.

In the acute episode, the injury sometimes has to be treated as an emergency if the circulation in the leg has been badly disrupted. If you feel that your leg has gone numb, or feels hot and hardened after you have had a sudden injury like a bad knock against the leg muscles, you should be treated by your doctor or the local casualty department as quickly as possible. If the injury is a gradual, ongoing process, the diagnosis of the problem may simply be made on the basis of the pain pattern and an assessment of the balance of your leg muscles. If conclusive tests are needed, you may have stress tests done on the muscles, in which the pressure changes in your muscles are measured before and after you do some running.

The modern treatment for the compartment syndrome as an overuse injury is usually slow-pulse electrical muscle stimulation, which is often called functional electrical stimu-

Functional electrical
stimulation to treat
compartment syndrome.

lation (FES). This improves the condition of your slow-twitch underlying postural muscles relative to the faster overlying muscles, which are those most commonly affected by the compartment syndrome. It also improves your circulatory flow. After an initial phase of acclimatization, the electrical stimulator may be used on a daily basis for about an hour or more (not necessarily continuously). You have to rest from running while you are having the treatment, but you should be doing stretching exercises for the shin and any painless exercises, including weight training, swimming or cycling, during the recovery phases. Specific remedial exercises are based on slow, controlled movements, to enhance the tone in your underlying postural muscles. If deficiencies in your foot biomechanics have contributed to the problem, you may be fitted with orthotics by a podiatrist.

Full recovery may take up to three months, depending on the details of the problem, and how long you have been suffering. If it does not settle with conservative treatment, especially the slow-pulse electrical muscle stimulation, you may need surgery. The operation usually involves making a cut in the muscle sheath in order to allow the muscles inside more freedom, so that the previous tension and restriction are reduced. Following surgery, you have to re-train your leg muscles with remedial exercises, preferably under the guidance of a chartered physiotherapist (physical therapist) to avoid any recurrence of dangerous muscle imbalance.

Exercises for shin problems

The detailed exercises you will be prescribed for any shin problem will depend on what type of injury you have, and what stage it is at. The following exercises are movements which you should be able to do well and without any pain before you think of re-starting running.

1 Standing on the outer edges of your feet, walk forwards, backwards and sideways, about twenty steps in each direction.

2 Standing on one leg, go up on your toes as high as you can, slowly, then reverse the movement, with full control. Try to do five or ten repetitions on one leg, then repeat with the other.

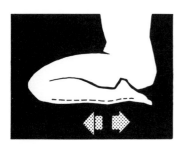

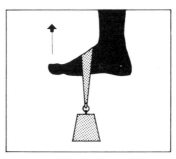

3 Kneeling down, sit back on your heels to stretch the front of the shin. Hold the position still for a count of six, then relax. Repeat five to ten times.

4 Sitting on a high support or table, with a weight over the top of your foot or a weights boot on your foot, slowly lift your foot upwards as high as you can, keeping your knee still and bent to a right angle, then reverse the movement, maintaining full control. Repeat five to ten times with one foot, then the other.

5 Standing on your heels with the balls of your feet held off the ground, walk forwards, backwards and sideways, about twenty paces in each direction.

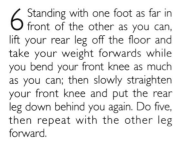

6 Standing with one foot as far in front of the other as you can, lift your rear leg off the floor and take your weight forwards while you bend your front knee as much as you can; then slowly straighten your front knee and put the rear leg down behind you again. Do five, then repeat with the other leg forward.

TIBIAL TUBERCLE INJURIES

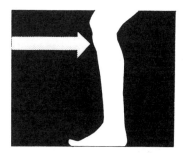

In young runners, the bone growth point at the top of the shin-bone, where the patellar tendon is attached, is vulnerable to overuse injury. Too much running (or jumping, football or basketball for that matter) can cause excessive strain through the patellar tendon against the tibial tubercle, and this can pull the growth area of the bone away from the main shin-bone. This sets up a pattern of gradually increasing aching and pain, associated with continuing running, jumping and kicking. This problem, technically called an apophysitis, has the special name, Osgood-Schlatter's 'disease', although it is not an illness as such. It happens, more to boys than to girls, between the ages of about ten and fifteen.

In older runners, a similar type of pain can be experienced through too much running, but it may be caused by inflammation between the patellar tendon and the tibial tubercle, or by a stress fracture in the tibial tubercle.

Once the problem has started, any activities which stress the patellar tendon cause pain. The pain may subside with a few days' rest, but it reappears very quickly if normal sports are resumed before full recovery has been reached. Treatment is generally directed towards the muscle balance in the lower leg and knee, so remedial exercises are set out, which may follow the pattern of the basic exercises for knee problems (see pp.178–9), with special emphasis on calf, front-thigh and hamstring stretching. Electrical muscle stimulation may be used for vastus medialis obliquus (p.191), to protect the kneecap joint. Especially in young patients, other forms of electrotherapy, such as ultrasound, are generally avoided. Ice treatments are probably the best way to relieve any special pain and tenderness.

If the problem is allowed to develop to a severe stage, the tibial tubercle may be pulled away from the main shin-bone by the pressure from the patellar tendon. If this happens, the bone has to be re-attached surgically. More often the problem can be easily controlled and treated conservatively. Rest from any painful activities is the main part of the cure. It is only safe to re-start running once the tibial tubercle is no longer tender or warm to touch, or painful when the knee is bent and straightened under load, for instance when you squat down. Meanwhile, any activities which can be done without pain are continued: these may include cycling and swimming. When your practitioner allows you to resume running, you must re-start in very easy stages and be sure to stop at any sign of a recurrence of the pain.

For the child going through the early teenage growth spurts it is particularly important to cultivate good muscle balance, and to prevent weakness in vastus medialis obliquus or tightness in the hamstrings. If these develop as an after-effect of Osgood-Schlatter's 'disease' they may lead to a series of secondary injuries, including kneecap joint pain (see p.185), thigh muscle injuries, and hip problems. In the worst of cases, there may even be long-term effects of continuing or recurring pain even after maturity has been reached. Once a young runner has suffered from Osgood-Schlatter's 'disease', protective knee exercises should be continued on a regular basis.

Knee joint problems

11

WHAT YOUR KNEE IS AND WHAT IT DOES

The main knee joint between the shin-bone (tibia) and the thigh-bone (femur) is technically called a condylar joint rather than a hinge, because it can twist on itself slightly, as well as moving backwards and forwards. The knee is fluid-filled: like other moving joints, it has a synovial lining which produces fluid for friction-free movement. It combines strength with mobility. Although the bones are not shaped to fit into each other closely, the knee is protected by very strong ligaments, which are specially thickened parts of the joint capsule. Right in the middle of the joint are two very strong bands, called cruciate ligaments because they cross over each other. On the inner side is the medial ligament, on the outer the lateral ligament, both of which are much stronger than the ligaments binding the back of the knee.

The kneecap lies over the front of the knee, forming its own (patellofemoral) joint, and the tip of the kneecap is linked to the top of the shin-bone at the tibial tubercle by the patellar tendon, which is the binding element of the quadriceps muscles on the front of the thigh. Inside each knee are two soft buffering pads called semilunar cartilages or menisci. (These soft cartilages are quite distinct from the harder cartilage which lines the bone surfaces within every joint.)

The knee is a vital weight-bearing joint when you walk, jump and run, whether in straight lines or changing direction (cutting). Besides helping body propulsion, it is also part of the shock-absorbing mechanism of your leg. When you run on slopes or steps, the knee takes most of the pressure through the action of your thigh muscles. When you run round bends on a track, the knee has to co-ordinate with the foot, ankle and hip as you lean into the bend.

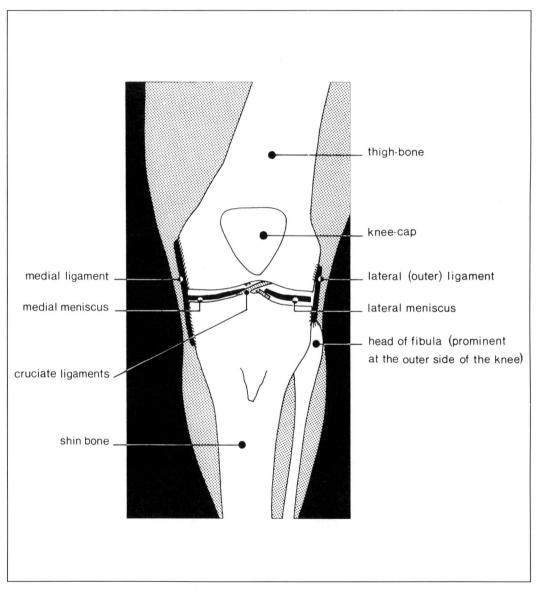

Knee structure, left knee from the front.

Traumatic and overuse injuries to the knee

How the knee can be injured

Because of its mobility, the knee is less stable than the ankle or the hip. It is particularly vulnerable to twisting or shearing strains. These can happen during running, if you stumble or fall, especially if you catch your foot at the same time. Traumatic knee injuries are more likely to happen through activities which place severe stresses on the joint, especially skiing, soccer, American football, rugby and motorcycling. A traumatic knee injury which has happened through a different sport or through an accident will inevitably affect your running. Running, in itself, tends to cause overuse knee problems rather than traumatic injuries. Over-pronation at the foot, whether caused by foot biomechanics or because of faulty shoes, can put extra stress on the inner side of the knee during running, perhaps causing strain in the medial ligament or the tendons which are attached just below the knee (the pes anserinus). Over-supination puts pressure on to the outer side of the knee, perhaps affecting the lateral cartilage, lateral ligament and the iliotibial tract.

What damage can happen?

A major injury can cause a break or fracture in the knee bones, or dislocation of the whole joint. It is usually obvious when the knee has suffered a serious injury, as there may be severe bleeding, excruciating pain and visible deformity in the bones. Other structures of the knee can suffer together with the bone damage: for instance, one or sometimes even both of the cruciate ligaments may be partly or completely torn; one or both of the soft cartilages (menisci) may split or fray; there may be tears or part-tears in the medial or lateral ligament.

Most traumatic knee injuries are less serious, even though they can be very painful at the time. If you twist or jar your knee you may feel immediate pain, and the knee may swell up instantly. In some cases, the knee feels all right immediately after the injury, but pain, stiffness and swelling develop later or overnight. There may be soft cartilage damage, cruciate injury, or medial or lateral ligament strains or tears. Quite often it is not obvious in the early stages of the injury how much damage has been done, or which tissues have been injured.

Overuse injuries can cause attritional damage to the same tissues. There may also be bone damage: repetitive strain can cause cracks in the bone, or stress fractures; chips of bone can break away in an avulsion fracture, where a strained ligament or tendon pulls too hard against a bone; in young runners, the bone cartilage surface can be damaged, causing osteochondritis; and in older runners wear and tear can cause a gradual breakdown (osteoarthritis) in the bone and cartilage surfaces forming the joint. Any knee injury at a young age can give rise to later osteoarthritis – although this does not necessarily happen.

What you feel

If you break any of the bones in a traumatic knee injury there is instant pain, and you cannot put weight on your leg to walk. There is usually immediate swelling, and sometimes visible bruising as well.

In the absence of major bone damage, however, pain in the knee is often a very imprecise guide to what is injured, or how bad the injury might be. You may not realize that there is internal damage until weeks after the injury has happened. For instance, total rupture of a cruciate ligament may cause only momentary pain, so the severity of the injury is not obvious until you realize that the knee is unstable. The instability is usually most noticeable when you turn slightly sideways while standing up.

A torn cartilage might only cause pain when the knee is bent and twisted in a certain direction. Sometimes a torn

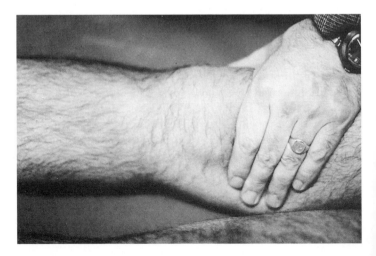

Knee swelling may be very slight, but it should never be ignored.

cartilage does not cause pain at all, but blocks knee movement with a 'locking' sensation when the joint is in a certain position. Once the knee has 'locked', you may have to free it by flicking the leg, or by manipulating the knee gently with your hands. Knee injuries can involve combinations of damage, so that, for instance, cartilage tears can happen together with ligament tears or strains. The structures on the outer parts of the knee give more localized pain when they are injured in themselves. If the medial ligament is strained or torn, you feel pain and tenderness directly over the inner side of the knee. Strains to the pes anserinus may feel similar to medial ligament injuries, but the tenderness is just below the knee joint. Patellar tendon injuries cause pain over the front of the joint, while lateral ligament and iliotibial tract injuries give pain over the knee's outer side.

The symptoms of overuse injuries are usually those of gradually increasing pain, sometimes together with slight swelling, which come on after or during running. As the injury gets worse you notice the pain at other times during your everyday activities apart from when you run.

In both traumatic and overuse knee injuries you may also notice that the joint feels warm to the touch, and sometimes looks reddened.

In every knee injury the most important damage is done to the nerve systems which control the joint's 'self-awareness', or internal co-ordination mechanisms, technically called proprioception. When the proprioceptive mechanisms are disrupted, the knee's controlling muscles no longer work efficiently. They become inhibited: vastus medialis (see p.185) stops working almost immediately, so you find it hard to straighten your knee fully. The other major muscles all round the thigh lose strength rapidly, and can shrink (technically atrophy) by about one inch in the space of twelve hours.

Surgery for the injured knee

Major traumatic injuries in which there is obvious damage have to be treated as emergencies: the victim must be treated with first aid and transported to hospital as quickly as possible.

After any significant injury to your knee, you should attend the hospital casualty department or consult your doctor as quickly as possible. If there is swelling it may be necessary to drain off (aspirate) the fluid, partly to relieve the pressure

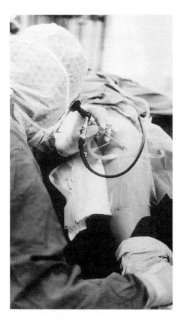

Arthroscopy of the knee.

on the knee, and partly to ensure that, if the excess fluid contains blood, it does not remain in the joint, as it would damage the bone cartilage surfaces. If it seems likely that the knee has suffered internal damage, such as a soft cartilage (meniscal) tear, the casualty officer or your doctor will refer you to an orthopaedic specialist surgeon.

The specialist may order X-rays and investigations such as an arthrogram (a special X-ray taken when dye has been injected into the joint to show up the soft tissues) or a magnetic resonance imaging (MRI) scan, which uses magnetic and electromagnetic fields to produce signals showing the state of the inside of the joint. Alternatively, the orthopaedic surgeon may decide to look inside the joint with a special instrument called an arthroscope. It may be possible to repair, trim or remove the torn cartilage through the arthroscope.

Surgery may be needed for other types of damage in the knee. When a cruciate ligament is torn, the surgeon has to decide whether it is better to reconstruct the ligament, either by stitching the torn ends or by inserting an artificial ligament, or by using part of another tissue such as the patellar tendon to make a 'new' ligament. If the medial ligament is completely torn, it usually has to be mended. A totally ruptured patellar tendon has to be mended as a matter of urgency. When the patellar tendon is badly strained, a painful cyst can form within its fibres; this usually has to be removed surgically, and very often the surgeon then reinforces the tendon with stitching.

If surgery is likely to be needed following any knee injury, it should be done as quickly as possible. Delay risks causing further damage to the joint surfaces, which in turn is likely to lead to osteoarthritis later on. There is no benefit in waiting to see whether the knee might get better, rather than seeking specialist help for accurate diagnosis and treatment. Since the development of arthroscopy it is now relatively simple to diagnose and operate on most sports injuries: the sooner the better, as early treatment makes the rehabilitation programme much easier and quicker to complete.

Treatment and rehabilitation

After surgery, or if there has been no immediate need for specialist treatment, you should treat any swelling in the knee with ice packs or cold compresses (see p.77) for as long as it lasts. You should also take care that food intolerance reactions do not contribute to the swelling (see pp.91–6). If the knee continues to swell for a long period after the operation or injury, especially if it is painful, you should ask your doctor to refer you to an orthopaedic specialist for a further assessment. If possible internal damage such as a torn cartilage has been missed, or if there has been a further injury, it should be dealt with as quickly as possible, to prevent continuing damage to the knee's bony surfaces. In some cases, such as medial ligament injury, an injection may help to reduce the pain and inflammation; electrotherapy treatments such as ultrasound can also help. However, any internal damage, such as a cartilage tear, will not be cured by this type of treatment, so it is unlikely that your specialist would try to inject the joint if internal damage is suspected.

Painless exercises have to be started almost immediately after the injury or operation: where possible, I always use electrical muscle stimulation to re-educate vastus medialis (see p.191). For most injuries, the exercise regime in the first phase of recovery is precisely the same as that for 'runner's knee' (see pp.178–9). The major exception to this is after cruciate ligament rupture, where special emphasis is placed on hamstring work, and the first phase of exercises usually gives priority to isometric contractions for the hamstrings holding the knee bent (see p.182). Remedial exercises should always be done under the guidance of a chartered physiotherapist, who can monitor your progress back to running.

THE ILIOTIBIAL TRACT FRICTION SYNDROME

This is an overuse injury which is sometimes also called 'runner's knee', although I prefer to reserve this name for anterior knee pain or kneecap joint pain (see p.185). Pain on the outer side of the knee, just above the joint line, is a common problem among distance runners.

What is the iliotibial tract?

The iliotibial tract or band forms a strong fibrous stabilizing structure down the length of the outer thigh, linking the outer hip muscles with the top of the outer part of the shinbone (tibia) and of the fibula. The tract moves forwards and backwards as your leg moves through the different phases of the running action. As the leg bends, the iliotibial tract helps

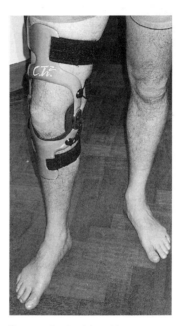

Support for the injured knee: a stabilizing brace is a must after certain knee injuries, especially cruciate tears. If possible, supports which totally enclose the knee should be avoided, although they may be necessary initially to control swelling.

the hip and knee to maintain the flexed position. When your knee is locked fully straight you can (usually) see and feel the iliotibial tract as a tense cord at the lower end of the outer thigh, because it stabilizes the knee in full extension.

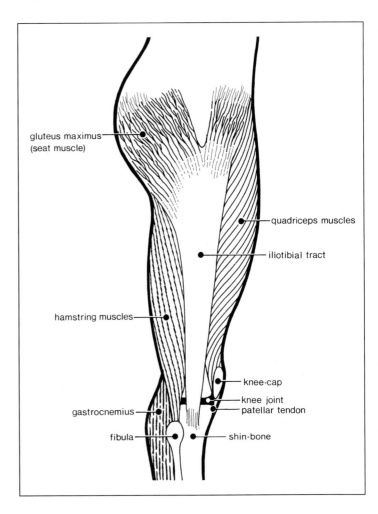

gluteus maximus
(seat muscle)

quadriceps muscles

iliotibial tract

hamstring muscles

knee-cap

knee joint
gastrocnemius
patellar tendon

fibula

shin-bone

Iliotibial tract on the outer side of the right thigh.

What causes the iliotibial tract friction syndrome (ITFS)?

As the iliotibial tract moves backwards and forwards close to the bone at the lower end of the thigh, inflammation can be caused by the repetitive rubbing of the tract against the bone. This is sometimes simply due to excessive running, especially if you have just built up your mileage. More often the friction syndrome is associated with a fault or a change in your running mechanics.

Any kind of abnormal stretch over the outer side of your leg, combined with the repetitive movements of running, can cause the problem. Causative factors can include hip, knee or ankle stiffness, over-supination of your feet, and running on camber or hills. The problem of over-supination can be caused or aggravated by shoes with too much padding under the arch of your foot, or which have become very worn in the outer parts of the soles. A blister or pain under the big toe or the ball of the foot can lead to over-supination, as can running on a slope or camber which forces the outer side of your foot downwards. Bow legs (genu varum) tend to stress the outer sides of the knees: while bow legs can develop from childhood, in the older runner they can develop as the result of osteoarthritis, or following earlier injuries to the knees.

The pain is caused by inflammation either in the fibres of the iliotibial tract itself, or in the bursa (natural fluid-filled cyst) which lies between the tract and the lower thigh-bone.

Because the lower end of the iliotibial tract is also attached to the outer side of the kneecap, tightness in the tract and friction syndrome pain can be closely associated with anterior knee pain (see p.185).

What are the signs and symptoms of ITFS?
Sometimes the first sign of trouble is pain over the outer side of the knee *after* running. More typically, the pain occurs after a certain time of running, perhaps after ten minutes or so. The pain is usually felt over one well-defined spot, but you might feel it radiating upwards and downwards along the thigh. At first, you may be able to run through the pain without too much discomfort, and you feel little or no pain after running. However, if the problem is allowed to get worse, the pain can become severe enough to stop you running. You might feel better with a few days' rest, but the pain can recur each time you try to run again. You may notice a swollen spot to the side of the knee, and there may be localized tenderness.

How is the problem of ITFS diagnosed?
You should consult your doctor in the first instance. You may then be referred to a physiotherapist, sports doctor or surgeon. Problems other than ITFS can cause similar-seeming

pain at the outer side of your knee, so your practitioner has to decide what the injury is, firstly through your description of the pain and how it comes and goes, secondly by a physical examination of the knee, thigh and hip, and thirdly, if necessary, through tests such as X-rays, scans or blood screening.

Your description of the pain is a good guide, because the pattern of the iliotibial tract friction syndrome is usually typical. Don't forget to mention any changes you have made to your insoles, shoes or training.

Your practitioner might test your leg for tightness in the iliotibial tract. In Ober's test, you lie on your side with your knees slightly bent; the practitioner bends your upper knee to a right angle, draws your leg back in line with your body, and then allows the leg to rest downwards to see how far it can drop from the hip. To test for localized tenderness, you are placed lying on your back with your knee bent to a right angle, and the practitioner presses against the lower part of the iliotibial tract while straightening your knee out. This is called Noble's test, and it is positive if you experience tenderness when the knee is brought to an angle of about 30 degrees.

What is the treatment for ITFS?

The first line of treatment is conservative, rather than surgical, and involves correcting any known causative factors, combined with physiotherapy to try to reduce the localized pain and inflammation. I have successfully used a mixture of several modalities: ultrasound, interferential therapy and Diapulse in succession during the treatment session, plus ice, massage, and electrical muscle stimulation for vastus medialis (see p.191). Recently I have been using ice, massage and possibly ultrasound to the painful spot, plus electrical muscle stimulation for the iliotibial tract and vastus medialis.

If the injury has been present for a long time, and there is very severe inflammation or damage to the iliotibial tract or the underlying bursa, surgery may be needed to solve the problem. This is followed by remedial exercises and a very cautious return to running.

Iliotibial tract exercises

In all cases, the patient has to do stretching exercises for the iliotibial tract, concentrating on those which give a good sensation of painless pulling over the outer thigh:

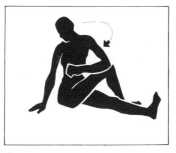

▲

1 Sitting on the floor, bend your injured leg up and place the foot on the outer side of your other knee. Gently press your injured knee over the other leg with the opposite elbow; hold for a count of six, then relax.

3 Standing, supporting yourself with one hand (on a wall-bar or table), move your injured leg in front of the other leg, hold for six, then relax.

▲

2 Lying on your back on a firm surface, pull your injured leg up with your hands towards your chest and over towards the opposite shoulder. Hold for a count of six, then release.

4 Standing alongside a wall with your injured leg closest to the wall and your arm and hand placed outstretched for support against the wall: bend your trunk sideways towards the wall, hold for six, then relax.

The stretching exercises should be done about six times each, three or four times a day at least, if possible. They should also be done before and after any exercise session.

Running has to be limited to the amount you can do without incurring any pain. You may have to alter your shoes or insoles, or invest in new shoes which correct any tendency for your feet to over-supinate. You have to avoid hills or camber, for the time being.

Do alternative training: you should be able to swim and do workouts in a gym. It is especially useful to do varied exercises for mobility and strength all round the hips and knees. You may or may not be able to cycle, depending on how severe the ITFS is. If you can cycle without pain, remember to have the saddle high to encourage full knee extension as you pedal.

How long does recovery take?

If the problem is at a minor stage, and you correct the causative factors accurately, you may only need one or two treatment sessions and a couple of weeks of reduced running to get over it. On the other hand, if the inflammation is severe to the extent that you cannot run at all without pain, it will certainly need several weeks' rest followed by a very gradual return to running.

As this injury does not in itself affect the main knee joint, it is unlikely to have any long-term consequences. For this reason, if there is an important event coming up, you can sometimes take the risk of running in it, even if you know you will feel pain during the race. This will certainly delay your full recovery for a while, so you have to weigh up exactly how much you really want to compete or participate, and whether it is worth the setback.

You must always be guided by your practitioner as to when you can run, and how much you can safely do.

OSTEOARTHRITIS, THE KNEE AND RUNNING

When wear and tear degeneration, technically called osteoarthritis or osteoarthrosis, happens in the knee, the damage on the joint surfaces is more or less irreversible: it can only get worse if you do activities which might harm the joint. Osteoarthritis can happen because of hereditary factors, but it is often a late after-effect of injury, especially if you did not make a full functional recovery. Wear and tear also happens as a natural part of the body's ageing process, and it can reflect your normal, habitual patterns of movement, especially if you have done a repetitive weight-bearing sport like running over many years.

Both the main (tibiofemoral) knee joint and the kneecap (patellofemoral) joint can be affected by wear-and-tear degeneration. The signs of osteoarthritis are slight swelling, especially after exercise; aching or pain during or after exercise, or at night; a tendency to ache when the weather changes, especially when it is damp or cold; and a gradual stiffening in the joint, which makes it look out of shape. In most cases, the arthritic knee tends to become bent (technically in fixed flexion deformity), and it may look bowed (genu varum) if the inner joint surface is badly damaged, or bent inwards (genu valgum) if the outer part of the joint is the worse affected. The kneecap can become very stiff, so that it feels as though it is glued to the bone underneath.

Exercise to maintain good strength, mobility and blood flow for the knee is vital to prevent osteoarthritis from getting worse. It is also vital to take regular exercise to avoid obesity. On the other hand, running, on its own and in itself, is not good for this purpose, because the movement of running only takes the joint through a limited range, and it involves jarring forces. This combination means that certain parts of the weight-bearing joint surfaces are subjected to extra pounding pressure, compared to other parts, and this can accelerate wear-and-tear degeneration.

Diet is also an important factor in controlling the pain of osteoarthritis, partly because you have to avoid overeating in order not to be overweight, and partly because your osteoarthritic joint(s) might be more vulnerable to food intolerance reactions (see pp.91–6).

For the middle-aged or veteran runner who is known to have osteoarthritis in the knee, the priority is to protect the joint as much as possible. This probably means that you have to give up marathon running, if that has been your event, although you may well be able to continue shorter distances. Your running shoes should have good shock-absorbing insoles, if you do not use custom-made orthotics. The shoes themselves should not be too thick, and should not aim to be corrective. You should do daily remedial exercises, using the early-phase programme (see pp.178–9) as the basis for a regular routine. You should also do alternative training, or cross-training, including cycling and swimming, for overall fitness.

In the worst of cases, the severely arthritic knee joint may have to be replaced surgically. This is a relatively routine operation nowadays, although less so than hip joint replacement. You can expect to stand and walk comfortably afterwards, but there is no guarantee that you will be able to run for training or competition again after the operation. So the best option is to preserve your own knee joint by treating it sensibly at all times.

Vital factors for controlling and preventing osteoarthritic pain

- Limit your running to one or two sessions a week.
- Limit the distance you run to the amount you can do without suffering any reaction of pain or swelling.
- Do an all-round programme of protective knee exercises every day.
- Watch your diet, and make sure it is well balanced.
- Cross-train, using a wide variety of exercise programmes.

Basic early-stage remedial exercises

1 Standing with your legs straight, or sitting on the edge of your chair with your leg stretched straight in front of you and the heel on the floor, or sitting with your legs up, practise tightening and relaxing your thigh muscles to twitch and relax your kneecap, three to five times, every hour.

2 Sitting on a mat on the floor, legs straight in front of you, or on the edge of your chair with one leg straight, heel on the ground, with your toes pointing vertically upwards, straighten your knee hard (backwards). Hold for a count of two, then relax completely for a count of six. Five times, at least three times a day.

3 Sitting on a mat on the floor, with your legs straight, toes pointing upwards, and a rolled towel or a small block under your heel, straighten your knee hard, pushing the back of the knee down on to the floor. Hold for a count of two, then relax for a count of six. Five to ten times, two to three times a day.

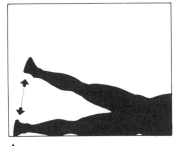

▲ 4 Lying on one side (opposite to the injured leg), keeping your body straight, lock your upper knee and lift your leg straight upwards, then slowly lower and relax. Do one to three sets of five to fifteen repetitions, two to three times a day. Use a heavy boot or gradually increasing ankle or foot weights when you can do this with perfect control.

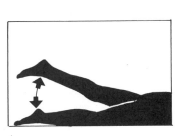

▲ 5 Lying on your stomach, lock your knee straight and point your toes downwards in line with your leg; lift your leg straight backwards a little way, lock the knee straight again, then slowly lower and relax. Do one to three sets of five to fifteen repetitions, two to three times a day. Add weights when you can do the movement accurately.

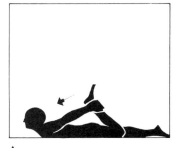

▲ 6 Lying on your stomach, with a folded towel under your thigh if you feel any discomfort over the kneecap, bend one knee and gently pull your heel towards your seat with your hand. Do not pull the knee into a painful range. If you cannot reach your heel with your hand, support the lower leg with the opposite ankle and lift it carefully backwards, or put a belt round the ankle and pull gently on that. Hold the stretch for a count of six, then relax completely. Repeat five to ten times, two to three times a day.

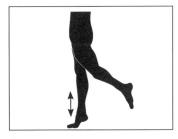

▲ 7 Standing on one leg, go up and down on your toes, keeping your knee straight. Do one to three sets of five to fifteen repetitions, two to three times a day.

◄ 8 Standing with one leg behind the other, keeping the back knee straight and back heel on the ground, bend the forward knee until you feel a gentle stretch on the hind calf. Hold the stretch for a count of six, then relax completely. Repeat five to ten times, two to three times a day.

Exercises for the stiff knee

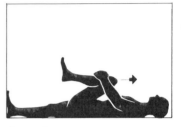

1 Sitting on a high support, let your knee swing backwards and forwards as far as it can without pain, twenty times.

2 Lying on your stomach, place the ankle of your uninjured leg under your injured leg. Gently bend your knees in a rocking movement backwards and forwards, as far as you comfortably can, twenty times.

3 Lying on your back, bend your injured leg up towards your chest, with your hands clasped round the top of the shin; gently pull your knee towards your chest, pushing it to bend at the same time. Repeat ten times.

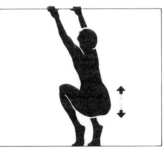

4 Sitting on a mat with your legs straight in front of you and a support under the heel of your injured leg, press down on your thigh to straighten your knee with a gentle rocking movement, ten times.

5 Standing up, holding on to a support, bend your knees in a bouncing movement as far as you can, twenty times.

6 On an exercise bicycle, with no resistance, set the saddle just below normal height, and pedal backwards and forwards to the limit of your knee's range. When you can make a complete turn backwards, practise until you can turn the pedal forwards. Then reduce the height of the saddle by one notch and repeat the process.

Strengthening exercises involving knee bending movements

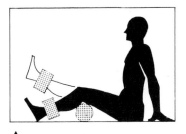

1 Use a leg press machine, if possible one leg at a time, although you may have to start by using both legs together. Start using small range (from about 30 degrees to full extension) then full range, straightening out the knee from the fully bent position. Do three sets of ten in each position, then gradually increase the weights.

2 Sitting on a mat with your legs straight in front of you, and a small support under your knee, with a light weight on your foot or ankle, straighten your knee fully, then slowly lower your foot. Build up to three sets of ten, then increase the weight slightly.

3 Lying on your stomach on a mat with a weight on your foot, or on a hamstring curl machine (with a folded towel under your thigh if your kneecap is sore in this position), bend your knee fully, then slowly straighten it out again. Do three sets of ten, then gradually increase the weight.

4 Sitting on a bench with a weight on your foot, or on a knee extension machine, with a rolled towel or wedge support under your knee, straighten your knee fully, then slowly reverse the movement. Do three sets of ten, then increase the weight in gradual stages.

5 Standing straight, go up on your toes and squat down quickly as far as you can without pain (keeping as relaxed as possible), then straighten up quickly and lock your knees. As you get stronger and more confident, vary the exercise by squatting down as slowly as you can, but still straightening up fast. Do one to three sets of five to fifteen repetitions. Gradually progress to holding light weights in your hands.

6 Standing on your injured leg, slowly bend your knee as far as you comfortably can, then straighten up fully again. Do five to ten repetitions with full control.

The hamstring-emphasis programme for cruciate ligament deficiency

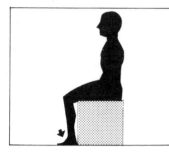

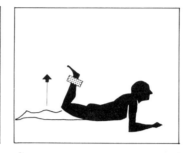

▲

1 Sitting on an upright chair, barefoot or in shoes, press your heel back against the chair leg, turning your foot slightly outwards at the same time. Hold for a count of three, then relax completely. Repeat five to ten times.

▲

2 Lying on your stomach on a mat, with a weight round your ankle, and your knee bent to a right angle, lift your leg backwards a little way from the hip, then slowly reverse the movement, keeping the knee bent. Repeat ten times, then straighten the knee. Build up to three sets of ten, then gradually increase the weight.

3 Lying on your stomach on a mat, with your knee bent to a right angle and a weight round your ankle, lift your leg backwards from the hip a little way, then take the leg out sideways, keeping your knee bent throughout. Repeat ten times, then rest. Build up to three sets of ten, then increase the weight gradually.

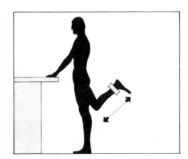

▲

4 Standing on your uninjured leg, with a weight round the ankle of the other leg, bend your knee as far as you can, keeping your back straight and your hip well forward, then slowly reverse the movement. Repeat ten times, then rest. Build up to three sets of ten, then gradually increase the weight.

▲

5 Standing on your uninjured leg, with the other knee bent and a weight round the ankle, take the injured leg backwards a little way from the hip, keeping the knee bent. Repeat the movement five to ten times, and build up to three sets of ten, gradually increasing the weight.

6 Standing with your back to a step, put your injured leg on to the step and step up on the one leg, then step down again, but do not put your other leg fully on to the floor. Repeat the movement five to ten times without a pause. Gradually build up to three sets of twenty.

Advanced-stage knee exercises

1 In shoes or barefoot, crouching on the floor resting your weight on your hands with your elbows straight, and your legs straight·out behind you; bend one leg to bring your knee towards your chest, then kick that leg straight behind you as you bend the other leg. Repeat the sequence in quick succession, alternating legs, twenty to thirty times.

2 Standing barefoot on a wobble board on your injured leg, slowly bend and straighten your knee, keeping your balance. Try to do five to ten repetitions.

3 In shoes, from standing up, bend your knees and touch the floor with your hands, kick your legs straight out behind you, bend your knees again, then spring upwards as high as you can, bending your knees again as you land, so that you repeat the sequence in quick succession. Try to do twenty to thirty repetitions.

4 In shoes, hop ten to twenty paces, first forwards, then backwards, then sideways.

5 In shoes, hop upwards on to a step (low at first), then hop down to land on the same leg. Start with five repetitions and gradually increase the number.

6 In shoes, run up and down stairs, leading with your previously injured leg. Start with ten steps, gradually increase the number, and then, if possible, try going up two steps at a time.

RETURNING TO RUNNING AFTER A KNEE INJURY

As the knee is a major weight-bearing joint, it has to recover full function before you can safely subject it to jarring stresses again. I strongly discourage any runner from simply putting on a bandage or brace in order to try and carry on training. Wearing an enclosing bandage can weaken the knee, making it more susceptible to further damage. And failure to regain full strength and mobility in the joint only

Uneven squatting: the full bend should be recovered through exercises if at all possible.

stores up trouble for later on. Apart from the long-term risks to the knee joint itself, there is the added, very real, danger of over-stressing the hip joint through compensatory movements and loading.

You are safe to return to running when:

- you can lock your knee straight, fully, and with control
- you can bend the knee fully when you lie on your stomach
- you can stand on the injured leg and go up and down on your toes, keeping the knee straight
- you can squat evenly with both knees.

There are situations when total recovery from knee problems is not possible. This might happen after a major cruciate ligament injury, for instance. In this case, your surgeon may recommend you to use a supportive, custom-made brace for sports. At the same time, you will have to maintain a consistent daily routine of remedial exercises to protect the knee. Running is one of the activities which may have to be limited, as the repetitive jarring involved can be damaging to the joint.

'Runner's knee'

'Runner's knee' is the term used to describe pain over the front of the knee, arising from the kneecap's joint with the thigh-bone (femur). The more technical names for the same problem include patellofemoral (joint) pain, patellofemoral pain syndrome, patellofemoral dysfunction, retropatellar pain, anterior knee pain, and chondromalacia patellae.

'Runner's knee' is a mechanical problem: if the kneecap (patella) deviates from its proper track when you bend and straighten your knee, it stops gliding smoothly, and sets up a typical pattern of pain. In the vast majority of cases the kneecap deviates outwards (laterally).

The most significant factor in 'runner's knee' is the failure of the muscles controlling the kneecap to hold the bone in its proper track. The kneecap is a small bone lying within the lower end of the quadriceps muscle group (part of the front-thigh muscles). It is anchored, together with those muscles, by the patellar tendon which links the lower tip of the kneecap to the upper shin-bone through the tibial tubercle. The key muscle for kneecap control is the only one to hold the kneecap from its inner edge: vastus medialis obliquus (often referred to as the VMO for short).

WHAT ARE THE SIGNS AND SYMPTOMS OF 'RUNNER'S KNEE'?

'Runner's knee' can affect one knee only, or both. It causes an ache or pain over the front of the knee, which feels as though it is right inside the joint. Very often it comes on gradually, and you begin to notice an ache over the front of the knee when you are squatting, crouching or kneeling. Sitting still for long periods can cause similar pain: this is often called the 'cinema (moviegoer's) sign'. Sometimes the knee gives a sharp pain when you stand up from sitting. It is usually painful on stairs, either going up or coming down, or both ways.

The pain may also come on suddenly and severely. It can either give you consistent pain while you are doing certain movements involving the knee, or it can occur as a sudden stab of pain which appears to happen at random during normal activities such as walking or running.

Sometimes the knee might feel as though it is giving way, although it does not buckle completely, and you do not actually fall over.

You will probably feel a grating or creaking sensation around the kneecap when you bend and straighten the knee. You might even hear cracking noises, especially on stairs. There is usually little or no swelling, although you may notice some puffiness on the front of the knee around the kneecap. In most cases the knee is not painful in bed at night, although it may catch if you turn over awkwardly.

If the problem has been going on for some time, you may notice that it is increasingly difficult for you to straighten the knee, and the back of the knee may become tight and tender to touch.

WHY DOES 'RUNNER'S KNEE' HAPPEN?

'Runner's knee' can happen to anyone, at any age. Sports, movements or postures that work or hold the knee bent without allowing it to straighten out properly can trigger the pain.

Training error is an important cause of 'runner's knee'. If you do too much of any exercise or activity which involves bending the knee under load, you create an imbalance in the knee's controlling muscles by over-exercising the major thigh muscles and under-exercising the VMO. This can happen through slow jogging, practising running round bends on the track in one direction only, walking or running on hills, slopes, stairs or camber, or doing excessive hopping and bounding exercises.

'Runner's knee' can also happen if you do weights exercises on a leg press or squat machine without locking the knees fully straight after bending them. Doing leg extensions without a support under the knee can block the joint from straightening fully. Cycling with the saddle too low, whether on a moving cycle or a static (exercise) bike, can cause the same problem. Similarly, the pain can result from staying in the saddle while pedalling up hills on a road bike, instead of standing up on the pedals.

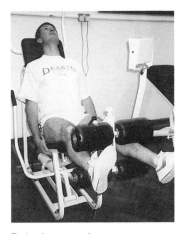

Doing leg extension movements without locking the knees fully straight can cause 'runner's knee'.

Muscle imbalance due to insufficient or inappropriate training can set up the conditions for 'runner's knee', especially if your calves, hamstrings and/or front-thigh muscles are weak or tight. If the iliotibial band on the outer side of the knee is tight, it contributes to the problem by helping to pull the kneecap outwards. Running down hills is a common cause of 'runner's knee', as few runners do enough eccentric training for the front-thigh muscles to mitigate the pressure taken by the kneecap joint. In some patients the problem occurs in the dominant leg, because it takes most weight; in others the non-dominant leg might be affected because it is weaker. Occasionally the problem happens in both knees simultaneously.

Body mechanics can play a part in the problem, including excessive foot pronation and stiff, in-turned hips. Growth spurts can also contribute, especially in teenage girls during the phase when their leg bones lengthen and their hips widen while the leg muscles remain relatively weak. 'Runner's knee' can follow an injury to the opposite leg, through overloading because you have favoured that leg.

Inactivity can also undermine vastus medialis obliquus and bring on 'runner's knee', if you simply hold the knee bent for too long without straightening it out, for instance if you have to sit still during a long aeroplane journey, or in a low armchair.

A direct blow to the kneecap can bring on instant 'runner's knee' pain, because VMO is immediately inhibited in this situation. Dislocation or subluxation of the kneecap can leave a legacy of kneecap pain, because of disruption to the VMO. In fact, any injury to the main (tibiofemoral) joint causes inhibition of VMO, so 'runner's knee' can be a secondary result of twisting injuries which cause internal damage, for instance to the knee cartilages or ligaments.

VMO wastes (or atrophies) more quickly than the rest of the thigh muscles, which can themselves reduce by up to an inch in the first twenty-four hours after a knee injury. It is also much slower to recover once muscle re-education exercises begin. Indeed, it is possible to strengthen all the other thigh muscles without affecting VMO at all, if you just do exercises such as straight-leg-raising upwards, or leg extensions. Because of this danger, it is vital to re-train VMO accurately after any knee injury, before returning to normal sport.

WHAT HAPPENS INSIDE THE KNEE IN 'RUNNER'S KNEE'?

The curious thing about kneecap pain is that the pain you feel rarely corresponds directly to any visible damage on the surfaces of the kneecap or the knuckle of the thigh-bone (femoral condyle). There may be obvious damage to the joint surface, such as chondromalacia patellae (degeneration in the bone cartilage), or osteoarthritis (osteoarthrosis), which is wear-and-tear degeneration of the joint surfaces. However, there may also be visible damage in the kneecap joint, but the joint can be free of pain. Conversely, there can be pain without any obvious joint damage.

The pain pattern of 'runner's knee' relates directly to the abnormal mechanics of the kneecap joint. As long as the kneecap tracks badly, you will notice pain in the situations described above. Once the mechanics of the kneecap joint are corrected, the pain disappears.

HOW IS 'RUNNER'S KNEE' DIAGNOSED?

What you say about the pain pattern and how it started suggests to your doctor or specialist whether your problem might be 'runner's knee'. Other possible problems may need to be excluded, such as inflammatory arthritis, infection, referred pain from the hip or back, stress fracture in the kneecap, hip injury (especially in young runners), or other types of damage affecting the kneecap joint surfaces, such as osteochondritis (see p.99).

The doctor or specialist may order X-rays, especially so-called 'sky-line' views done with the knees fully bent, to show whether the kneecap is drawn down and sideways when your

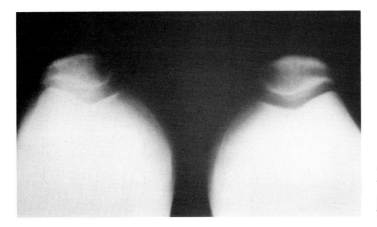

'Sky-line' views of the knee caps. The knee cap on the left of the picture is tethered slightly and tilted towards its outer side.

knee bends fully. Other tests such as blood checks may be done if there is a suspicion of inflammation or infection.

The physical tests done might vary according to the individual practitioner, but a general pattern could include tests and observation while you are standing up, lying (prone) on your stomach, lying on your back, and finally sitting up (reclining) on the couch.

When you are standing up, the practitioner checks whether:

- there is any obvious swelling
- your feet and legs align normally
- you can tighten and relax your thigh muscles to move your kneecap up and down with control
- you can hold your balance standing on the one leg
- you can balance on the leg, while lifting your other leg sideways a few times
- you can go up and down on your toes standing on the one leg, keeping your knee locked straight
- you can squat down fully, and without pain

You may then be asked to lie down on your stomach on the couch. If you experience pain when lying with pressure directly on the kneecap, the practitioner will place a support, such as a folded towel, under your thigh to lift the kneecap clear of the couch. The examiner then checks whether:

- the back of the knee is tight or tender
- your knee can be bent fully, passively (by the practitioner), without pain, and equally with your other knee
- you can lift your leg up backwards from the hip, keeping your knee firmly locked straight

When you turn over to lie on your back, the practitioner checks whether:

- your hips splay out symmetrically
- there is any limitation in the hip when it is pressed into the extreme angles of its range of movement
- pressure on the hip re-creates pain in your knee

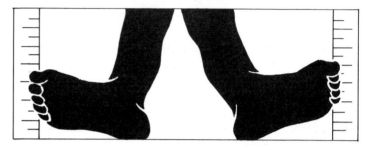

Checking foot splay to see whether the hips turn out evenly.

For the last part of the examination, you usually sit up to recline against the back-rest of the couch, with your legs straight in front of you. The practitioner tests whether:

- there is any warmth or swelling in your knee
- your knee is tight or lax as it is pulled passively (by the practitioner) into its straightest position
- your kneecap glides properly in its track as you tighten and relax your thigh muscles to straighten your knee
- you can control your thigh muscles to straighten your knee
- you can lock your knees fully straight
- the kneecap is painful if it is pressed down against the thigh-bone
- there is pain if the practitioner blocks the top of the kneecap while you try to contract your thigh muscles to straighten the knee, drawing the kneecap upwards (this is called 'Clarke's sign')

How is 'runner's knee' treated?

The usual line of conservative (non-surgical) treatment is to try to correct the faulty kneecap mechanics which cause the pain of 'runner's knee'. Passive treatments aimed at 'curing' the damage, such as perhaps ultrasound or hydrocortisone injections, are very rarely used nowadays. Practitioners may use different treatment systems. One very popular method is the 'McConnell technique', which involves taping the kneecap and practising controlled eccentric exercises. If faulty foot mechanics have a part in the problem, orthotics may be fitted by a podiatrist (although the orthotics are unlikely to effect a cure by themselves).

Surgery might be needed if the pain is long-standing and severe. The most commonly used operation for 'runner's knee' is probably the lateral release, in which a small cut is made internally to free the tissues which hold the outer side of the kneecap, in order to allow the kneecap greater freedom of movement. It is rare for surgeons to scrape the back of the kneecap smooth any more, as this tends to create a lot of pain in itself. If the knee alignment is particularly poor, the surgeon may perform a more complicated operation, to move the attachment of the patellar tendon over, to allow it to pull the kneecap in a straighter line.

After any surgical procedure for 'runner's knee', accurate rehabilitation is vital. It is all too common for a well-performed operation to fail simply because the rehabilitation has been inadequate.

My own treatment regime is to use electrical muscle stimulation to revive the VMO muscle, whether the patient is being treated conservatively (without surgery) or after an operation. If at all possible, when a patient is due to have surgery, I try to start the process pre-operatively, before the patient actually has the operation. If there is tightness at the back of the knee, or in the iliotibial band at the side of the thigh, I release this with massage. If there is noticeable puffy swelling around the kneecap I use ice treatment (cryotherapy) or sometimes diadynamic electrical currents to reduce it. When the kneecap is especially stiff, or tilted downwards (usually towards its outer side), I manipulate to free it.

I use the electrical muscle stimulation to encourage precise function in VMO. With the electrical current giving intermittent impulses, the patient performs three different kinds of muscle work. One is to tighten the thigh muscles just enough to twitch the kneecap, without activating the outer (lateral) thigh muscles. The second is to straighten the knee hard (into hyperextension), pressing the knee down while the foot is pointed upwards: the heel should lift slightly off the couch. The third is to do the same active hyperextension effort, with a support under the heel to give some leverage, so that the patient actively presses the back of the knee into the couch.

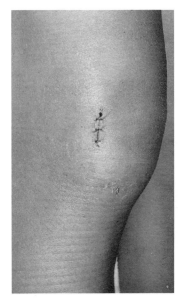

The scar from the lateral release operation.

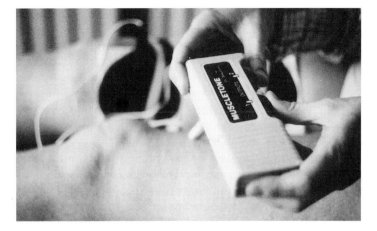

A small muscle stimulator suitable for home use.

In all cases, the muscles have to relax fully after each contraction. The patient works in sets of four to six contractions, with a rest between sets, for anything up to forty-five minutes, once he or she is used to this type of active treatment.

The electrical muscle stimulation may be repeated on a daily basis, or just once a week or fortnight, depending on how badly VMO is inhibited or weakened. For long-standing cases where recovery threatens to be slow, I often recommend the patient to use a small muscle stimulator at home. The muscle work is backed up by a routine of remedial exercises designed to help VMO gain proper co-ordination with the rest of the thigh and calf muscles. These early-stage exercises, in fact, form the basic programme for most knee injuries (see pp.178–9). Once VMO is working properly, so that the kneecap tracks better and there is no pain on such movements as going up and down stairs, controlled exercises working the knee through the bent position are added to the exercise programme. The early-stage, so-called 'straight-leg', regime has to continue until full recovery is achieved, and preferably indefinitely beyond that, if possible. The problem is over when you can do all the previously painful movements without pain, especially the full squat.

Recovery may be quick, within a day or two of starting the remedial programme, or slow, extending over ten or twelve weeks, perhaps even longer. If there seems to be no progress, you may be referred to a specialist for further checks, in case you are one of the small percentage of patients who will need surgery, or in case you have a more complicated problem than 'runner's knee'.

Self-help measures for 'runner's knee'

1 Avoid any painful activities. You may have to stop running, unless you can do short, fast sessions without pain.

2 Use ice to control any soreness, pain or swelling.

3 If you have to sit down for long periods, try to stretch your legs out at frequent intervals.

4 Try to sit on high upright chairs, rather than low lounge seating or sofas.

5 When you go up stairs, lead with your 'good' leg, and try to push off your toes to straighten the knee on your painful leg.

6 Going down stairs, walk slightly sideways to avoid full pressure on your kneecap.

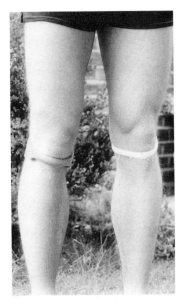

7 Use a patellar strap (which can simply be a small strip of rolled-up tubular bandage), just under the tip of the kneecap, if this relieves your pain.

8 If you normally cycle to school or work, raise your saddle as high as possible. Stand up in the pedals whenever you ride up a hill. If cycling still hurts, you should try to avoid it for the time being.

9 If driving a car or van causes pain, extend the car seat backwards as far as possible, so that your leg is almost straight as you depress the pedal or foot brake. It may help to sit on a cushion, so that your legs extend slightly downwards towards the pedals. If driving a manually operated (gear-shift) car causes problems, you may have to try driving an automatic, or you may have to avoid driving.

10 Do your remedial exercises regularly. Even if both knees are painful, do them on one leg at a time at first. When you have gained good control of VMO on both legs, you can then exercise them simultaneously.

11 Use your electrical muscle stimulator regularly, if you have been advised to do so by your physiotherapist or other practitioner.

12 Do not try to progress to harder exercises or running before your practitioner allows you to. If in doubt or pain, refer back to your practitioner.

Avoiding recurrence of 'runner's knee'

Once you have returned to running, the problem of 'runner's knee' may recur, if you neglect some safety factors:

1 Run fast, or relatively fast, for at least some of your programme, rather than jogging slowly all the time.

2 On longer runs, run sideways in each direction for short spells.

3 Avoid hill running, practising bends on the track or running on camber, in the early stages following recovery.

4 If you do sessions involving hills or track bends, space them out, never try to repeat them on consecutive days, and try to end each session with some of the early-stage remedial exercises, or a session using the muscle stimulator for VMO.

5 Be careful not to overdo other activities which place a lot of load on the bent knee, such as squash, field hockey, aerobics, fencing, or riding a bicycle. Try to do your remedial exercises after any sessions of these.

6 If you ride a bicycle, whether pushbike, racer or static exercise bike, keep the saddle as high as possible, and stand out of the saddle whenever you are pedalling hard or going up a hill.

7 Try to balance any knee-bending activities with knee-straightening movements, if possible.

8 Try to maintain the basic 'straight-leg' exercises, or a session using the muscle stimulator for VMO, especially if there is any hint of the pain recurring.

9 If you cannot relieve any soreness with the exercises, and perhaps muscle stimulation at home, refer back to your practitioner as quickly as possible for advice and treatment.

Hamstring injuries

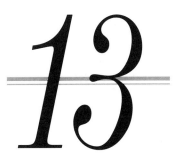

WHAT THE HAMSTRINGS ARE AND WHAT THEY DO

The hamstrings are three muscles with long tendons which link your seat-bone (ischial tuberosity) with the back of your knee, stretching over the length of the back of the thigh. They cross two joints, and act to draw the hip backwards (technically into extension), and to bend the knee (into flexion).

Hamstring efficiency is vital for a smooth running action. When one foot makes contact with the ground, the hamstrings work to provide stability for the knee and to extend your hip, as your weight is transferred forwards. As the leg is lifted off the ground, the hamstrings contract and shorten to bend the knee – this movement is often referred to as 'picking your knees up'. As you bring your leg forwards through the air towards the next heel-strike (or toe-strike), your hamstrings pay out (technically they act partly *passively* and partly *eccentrically*) as your front-thigh muscles come into play, but they then have to work actively again to bring your leg backwards from the hip and to control your leg as your foot reaches the ground. In sprinting, during the final phase of this eccentric contraction, the hamstrings contract extremely hard to decelerate the leg before the foot strikes the ground.

The efficiency with which you can kick your heels upwards to your seat during the leg-swing phase when your foot is off the ground is an important factor determining your speed. The closer your heel comes to your buttock before your leg swings through to strike the ground again, the faster you run. If your hamstrings become fatigued in the course of a run, your heel-kick becomes less effective, and you slow down.

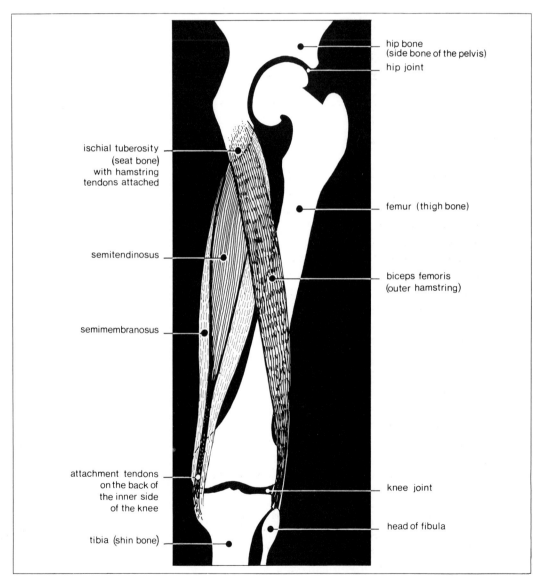

Hamstrings, back of right thigh.

REASONS WHY HAMSTRING INJURIES HAPPEN

The hamstrings are active through each phase of the running action, and they have the complicated role of acting both to draw your leg backwards and to bring your heel towards your seat. Because of this, they tend to become both fatigued and shortened, if you do a lot of running. This is why hamstring injuries are so common among runners. Sprinters tend to get sudden tears, whereas distance runners suffer niggling overuse injuries.

Usually there are several background factors involved in hamstring injuries, which can include:

- Tightness in one or more of the hamstring muscles. This might be because you have not been training regularly, especially if you have to sit down most of the time for studies or your job. Cramp can contribute to hamstring tightness, so you must make sure you are drinking enough plain water, perhaps combined with some electrolytes, all day, every day. If the hamstrings are relatively short, and you try to stretch your leg fully forwards, forcing your hip to bend and extending your knee, part of the muscle group may be over-stretched, causing it to strain or tear. This might happen if you are trying too hard to stretch the hamstrings, or if you are running fast and over-striding.

- Weakness in the hamstrings. This can contribute to strains or tears through overuse. The problem is greater if the front-thigh muscles are relatively strong compared to the hamstrings, making you think that you can run further or faster than your hamstrings can in fact manage. You may not realize how much of a limiting factor your weak hamstrings are.

- Fatigue. This can be linked to muscle weakness: if you have run further or faster than your hamstrings' capacity for endurance, part of the muscle group may strain or tear.

- Inadequate warm-up.

- Previous injuries to other leg muscle groups. Secondary injuries in the hamstrings can follow other muscle injuries. If you do not regain full strength and co-ordination after calf muscle or Achilles tendon injuries, for instance, you will almost certainly use compensation and cause overload in the hamstrings if you try to do normal running training.

- Joint problems. Injuries to the back, hip or knee can affect the way the hamstring muscles work. Both back and hip problems can lead to referred nerve pain affecting the back of the thigh, which can contribute to hamstring muscle tightness and weakness. Any knee injury causes inhibition and weakening in all the thigh muscles: if you concentrate on re-strengthening the front-thigh muscles alone, without also working on the hamstrings, you create a potentially damaging muscle imbalance.

- Training errors. A common mistake is to neglect specific training for the hamstrings, and to do too much overload training involving the front-thigh (quadriceps) and seat (gluteal) muscles, such as hill running, hopping, bounding, or squats with weights.

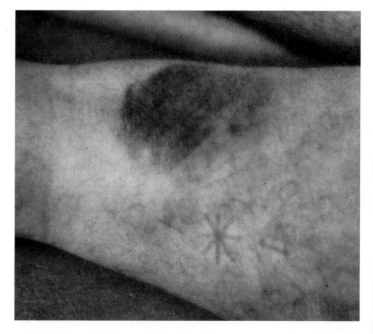

Bruising from a hamstring tear has tracked away from the injury, which is marked by a star.

How do hamstring injuries happen?

Sudden tears in the hamstrings can happen in explosive events like sprinting. The runner feels a sudden very sharp pain, and may even hear or feel a 'bang'. When this happens, the pain pulls you up short, and may even cause you to fall over.

Overuse strains or 'pulls' can happen to sprinters, longer-distance runners and joggers. The runner feels an ache or pain over the back of the thigh, either during running or immediately afterwards. Once the problem has started, you usually feel increasing pain with every run, and during any activities which stress or stretch the hamstrings. You may even feel a soreness if you sit still on a hard upright chair.

How are hamstring injuries diagnosed?

When you consult your doctor or physiotherapist with pain in the back of your thigh, the first clue to what you have done comes from your description of how the pain started, exactly what you were doing at the time, and what you felt. If one or more of the hamstrings are strained or torn, you will be able to describe the exact time and place when the injury happened. On the other hand, if the pain has come on more subtly, and you have felt it in different situations, such as sitting down, or resting at night, then your practitioner might suspect that your back or hip could be involved.

When your doctor or physiotherapist examines you, your leg will be tested through different kinds of stress. You may be asked to do balancing and knee-bending movements standing up: these tests show the extent of any hamstring damage, and whether the hip or knee might be involved. Lying on your stomach on the couch, you may be asked to work the hamstrings against the manual resistance of the practitioner's hand: you might bend your knee first, then lift your leg straight up backwards from the hip, and then lift the leg up from the hip with the knee held bent. Any or all of these movements may cause pain if there is injury to the hamstring muscles. With you lying on your back, the practitioner may lift each leg in turn gently up in the air, keeping the knee straight, to test whether there is tightness and painful restriction in the injured leg. If there is, the practitioner will probably also do checks on your hip and back to see whether you might have referred pain from a joint problem together with or instead of a hamstring injury.

HOW ARE HAMSTRING INJURIES TREATED?

Most hamstring injuries can be treated by a chartered physiotherapist (physical therapist). In the acute stage, when the injury has just happened, taping may be used to restrict movement and protect the muscles, if you are in severe pain. You might even have to use crutches for the first few days.

You should use ice over the injury, and your physiotherapist might use ice massage or ice packs as part of your treatment sessions. Various electrotherapy treatments might be used in the early stages, such as ultrasound, diadynamic therapy, interferential, electromagnetic energy, or low-intensity electrical muscle stimulation.

You have to start carefully controlled stretching exercises as soon as the initial discomfort has subsided enough to allow painless movement.

For the milder tear, the overuse strain, or the later stages of the traumatic tear, the treatment might be massage around and over the injured area, and electrical muscle stimulation combined with painless active hamstring contractions. (Ultrasound, for instance, is usually not used after the very first stages of the injury.)

If your back and/or hip are also involved in the injury, your practitioner will do appropriate treatments according to the situation. You might have lumbar traction, in which your back is gently stretched on a special couch to relieve pressure on the nerves. Or you might be treated with different kinds of manipulation.

Surgery is needed in a very small minority of cases. For instance, if there is a tear at, or close to, the attachment point of the hamstrings on the seat-bone, a chip of bone can be broken off in an avulsion fracture, and this may need to be fixed or removed.

Exercise therapy

In all cases, the injured hamstrings have to be properly re-
trained before it is safe to start running again. The rehabilitation programme combines stretching with strengthening
exercises. The stretching exercises are the start of the remedial programme. Later on, they are done before and after any
strengthening exercises, and similarly before and after any
other type of exercise or training session. The strength
training usually starts with isometric contractions within pain
limits (see p.87), followed by active concentric and eccentric
contractions against increasing loads or weight-resistance,
and culminating in dynamic exercises which progressively
test the hamstrings. The exercises are primarily for the injured leg, but they can also be done with the uninjured leg,
for balance, if you take care to do more exercises and repetitions on the injured leg.

The exercises are usually devised to protect the back, as it
is all too easy to strain the back by carelessly over-stretching
the hamstrings. You may also be prescribed back exercises
(see pp.232–4), if the hamstring injury has involved the spine.
At all stages of recovery you have to take care to avoid any
painful movements, and only to do your remedial exercises
within pain limits. If in doubt, always be guided by your doctor, chartered physiotherapist or the particular practitioner
who is treating you.

REMEDIAL HAMSTRING EXERCISES

Stretching exercises

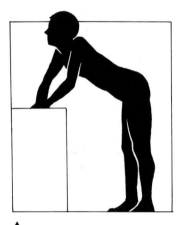

▲
1 Standing up, lean forwards to rest your hands on a support (such as a bar or table); lock your knees straight and lean gently forwards, keeping your back straight, head up, legs as vertical as possible (don't let your seat drift backwards). When you feel a gentle stretch at the backs of your thighs, hold the position for a count of six, then relax. Repeat three to five times.

▲
2 Standing with the foot of your injured leg on a low support, about six inches off the ground, lock your knee straight, point your toes upwards and lean gently forwards keeping your back straight and your head up. Hold for six, then relax. Repeat three to five times.

3 Standing in the same position as for (2), turn your leg outwards to localize the stretch on to the outer hamstring muscle (biceps femoris): lean gently forwards, keeping your back straight, head up, toes pointing upwards. Hold for six, then relax. Repeat three to five times.

4 Standing as for (2), turn your foot inwards to localize the stretch to the inner hamstrings: lean gently forwards, back straight, head up, and toes pointing upwards. Hold for six, then relax. Repeat three to five times.

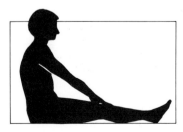

◀
5 Sitting with your legs straight in front of you, toes pointing vertically upwards; lean gently forwards, keeping your back straight, head up. Hold the stretched position for a count of six, then relax. Repeat three to five times.

Strengthening exercises

1 Lying on your stomach, with a pillow under your hips, lift the injured leg backwards from the hip a little way, keeping the knee locked straight; slowly lower. Do five to fifteen repetitions. Once the exercise feels easy, you can use (gradually increasing) weights round your ankle or foot.

2 Lying on your stomach with a pillow under your hips, bend the knee of your injured leg, then slowly lower the leg back to the starting position. Repeat five to fifteen times. Add ankle or foot weights when the exercise is easy, or progress to using a hamstring curl weights machine in the gymnasium.

3 Lying on your stomach with a pillow under your hips, bend the knee of your injured leg backwards as fast as you can, trying to touch your seat with your heel, straightening the leg out fully on the reverse movement. (If you cannot reach your seat with your heel, put a cushion or thick book on your buttocks and kick back to touch that.) Repeat twenty times in quick succession.

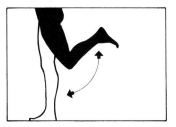

4 Lying on your stomach with a pillow under your hips and the knee on your injured leg bent, lift your injured leg backwards from the hip, keeping the knee bent, then slowly lower. Repeat five to fifteen times, and add ankle or foot weights when the exercise feels easy.

5 Kneeling on all fours, lift your injured leg backwards from the hip five to fifteen times in quick succession, returning to the starting position between each movement. Add foot or ankle weights when the exercise feels easy.

6 Standing, holding a support, extend the injured leg backwards from the hip, bend the knee to try to touch your heel to your seat, then slowly lower the leg to the starting position, keeping your back straight and slightly arched throughout the movement. Repeat five to ten times, and add foot or ankle weights when the exercise feels easy.

7 Pedal on an exercise bicycle, with the saddle as high as is comfortable. Start with five minutes at low resistance, building up to twenty minutes and gradually increasing the resistance over a few sessions.

8 Lying flat on your stomach, kick your heels to your seat alternately twenty times each, trying to keep a constant, rapid rhythm.

Co-ordination exercises

Hydrafitness step machine.

1 On a step machine (or stair climber), work for five minutes at medium pace, gradually increasing the time up to twenty or thirty minutes.

2 Run backwards, in a straight line. Start with short distances, slowly at first, then run faster. Take care not to bump into objects or trip over.

3 Run backwards in figure-of-eight patterns, gradually building up speed and distance.

4 Do 'strides', running forwards taking as long steps as you can, without over-stretching your leading leg.

5 In a pool, with water up to your waist or chest, or using a 'wet-vest' in the deep end, walk forwards and backwards, gradually increasing your speed. Pace yourself with short bursts of effort during a thirty-minute session, alternating the exercise with swimming, preferably crawl.

6 'Flick-ups': standing straight, run on the spot, kicking your heels as hard as possible towards your seat. Do ten to twenty movements, building up gradually to ten sets of twenty.

7 'Kick-backs': run forwards in a straight line, kicking your heels to your seat. Start with ten to twenty steps, then build up gradually to ten sets of twenty movements.

8 Hop forwards then backwards on one leg. Build up the number of hops on each leg.

9 Do bounding: drive off one leg, holding the forward leg horizontally as far as possible, so that you land rather flat-footedly to drive off again from the landing leg. Start with sets of ten bounds, and build up the number gradually.

Front-thigh injuries

THE MUSCLES OF THE FRONT-THIGH AND WHAT THEY DO

The main bulk of the front of your thigh consists of the quadriceps muscle group. These four muscles surround your kneecap and are attached to the patellar tendon. They act together to straighten (extend) your knee against a resistance or gravity. One of the quadriceps muscles, the rectus femoris, also crosses the front of the hip joint, so besides acting on the knee it helps to bend (flex) the hip. The vastus medialis is the only muscle in the group to act on the inner side of the kneecap, and its horizontal fibres have the special function of locking the knee fully straight and controlling the kneecap at the same time (see p.185). Acting to control a movement in the direction of gravity, for instance when you squat down, the quadriceps muscles work eccentrically, paying out and contracting at the same time.

Lying over the top of the quadriceps muscles on the thigh is the sartorius muscle, which passes over the hip joint, across the front of the thigh, to its attachment just below the inner side of the knee on the shin-bone. On the shin-bone, it is curved forwards slightly and is functionally linked to two other tendons, the gracilis and semitendinosus, to form a structure technically known as the pes anserinus or 'goose's foot'. Sartorius helps to bend both the hip and the knee, to twist the lower leg inwards at the knee, and it also acts to lift the thigh and twist it outwards at the hip.

When you run, the quadriceps muscles primarily control the knee. They extend the knee during the push-off phase,

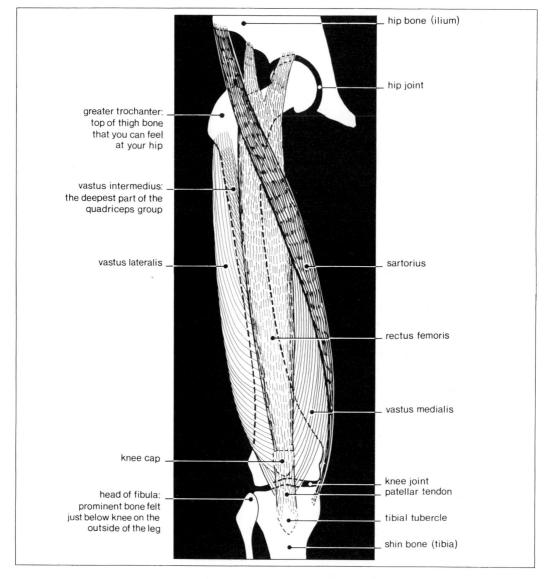

hip bone (ilium)

hip joint

greater trochanter:
top of thigh bone
that you can feel
at your hip

vastus intermedius:
the deepest part of the
quadriceps group

vastus lateralis

sartorius

rectus femoris

vastus medialis

knee cap

knee joint
patellar tendon

head of fibula:
prominent bone felt
just below knee on the
outside of the leg

tibial tubercle

shin bone (tibia)

Muscles on the front of the right
thigh.

and as your leg goes forwards towards the landing or strike
phase. The quadriceps muscles work concentrically when you
are running forwards in a straight line or up steps or a slope.
They work eccentrically when you run downhill. Sartorius is
especially active in the knee pick-up phase of running,
especially when you run uphill, as you bend your hip and
knee at the same time. Because of its structure as a two-joint

muscle going across the line of the main lever of the thigh-bone, sartorius' actions are more complex than those of the quadriceps group.

FRONT-THIGH MUSCLE INJURIES

The front-thigh muscles can be injured traumatically, if you fall over while your leg is blocked, or if you fall and get hit on the thigh. Traumatic tears of the front-thigh muscles usually affect the rectus femoris, because it is a two-joint muscle, but it is also true that any of the other quadriceps muscles can be torn in a sudden injury. Traumatic injuries to the thigh muscles may be referred to as 'corked thigh' or 'charley-horse', especially if there is obvious internal bleeding, visible as bruising, together with the symptoms of torn muscle. Hurdlers can suffer from repeated blows on the thigh of the trail leg if their technique is slightly out, and this can also cause bruising and strains or tears.

Runners more often suffer from overuse strains or partial tears in the front-thigh muscles. In young runners, overuse strains can be linked to 'growing pains' in the thigh bones. At any age, front-thigh injuries can be influenced by poor fluid intake. They can be linked to other injuries in the same or the other leg, to over-training, especially on hills, or to a badly planned training programme, especially if you have been doing a lot of drills involving driving off one leg, or hopping and bounding.

In the first instance, the practitioner has to differentiate the supposed muscle injury from the other possible causes of gradual thigh pain. A bone tumour is one of the very serious, and fortunately rare, conditions which might cause un-explained pain and swelling in the thigh region. Circulatory problems can cause thigh cramping and pain, and can con-tribute to muscle tightness, leading to strains. A more com-mon cause of thigh pain is a so-called 'trapped nerve', which transmits pain into the thigh from the hip or back. The symptoms of this type of referred pain can mimic those of a strained muscle very closely, except that you might notice more pain when you are sitting or lying down at rest than you would with a simple muscle injury. You may also have both trapped nerve pain and a muscle injury at the same time. Stress fractures in the thigh-bone can also cause pain similar to muscle cramping and strain.

Treatment for any immediate thigh muscle tear is simply ice and rest. On no account should the area be massaged, as there is a strong risk of bone formation, technically called myositis ossificans, in the injured muscle. If the injury is severe it should be checked by a doctor as quickly as possible, to rule out any bone fracture or joint injury. Even if a thigh muscle is torn completely, leaving a visible and palpable defect, it is unlikely that an operation is necessary, as the muscle can usually heal functionally quite adequately without surgery.

Once the injury is identified as a thigh muscle tear it may be supported with light bandaging, but it should be treated cautiously for the first few days. After the initial phase, the chartered physiotherapist (physical therapist) might start gentle massage techniques to reduce the pain and any swelling, and to help the circulation. Any qualified practitioner treating this kind of problem will use great care to avoid the risk of further damage to the tissues. In the later recovery phases of thigh muscle tears, the pattern of treatment is similar to that for overuse injuries.

I usually treat overuse injuries to the front-thigh with massage and electrical muscle stimulation, partly to restore good co-ordination in the injured part of the quadriceps group, and partly to make sure that the VMO does not become weakened, causing secondary kneecap pain problems (see p.185). If there is continuing pain, I use ice to control it. If there is a coexisting problem in the hip or back, this has to be treated simultaneously with the damaged muscle.

The remedial exercise programme for front-thigh muscle injuries usually consists of stretching exercises, a gradual strengthening programme, an eccentric strengthening programme, and then co-ordination exercises, done within pain limits at every stage. The stretching exercises are maintained as the first and last parts of any exercise session for a long time after complete recovery from the injury. If there is involvement of the back or hip in the injury, exercises directed at these areas have to be included as well.

REMEDIAL FRONT-THIGH EXERCISES

Stretching exercises

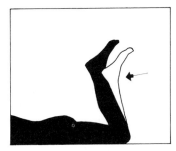

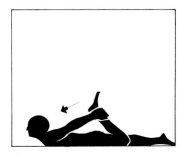

▲
1 Lying on your stomach, support the injured leg with your sound leg under the ankle, and gently bend your knees to bend the injured leg as far as it can go without pain. Hold for a count of six, then relax and lower down. Repeat five to ten times.

2 Lying on the side of your uninjured leg, gently bend your injured leg and hold the ankle with your hand; pull the ankle towards your seat and bring the leg behind you, keeping the hip forwards, as far as you can without pain. Hold for a count of six, then relax. Repeat five to ten times.

▲
3 Lying on your stomach, bend the knee of your injured leg as far as is comfortable, either with a belt round the ankle, or pulling the ankle with your hand. Hold the stretched position for a count of six, then relax completely. Repeat five to ten times.

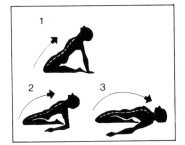

▲
4 Kneeling on a mat or cushion, with your knees slightly apart, lean gently backwards, keeping your hips well forwards and supporting yourself on your hands or elbows. Hold the stretched position for a count of six, then relax. Repeat five to ten times.

▲
5 Standing up, supporting yourself with your hand for balance, if necessary, bend your injured leg so that you hold the ankle behind you with one hand; pull your ankle gently towards your seat, keeping your hip well forward. Hold for a count of six, then relax. Repeat five to ten times.

Strengthening exercises

These include leg press and leg extension weights work, as described in the exercises for knee rehabilitation (see p.181). To emphasize the eccentric part of the muscle work, always remember to control the reverse movement as you return the leg to the starting position.

Eccentric strengthening exercises

1 Sitting with a weight over your ankle, or on a leg extension machine, lift the foot to straighten the knee hard, then slowly lower the leg downwards while counting to ten before the knee bends fully again. Repeat ten times.

2 Standing straight, slowly bend your knees as far as you comfortably can, counting to ten, then quickly straighten up again. Repeat ten times.

3 With your injured leg, step up on to a support about one foot off the floor, then slowly bend your knee to bring your sound leg to the floor (behind or in front of the step), as you count to ten before your foot touches the ground. Repeat ten times.

4 Standing on your injured leg, with your back to a table, slowly bend your knee to bring your seat level with the table, then straighten up quickly. Repeat ten times.

5 Standing on your injured leg on a step about eighteen inches off the floor, slowly bend your knee to bring your sound leg forwards to the floor, while you count to ten. Then lift your sound leg back on to the step as you straighten the knee on your injured leg. Repeat ten times.

Co-ordination exercises

These may include hopping, bounding, and balancing on a wobble board while you bend and straighten your knee slowly.

You can safely return to running, in gradual easy stages, as soon as you can stretch your injured front-thigh muscle(s) fully and can squat down fully on both legs without pain.

Groin and hip region injuries

THE FORMATION AND FUNCTIONS OF THE HIP REGION

The hip joint is one of the most stable in the body. The rounded head at the top of the thigh-bone (femur) faces a receiving surface, which is the cup-like acetabulum on the side of the hip-bone. The joint is firmly enclosed in its surrounding capsule, and the bonding is so secure that the pressure inside the capsule, which is filled with synovial (joint lubricating) fluid, is negative relative to the outside. The strong capsule is reinforced over its front by the iliofemoral ligament, one of the strongest ligaments in the body. The joint is deeply placed, so that the only part of the structure you can feel easily from the outside is the greater trochanter, which is the external ridge at the top of the thigh-bone, to the side of your hip.

The hip joint is a ball and socket joint, so it can move in virtually every direction, although its in-built stability means that it does not have the great freedom of movement that your shoulder does. The most limited movement, only about 15 degrees, is extension backwards. The adductor muscles from the groin down the inner side of your thigh draw your leg inwards, into adduction, towards the other leg. The hip flexors, which link the lower back to the front of the hip, bring your leg forwards, into flexion. The abductors at the side of your pelvis take the thigh outwards, into abduction. The hamstrings and gluteal muscles over the back of the joint take the thigh backwards into extension. Various muscles and tendons interact to twist the hip inwards and outwards, depending what position the leg is in.

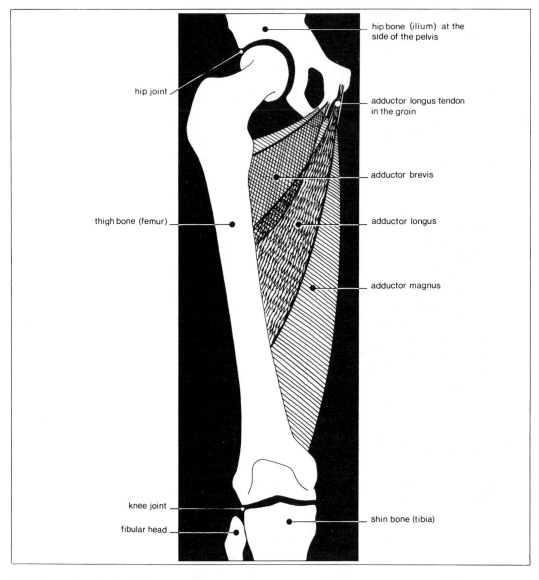

hip bone (ilium) at the side of the pelvis

hip joint

adductor longus tendon in the groin

adductor brevis

thigh bone (femur)

adductor longus

adductor magnus

knee joint

shin bone (tibia)

fibular head

Adductor muscles, front of right thigh.

Your hips function as a pair, but they are rarely symmetrical. You may be aware of the differences, as it may be more comfortable to sit with your legs crossed one way than the other, or you may habitually stand with your weight resting mainly on one leg. Your hips relate very closely to your pelvic joints and lower back, so postural or movement defects in the back or pelvis can cause secondary effects in the hip(s), and vice versa.

When you walk and run, you may turn one foot in or out relative to the other, and this may reflect an imbalance in your hips. You may find it easier to pick one knee up than the other, or one leg may extend backwards more readily than the other. One leg may be drawn across the other as you run, or both may be pulled inwards, so that your knees move in front of each other instead of side by side. If you have weakness in the hip abductor muscles on one side, your pelvis is not properly supported. When the weaker leg is on the ground, the pelvis tends to tip down sideways towards the opposite side as you bring that leg through in the leg-swing phase of running.

It is vitally important to protect the hips in young runners, and to investigate and correct, if possible, any noticeable imbalance in the joints. Hip deformities can happen at birth, for a variety of reasons. If they are bad enough, the baby is put in a special splint to help the hips to develop properly. However, even slight defects can lead to problems later on. The bones of the hip region grow gradually through the teenage years, and fuse at about the age of eighteen, so it is during this period that they are especially vulnerable to overuse or misuse injuries. In-turned hips during running are a tell-tale sign that the young athlete is running too much.

PAIN AND INJURIES IN THE HIP REGION

Inflammatory joint conditions can cause hip pain, either in isolation or in the context of pain in several joints at once. There may also be a burning and congested sensation in the region. Infections can cause the glands in your groin to become swollen and painful. Diseases like tuberculosis can also cause pain and damage in the hip joint, so in some cases your doctor has to screen you for these more serious possibilities, usually through a battery of tests including X-rays, bone scans and blood checks. Your description of your pain can help the doctor decide whether you have a simple injury problem or something potentially more serious.

Hernia

Groin pain can be caused by a hernia, which is a protrusion through the binding tissues which separate different areas of the body. Across the front of the groin region is the inguinal ligament, which separates the abdominal cavity from the thigh. There are natural gaps in the ligament to allow the main nerves and blood vessels to pass through. If one of these gaps becomes enlarged, other tissues may be pushed through the gap, causing pain and perhaps localized swelling. If the protruding tissue gets stuck, it is called a strangulated hernia. A hernia can be caused in a number of ways, including by heavy lifting, or simply by coughing violently. It can happen at any age, to anyone. One common cause of hernia among athletes is excessive abdominal exercises. Lifting both legs forwards and upwards with your knees straight as you lie on your back or hang from a bar is an exercise which carries the specific risks of causing a hernia or back pain, or both.

The pain of a hernia can be difficult to distinguish from pain caused by adductor tendon strain or referred from the lower back. The initial diagnosis may be made on the basis that you feel pain when you cough, and the doctor can feel the tender lump on direct pressure over the groin. If the hernia is causing continuing pain, or if a large protrusion has developed, surgery is needed to mend the defect. After the operation you have to be very careful not to do activities which increase the pressure in your abdomen, so you must avoid demanding abdominal exercises and heavy lifting for several months. Your return to normal training has to be dictated by your doctor or surgeon.

Referred pain

A 'trapped nerve' in the lower back can cause pain radiating into the groin region. If your practitioner suspects that this might have happened, your lower back will be tested at the same time as the groin region itself is tested. Treatment is then directed not only to the groin but also to the lower back, to relieve the pressure on the nerve. If you have this type of problem it is especially important to remember to sit and stand straight at all times, and to alter the position of your head and spine if you feel the pain when you are sitting or standing still.

Hip joint problems themselves can cause referred pain, which usually radiates down the outer side of the thigh, sometimes to the ankle. Sometimes the pain can be transferred into the groin, or down the front or the back of the thigh. The first priority is to identify the source of the pain, so that treatment can be accurate. Referred pain, characteristically, occurs not only when you are moving the painful area, but also when you are at rest with your hip in certain positions.

Hip joint problems

In young runners, especially between the ages of twelve and seventeen, the growth area of the head of the thigh-bone can become softened, sometimes for no known reason, sometimes as a result of injury or attritional damage. This can cause a limitation in the joint movement, and can damage the proper development of the joint's bones, leading to a condition technically known as a slipped epiphysis, because the growth area of the head of the thigh-bone tends to buckle slightly under the body's weight. The first sign of this problem may be slight pain, and it may only be felt in the knee, although it can be felt in the hip region itself, and sometimes in both the hip and knee. In some cases there is no pain at all, but the athlete starts to limp, without knowing why. At the first sign of potential trouble in the hip region, the young athlete should be checked by the doctor, who may refer him or her to a paediatric orthopaedic specialist for tests and appropriate treatment. On no account should the athlete be allowed to continue running or other sports until the problem has been identified and treated.

In older runners the hip joint can suffer from osteoarthritis (or osteoarthrosis), which is wear-and-tear degeneration. The problem can be hereditary, but it can also be influenced by excessive running training, previous injuries to the leg or back, and dietary factors involving food intolerance (see pp.91–6). There is gradual damage to the joint surfaces, and the joint's range of motion becomes limited, especially for twisting movements. The affected hip may be drawn forwards and inwards, technically into flexion and adduction, so that it becomes increasingly difficult to stretch it out sideways or backwards. Alternatively, the joint may gradually splay outwards, making it harder to turn it inwards towards the other leg. Sometimes both legs are affected simultaneously and equally, but more often osteoarthritis tends to affect one hip. Once one hip has been affected, however, the other might develop wear-and-tear degeneration through overloading due to compensation.

To limit the pain of osteoarthritis you should avoid excessive running, and this probably means that you have to restrict your mileage, and to run only a certain number of times per week. The amount you can do depends entirely on how much you can achieve without limping or incurring pain. You should do remedial exercises every day, to maintain and improve the muscle strength and flexibility and the hip joint mobility. Cross-training for general body balance and conditioning is vital. You can usually use swimming, cycling, stretching exercises and fixed-weights systems without problems. You should also pay attention to your diet, avoiding any foods or drinks to which you know you react (see p.95), and drinking plenty of plain water every day. You must also be careful to maintain good posture at all times, to protect both your hips and your back.

Osteoarthritis can occur very early in the hip joint, sometimes through congenital defects, but often as the result of over-training during the critical teenage growth years. The teenager who has done too much specialized running in the middle teen years can develop hip-related pains in the early twenties, and might even need corrective hip surgery by the age of thirty.

For the young patient, any hip surgery is likely to be reconstructive, so that the surgeon tries to rearrange the bones to make the hip formation better and more functional. For the older patient suffering from severe pain through osteoarthritis, the hip joint may eventually need to be replaced with an artificial joint. This is a relatively routine operation nowadays, although it cannot be guaranteed that you will be able to run again afterwards. Usually, running to a certain level is possible following hip replacement surgery: long-distance training and racing may be out of the question, but you may be able to do some running a few times a week. To recover fully from this type of surgery it is vital to follow your surgeon's instructions to the letter, to do the remedial rehabilitation programme strictly, and to maintain a routine of protective hip exercises indefinitely in the future. Track runners have to be especially careful never to overdo bend running, and whenever possible should protect the hips and pelvis from the repetitive stress caused by running the 'wrong' way (clockwise) round the track.

Stress fractures in the hip region

Runners who do too much running can suffer stress fractures in the fine bone at the front of the pelvis, the pubic ramus, in the neck of the thigh-bone, or in the main thigh-bone itself. The stress fractures can happen to runners of any age and either sex, although the pubic ramus seems to be more vulnerable in female runners, especially if their body fat is very low and they have stopped having periods (technically this is known as amenorrhoea).

As with stress fractures in other bones, the pain may be slight at first, and felt only after a running session. It usually starts within about a fortnight of an increase in your running schedule, and gradually gets worse if you continue running, although the pain seems to subside if you have a few days' rest. If you try to continue running without allowing the bone to heal fully, there is a strong risk of the fracture becoming complete, so that the bone breaks through.

If you have a gradually increasing pain over a bone, and you know you have been doing more running, you must see your doctor so that the necessary checks can be done to identify whether or not you have a stress fracture, and, if not, what the problem is. If the stress fracture is confirmed, you will be given a programme of painless remedial exercises to do, to stimulate bone healing without disrupting the bone further. You will probably need about twelve weeks off running. If your diet is deficient, you may be advised to adjust it, perhaps under the guidance of a dietician or nutritionist, and mineral supplements may be recommended. Female runners going through the menopause may be recommended to take hormone replacement therapy (HRT), if there is a possibility that they are at risk of, or suffering from, osteoporosis. Once the bone has healed, you have to return to running in gradual, easy stages.

Osteitis pubis

The joint where the two halves of the pelvic ring meet in front to form the pubis is very tightly bonded. However, it can suffer from shearing stresses, especially in hurdlers and steeplechasers, although this is a problem that is most common among footballers. The pressure on the joint can set up chronic inflammation, causing continuing pain and tenderness whenever you try to do your sport. Once the problem is diagnosed, the doctor may try injecting the joint to relieve the inflammation, following which you have to do careful rehabilitation exercises to re-establish stability around the joint. In the worst of cases, surgery may be needed.

Hip flexor injuries

The hip flexor muscles are attached to your spinal bones, and spread across the sides of your pelvis to the front of the hips.

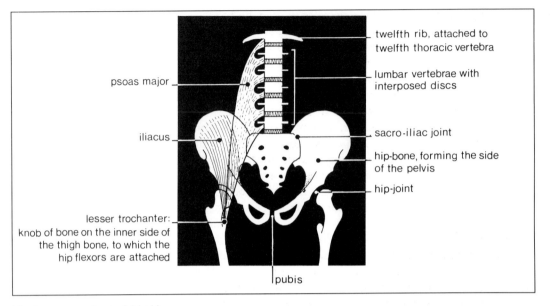

psoas major

iliacus

lesser trochanter:
knob of bone on the inner side of
the thigh bone, to which the
hip flexors are attached

twelfth rib, attached to
twelfth thoracic vertebra

lumbar vertebrae with
interposed discs

sacro-iliac joint

hip-bone, forming the side
of the pelvis

hip-joint

pubis

Hip flexors, over front of right hip.

The hip flexors tend to become tight through too much running, especially on hills. They can also tighten simply because you are getting older. If they are tight, they tend to hold your hip bent in flexion, and to pull your pelvis forwards, causing abnormal arching in your lower back. If the hip flexors on one side are tighter than the other there can also be a shearing effect on the pelvic joints, especially the sacroiliacs, causing a kind of twisting stress on the lower back. Once they are tight, the hip flexors can easily be strained if you run too much and they become fatigued. The hip flexors can also be injured traumatically, for instance if you fall over.

Hip flexor tightness can be tested when you lie on your back, and the practitioner bends one knee towards your chest until the straight leg begins to lift slightly off the couch. The tighter the hip flexors on the straight leg, the quicker the leg will begin to lift. The practitioner may judge this by eye, or may measure the distance each knee travels before the reaction in the opposite leg occurs. When the hip flexors are injured, you feel pain if the leg is drawn forwards from the hip against the resistance of the practitioner's hand.

Treatment may consist of ice, massage, and possibly electrical muscle stimulation or other electrical currents such as interferential therapy. The chartered physiotherapist (physical therapist) may do graded resistance exercises, technically called proprioceptive neuromuscular facilitation techniques, or PNF for short. You will have to do careful stretching exercises for the hip flexors within pain limits, building up to progressive strengthening exercises.

If the hip flexor injury has been quite severe, perhaps because you tripped and caught your foot as you fell forwards, the tendon can break off its attachment point at the top of the thigh-bone in an avulsion fracture. This may recover without interference, but if not it might need surgery to stabilize the area. After surgery, you should follow the detailed rehabilitation programme to recover full function in the hip flexors.

Failure to recover fully from hip flexor injuries leaves you at risk of subsequent problems in the hip or lower back.

Adductor muscle and tendon injuries

The inner thigh muscles, like the hip flexors, can become tight through over-training or simply as you get older. They can be strained or torn through a sudden accident, for instance if you catch your foot and fall sideways towards your other leg. The adductors are especially prone to overuse strains, which can be complicated by pain and spasm due to an underlying stress fracture, to a hip problem, or to symptoms referred from the lower back.

When the adductors are strained or partly torn, you experience pain when the practitioner stretches your leg out sideways as you lie on your back on the couch, and when you draw the leg inwards against the resistance of the practitioner's hand.

Treatment usually consists of ice, massage, PNF techniques, and perhaps electrical muscle stimulation combined with resisted adduction exercises. The remedial exercise programme might start with stretching exercises within the painless range, progressing to strengthening exercises. For chronic (long-standing) adductor strains, especially if the tendon close to the pubic bone is affected, progressive resistance exercises using PNF techniques may be essential to complete recovery.

The adductor longus tendon can tear off its attachment point at the front of the pelvis in a severe injury, and this may need to be stabilized by surgery if it does not recover with rest and graded exercises.

Abductor muscle injuries

Injuries to the abductor muscles, the gluteus medius and gluteus minimus, on the outer sides of your buttocks can lead to an imbalance in your pelvis, affecting your running action, your hips and your lower back. It is especially important not to try to run through injuries in this region, and to recover fully before re-starting running.

When the abductor muscles are strained, you feel pain if you stand on the other leg and lift the injured leg out sideways, and you also feel pain in the injury when you do the movement standing on the injured side and lifting the uninjured leg. The muscles give pain when you lie on the opposite side and lift the injured leg upwards against the resistance of the practitioner's hand. They also hurt when they are stretched, for instance if you lie on your back and pull the knee of the injured leg up towards the opposite shoulder.

Treatment usually consists of ice, massage and electrical muscle stimulation combined with active exercises. The remedial exercise programme generally starts with stretching exercises, progressing on to strengthening work. As the hip abductors have such a strong influence on both the knee and the lower back, the exercise programme may also include exercises for these areas as well as for the hip abductors themselves.

Bursitis

The tendons which pass close to the hip joint are all separated from each other and from the joint structures by bursae, or fluid-filled sacs which allow for friction-free movement. If one of these bursae becomes inflamed, perhaps because of awkward movements or undue pressure on a certain point, it sets up a localized pain spot which then causes pain whenever it is irritated by further movement across it. Sometimes the tendon over the bursa becomes tight, and causes a snapping sound or feeling as it moves: this is called 'snapping hip', and is fairly common in young runners, especially girls.

An inflamed bursa might be treated with ice, massage, and possibly electrotherapy techniques such as ultrasound or diadynamic currents. Your doctor might inject the area to reduce the inflammation directly. If the bursa has become very enlarged and painful, and does not respond to conservative treatment, it may be necessary to have surgery to remove it. Graduated remedial exercises are used to restore full movement and strength to the region, before running can be resumed.

REMEDIAL AND PROTECTIVE EXERCISES FOR THE HIP REGION

Stretching exercises

1 Hip flexor stretch. Standing with your injured leg behind the other, bend your front knee keeping your hind leg straight behind you, as far back as you can. Hold for a count of six, then relax. Repeat five to ten times.

2 Hip flexor stretch. Kneel on your injured leg on a cushion, with your knee bent so that the foot is in the air behind you; with your other leg bent up in front of you, foot flat on the floor, bend your forward knee to take your hips forwards, while you arch your back. Hold for a count of six, then relax. Repeat five to ten times.

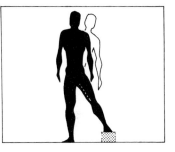

3 Adductor stretch. Standing with your feet wide apart, take your weight on your uninjured leg, and bend sideways over the injured leg. Hold for a count of six, then relax. Repeat five to ten times.

4 Adductor stretch. Sitting with your legs apart, feet turned outwards, lean gently forwards keeping your back straight and your head up. Hold for a count of six, then relax. Repeat five to ten times.

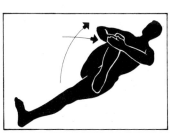

5 Abductor muscle stretch. Lying on your back, gently pull the knee of your injured leg up towards the opposite shoulder with your hands. Hold for a count of six, then relax. Repeat five to ten times.

6 Abductor muscle stretch. Sitting on a mat, bend the knee of your injured leg and place the foot by the outer side of your other knee; gently press the knee of the injured leg towards the opposite side with your opposite elbow. Hold for a count of six, then relax. Repeat five to ten times.

Mobilizing exercises

Pool exercises are probably the best way to improve mobility in the hip region: some of the exercises described below can be done in water as well as on land.

1 Standing on your uninjured leg, holding a support, swing your free leg backwards and forwards gently, twenty times.

2 Standing on your uninjured leg, holding a support, bend the knee of your free leg and swing that leg out and round in as big an arc as you can, twenty times. Take care to keep your back as still and straight as you can.

3 Lying on your back with your injured leg resting on a smooth board sprinkled with talcum powder, slide your leg sideways as far as you comfortably can, twenty times, quickly and rhythmically.

4 Lying on your back, bend the knee of your injured leg up so that the foot is flat on the mat, level with the opposite knee; let your bent knee move gently outwards and inwards rhythmically, twenty times (so that your hip is twisted mainly outwards).

5 Lying on your stomach, with the knee of your injured leg bent to a right angle, let your foot move outwards and inwards rhythmically twenty times (so that your hip is twisted mainly inwards).

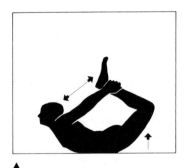

6 Lying on your stomach, bend your knees and hold your ankles behind you with your hands; rock gently backwards and forwards, twenty times.

Strengthening and co-ordination exercises

If possible, use weights machines for hip abduction and adduction movements, as well as leg press and hamstring curl exercisers. When you do free exercises standing up, remember to hitch your pelvis upwards into your waist before moving the leg on the same side.

Hydrafitness hip machine for abduction and adduction.

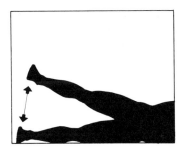

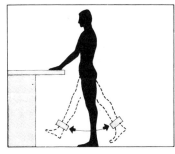

▲

1 Lying on your uninjured side, lift your upper leg upwards, keeping your knee and back straight, then slowly reverse the movement. Do three sets of ten. Add a weight on your foot or ankle when the exercise is easy.

▲

2 Holding a support if necessary, stand on one leg, with a weight over the ankle of the other leg, and move the free leg forwards and backwards ten times without pause. Repeat, standing on the other leg. Build up to three sets of twenty, then gradually increase the weights.

3 Stand on one leg, close to a support in case you need to steady yourself; lift your free leg out sideways, slowly lower without touching the foot to the floor, then lift again. Do ten movements in succession, then repeat with the other leg. Build up to three sets of twenty, then add a weight to the ankle of the moving leg.

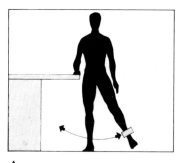

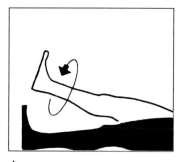

4 Lying on your stomach with a pillow under your hips, lift one leg a little way upwards (behind you), take it out sideways, then back to centre and slowly lower down. Do ten on one leg, then the other. Build up to three sets of twenty, then add weights over the foot or ankle.

5 Standing on one leg, close to a support in case you over-balance, with a weight on the ankle of your free leg, take that leg out sideways, then across in front of your other leg, then sideways again without touching the floor with your foot. Do ten movements in succession, then repeat with the other leg. Build up to three sets of twenty.

6 Lying on your back, with a weight over the foot or ankle of your injured leg, lift that leg straight up in the air, keeping the knee locked, and move the leg round in small circles. Do ten movements in succession, and build up to three sets of twenty, gradually increasing the weight.

Back problems

THE STRUCTURE AND FUNCTIONS OF THE BACK

At the tops of your legs the hip joints meet the pelvic ring, a basin-like bone formation which encloses and protects many of your vital organs. The hip-bones (ilia) which form the sides of the basin, just below your waist, meet the sacrum in the lowest part of your back, forming two sacroiliac joints,

The pelvis from the front.

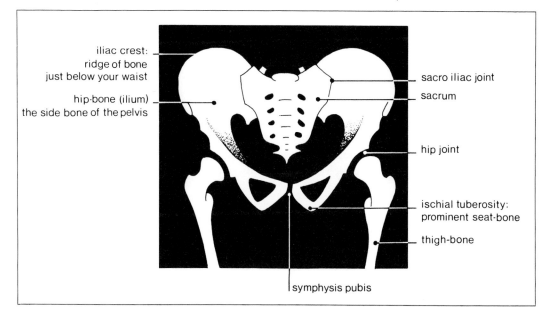

iliac crest: ridge of bone just below your waist

hip-bone (ilium) the side bone of the pelvis

sacro iliac joint

sacrum

hip joint

ischial tuberosity: prominent seat-bone

thigh-bone

symphysis pubis

one on each side of the midline. The sacrum itself is fairly flat and wedge-shaped, tapering downwards to where it is attached to your tail-bone or coccyx. The upper part of the sacrum supports the lowest lumbar vertebra. There are usually five lumbar vertebrae in your lower back, numbered from the highest downwards, so that the lowest is referred to as L5.

The vertebrae are blocks of bone which sit one on top of the other, linked together by ligaments and muscles. Soft-tissue discs lie between the main parts (bodies) of the vertebrae, and they act as shock-absorbers. Behind the vertebral bodies are finer struts of bone which form arches to protect the spinal cord. Gaps between the bones allow the networks of nerves to pass outwards from the spinal cord; from the lumbar spine, the nerves travel downwards into your legs and feet. Where the struts meet, they form facet joints.

Very little movement happens in the sacroiliac joints, although the bones glide slightly against each other as the hips and the lower back move. You cannot move the sacro-iliac joints at will, but their ligaments tend to loosen out automatically in females during the menstrual cycle, pregnancy and childbirth. The lumbar spine is designed to allow a greater range of backward and sideways movement than forward bending, and least for twisting. The movements between individual vertebrae are not very great, but the lumbar spine acts as a whole, and so has a reasonable degree of freedom.

Your trunk is supported by strong enclosing muscles all around. Against gravity or a resistance, the abdominal muscles bend the trunk forwards into flexion, while the back extensors along each side of your spine arch the back into extension. Bending sideways involves combined action between parts of the back extensors and the abdominals. Small rotator muscles close to the spinal bones act with the larger diagonal abdominal muscles to effect twisting movements, which happen mainly in the thoracic spine (middle back).

PRESSURES ON THE BACK

When you are upright, the back and the abdomen are subjected to strong pressures, some related to the effect of gravity, and some to your movements and activities. 'Abnormalities' in the structure of your back and hips may

make some of the loading greater, and potentially more damaging, especially if the trunk is asymmetrical. Some people
have six lumbar vertebrae. In some people the lowest vertebra is fused to the sacrum (although these variations in the
bone structure can be present without causing any problems).

The normal forward curve (lordosis) in your lower back is
more arched if the top of your pelvis is tilted forward, perhaps because of weak abdominal muscles or tight back
extensors. You may have a sideways twist and curve, called a
scoliosis, because the spinal bones are misshapen or the
muscles on either side have developed unevenly. If your legs
are different lengths your pelvis may tilt unevenly sideways,
stretching one side of your trunk and compressing the other.
Stiffness in one or both hips can cause distortion in the pelvis
and lower back.

When you are sitting upright, your trunk muscles have to
support the whole weight of your upper body and head
against the pressure of gravity, and all the loading is transmitted downwards on to L5, your sacroiliac and hip joints.
When you cough, sneeze or lift a heavy weight, there is a
huge rise of pressure in your abdominal cavity, which causes
a parallel rise in the pressure on your discs – this is why
coughing, sneezing and heavy lifting are so painful if you
have a disc problem. The pressure rise is reduced if you brace
your back first. Bending forward with your legs straight
while standing up causes pressure on the back, which can
reach dangerous levels if you have even a light weight in your
hand.

When you run, your pelvis and the lowest part of your
spine have to absorb some jarring pressures, but more
shearing pressures, because your legs twist the trunk one
way, against the contrary movement of your arms. The twisting forces are accentuated if you sprint hard, run round
bends on the track, run on camber, or up hills. Your running
style dictates, and is influenced by, the pressures your pelvis
and back have to absorb. Some runners stay very upright,
keeping the pelvis stiff and the back arched. Others bend forward, shortening the muscles over the front of the hips and
the abdominals. A tendency to drop one shoulder creates
stresses down the sides of the trunk. Weakness in the
shoulders and arms leads to extra work for the pelvis and
lower back if you are sprinting fast or running long distances.
It is usually because of weakness in the shoulders that
runners suffer from neck stiffness and pain.

BACK PAIN

Many factors can influence your vulnerability to back pain, such as fatigue, viral infection or some other type of illness, hormonal changes, and ageing. In women, the ligament laxity in the pelvic joints due to the menstrual cycle, HRT, or pregnancy can make the sacroiliac joints especially vulnerable to strains. In both men and women in the older, veteran age groups, wear-and-tear degeneration, or osteo-arthritis, can contribute to problems, or cause pain in itself.

Some illnesses actually cause back pain which mimics that of a 'normal' mechanical back injury. Inflammatory arthritic conditions can be a source of back pain. It also has to be re-membered that serious diseases such as cancer and tuber-culosis can cause back pain, although fortunately such cases are rare.

Ankylosing spondylitis is an inflammatory arthritic condi-tion which specifically causes progressive pain and stiffening in the body's joints. It usually starts in a sacroiliac joint, and then spreads up the spine into the shoulders and rib cage. It often affects the hip joints as well. It usually starts in the teen-age years, and tends to affect boys more than girls. It may not cause much discomfort at any stage, but in some cases it leads to severe disability, by restricting the victim's breathing as well as joint movement. In its acute phases the condition can cause flu-like symptoms. It often causes subsidiary symptoms such as plantar fasciitis and inflammation affecting the eye.

The disease is usually diagnosed on the basis of symptoms and blood tests, especially a test for the presence of the genetic factor HLA-B27. Very many people carry this factor without ever developing ankylosing spondylitis. However, it is possible that people who are HLA-B27 positive are espe-cially vulnerable to sudden episodes of acute back pain. There is no specific drug treatment to cure the problem of ankylosing spondylitis, but a well-balanced exercise pro-gramme is vital for maintaining joint mobility and preventing the spread of the progressive stiffness.

Back problems afflict most people, sometimes early on in teen years, more often from the early twenties. Some people are lucky enough not to suffer until they are quite old, but it is the very rare person who does not have at least one ex-perience of back pain or ache in the course of a lifetime. No matter whether you are sedentary or sporty, obese or thin,

you are equally vulnerable, because your spine is under constant pressure from gravity, your habitual posture and your
movement patterns. It does not take much to injure the back,
but you are more likely to suffer from more severe damage if
your job involves heavy lifting.

The fact that back problems are so common does not
make them any less unpleasant for the patient, or any easier
to deal with for the practitioner. Any of the spinal structures
can be damaged, including the bones, ligaments, muscles,
nerves and discs. Even though it is not always possible to
reach a certain diagnosis as to what damage has happened in
the back, any significant back pain should be properly treated according to a detailed assessment of the signs and symptoms. This is especially important in the case of young children, who, by rights, should not suffer from noticeable back
pain at all. If a child under the age of twelve complains of
back pain, it should always be investigated and solved, and
meanwhile the child should not be allowed to take part in
any activities which bring on or aggravate the pain.

A back problem can start off as a gradual ache, or as
acute, severe pain. The pain may be localized to one or other
of the sacroiliac joints, to the middle of the spine or to either
side of it. There may be associated leg pain which travels
down the back of the thigh, or down the side of the thigh, or
down the whole length of the leg, perhaps even into the foot.
This is called referred or radiating pain, and is caused by
damage to, interference with or compression against one or
more nerves, usually where they pass close to the spinal
joints. Pain in the lumbar spine itself may be felt where the
strain or damage is, but it is not necessarily precise, and may
radiate into one spot from another source.

BACK INJURIES AND DAMAGE

In most cases, the damage done to any tissues in your back
through injury is relatively minor, even though you might
have very severe pain. For instance, you might have strained
or partly torn a ligament or muscle. Any damage in the back
is automatically accompanied by some degree of muscle
spasm or tightening, which is a protective reflex forming a
natural splint over the affected area. The spasm restricts your
movements, and can in turn lead to extra pain.

More severe twisting or loading injuries can cause serious damage to the spinal structures. The discs are especially vulnerable if they are a little worn because of age and/or wear and tear. A minor rupture of a disc might cause little more pain and disability than a minor ligament or muscle strain. However, a major disc rupture or protrusion can cause unremitting pain in nerve pathways down one or both legs, with or without pain in the lower back. The affected leg may feel numb or painful by turns, and its muscles may shrivel, becoming very weak. Despite the fact that nerves are involved, it is *extremely* rare for paralysis to result from this type of injury: in most cases the nerve damage can be reversed.

Like any other bones in the body, the spinal bones can suffer stress fractures due to repetitive pressure and shearing. These can happen to runners, although they are more common in sports involving greater loading, such as rowing or tennis. The stress fracture (technically a spondylolysis) can happen in a strut on one side of the spine, and it usually causes an aching when you turn in a certain direction. Sometimes stress fractures can happen on both sides, in association with a slippage of the body of the vertebra. This is called a spondylolisthesis, and it may cause surprisingly little pain or severe pain, according to circumstances and luck. Traumatic fractures in the spinal bones are usually only caused by a major force, as in a bad fall from a height, unless you have brittle bones, or osteoporosis. A bad fracture carries the risk of disrupting or rupturing the spinal cord itself, which can cause partial or total paralysis below the level of the fracture. Fortunately, this is a type of injury which is not normally associated with running or most fitness activities.

HOW TO COPE WITH BACK PROBLEMS

If you have an acute back spasm or sudden pain, you should:

- apply ice over the painful area
- lie down to rest
- have frequent warm baths, if they ease the pain
- avoid sitting, especially in a low chair
- avoid any painful movements
- see your doctor (or practitioner) as quickly as possible.

To rest reasonably comfortably, you can lie face-down with a pillow under your abdomen, on your back with your knees bent, on your back with two or three pillows under your knees, or on your back with your legs resting up on a soft support which keeps your hips and knees at right angles (this is called 'Fowler's position'). You can also lie on your side, with your upper arm and leg supported on pillows. You must resist the temptation to twist your trunk in an effort to avoid pain. However comfortable a distorted position feels, it will leave you with extra pain when you have to get up or straighten yourself again.

When you consult your doctor or practitioner, be prepared to describe what has happened. You will be asked details of background factors, such as whether you have been ill recently, or had any digestive or urinary (waterworks) problems, or, in the case of females, whether the pain is related to your menstrual cycle or some hormonal changes such as pregnancy or a different contraceptive pill. You are likely to be asked the relevant questions about the pattern of pain, such as:

- Did it start in relation to your running?
- Does running make the pain worse or better?
- Do you have pain sitting or standing still?
- Do you have pain coughing or sneezing?
- Do you feel pain and/or stiffness in the early morning?
- Does your pain get worse during the day?
- Is the pain pattern constant or does it fluctuate?

For the physical examination, you will be asked to undress down to underwear, so you should be prepared for this, and be prepared to say if you feel nervous about it. The practitioner checks your movements in all directions, noting any pain and limitation. You are normally examined standing up, sitting on the edge of the couch, and then lying down on your back, side and stomach (not necessarily in that order). If any position is too painful for you to tolerate, it will be avoided for the time being.

The practitioner analyses your muscle balance, identifying areas of relative tightness or weakness. Your foot biomechanics are also taken into account, especially if your back pain is directly related to running. In many cases, the practitioner measures your leg lengths, to establish whether the bones are different lengths (this is called 'real shortening'), or whether perhaps the legs only *look* different lengths because one side of your trunk is in spasm and shortened, or because your hip is tight.

In most cases, a specific diagnosis cannot be made. It is impossible to tell from the outside exactly which tissue has been damaged, and whether a problem is definitely a strained ligament, muscle, disc, or any other type of tissue. Back pain is not usually caused by one damaged tissue in isolation, but by a combination of muscle spasm and joint damage, either of which can be caused by, or give rise to, the other. Your problem may be described as lumbago, backache, disc problem, facet joint injury, strained muscle or torn ligament: the diagnosis based on physical assessment is always informed guesswork, so you must not be puzzled if different practitioners use different terms to describe one problem.

For severe, chronic back problems, more precise diagnostic procedures may be used, such as different types of scan and X-rays. A myelogram is a special X-ray taken after a radio-opaque 'dye' has been injected into the spinal canal. It shows very precisely any disruption in a disc or any disease in the spine, but carries the disadvantage that it can cause severe headaches for several days after it has been taken.

Accurate analysis of a problem is essential where the pain has become so bad that an operation might be needed. Surgery is usually only needed where there has been bad damage to a disc, causing unremitting pain in the back and/or one or both legs. Most back problems are more simply

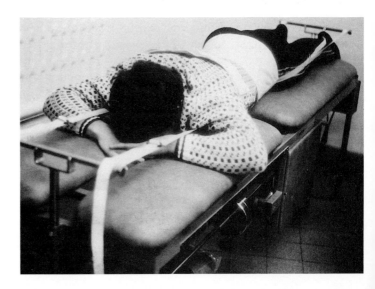

Lumbar traction to relieve nerve pressure in the lower back.

treated with physical techniques, such as manipulation, traction, massage, electrotherapy and, above all, exercise therapy. Especially when a patient is recovering from a back problem, I use electrical muscle stimulation to help the spinal muscles to work efficiently again. You may have to have a period of bed-rest when the problem is acute, and you may be advised to wear a firm or elastic corset to protect the lower back during normal activities, especially if you sit at a desk or do strenuous work. After a period of bed-rest, or after surgery, a progressive rehabilitation programme is vital before you can think of resuming any normal sporting activities. If leg length differences have contributed to your problem, you will probably be given a shoe raise or heel lift to help balance you properly during walking or running.

HOW TO PROTECT THE BACK

These are general guidelines, which can help to prevent back problems from getting worse. Always remember that bad postural habits, repeated throughout each day, can certainly aggravate back pain, delay or prevent recovery, and in some cases may actually cause back problems. Avoid any movements or exercises which aggravate your pain.

- Never sit with your legs crossed, or stand with your weight balanced on one leg.
- Avoid sitting in a chair or on the floor with your legs straight in front of you.
- Adjust any chair you sit in regularly, including car seats, so that your back is straight and your hips are higher than your knees.

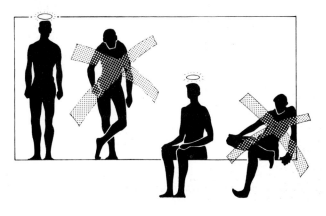

- If you sit at a desk, arrange the papers and equipment so that you sit straight, with your head up, and do not have to twist or bend in one direction all the time.
- Use a wedge cushion, if this suits you, and if your practitioner has recommended it.
- Do not slouch on a sofa or in bed with your trunk twisted (for instance so that you can read a book or watch television).
- Use the type of bed, hard or soft, that suits you.
- Avoid lifting heavy weights. If you lift even a light weight, always bend your knees and keep your back straight.
- Avoid carrying heavy weights; if you have to, try to divide the load into two bags, to carry in each hand.
- Brace yourself whenever you cough or sneeze.
- Never lie on your back and lift both legs upwards with the knees straight (double-leg-raises).
- Avoid forward-bending movements, such as toe-touching, especially with weights in your hands or on your shoulders, as in the 'good-morning' exercise.
- Avoid extreme back-arching, twisting or side-bending movements.

Remedial and protective back exercises

There are many different systems of back exercises. I favour a routine which works the different muscle groups controlling the spine, with the emphasis on stability through the joints. Never do any back exercises that cause or aggravate pain. Always be guided by your practitioner as to exactly which exercises you should be doing in relation to a problem.

1 Lying on your back on a mat with your knees bent, and your feet resting on the floor, flatten your back into the floor, then arch it gently to lift off the floor, keeping your hips and shoulders in contact with the floor throughout. Repeat ten to twenty times.

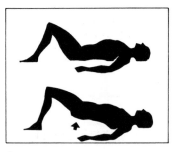

2 Lying on your back with your knees bent as in (1), raise your seat into the air, hold for a count of two, then slowly lower. Repeat ten to twenty times.

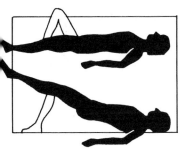

▲
3 Lying on your back, knees bent, feet flat on the floor, raise your seat into the air, straighten one knee to lift your foot into the air, bend the knee, replace the foot on the floor, and slowly lower your seat. Do ten movements on one side, then the other.

▲
4 Lying on your back, knees bent, feet on the floor, let your knees fall to each side in turn, creating a 'rolling' movement at your waist and hips. Repeat ten to twenty times continuously.

▲
5 Lying on your back, knees bent, feet on the floor, lift your head and shoulders to reach your hands forwards to touch your knees, keeping your elbows straight, then slowly lower back. Repeat ten to twenty times.

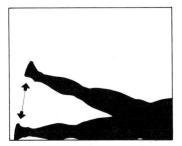

▲
6 Lying on your side, lift your upper leg upwards, keeping your knee straight and your hip well forward; hold for a count of three, then slowly lower. Do ten on one side, then repeat on the other side.

▲
7 Lying on one side, resting on your elbow, lift your hips upwards so that you are resting on the side of your foot and your elbow, then slowly lower. Do five to ten on one side, then repeat on the other.

8 Lying on your stomach with a pillow under your hips, arms alongside you, lift your head and shoulders backwards, just a little way, pressing your shoulderblades together; hold for a count of three, then slowly lower. Repeat ten to twenty times.

▲
9 Lying on your stomach with a pillow under your hips, lift one leg backwards a little way, hold for a count of three, slowly lower, then repeat with the other leg. Do ten to twenty on each leg.

◀
10 Kneeling on hands and knees, arch your back to hump it upwards as you bend your head downwards, then curve your back to hollow it out, as you raise your head up. Repeat ten to twenty times.

11 Kneeling on all fours, stretch one leg straight out sideways, turning your head to the same side to look at your foot; swing your foot round behind you, keeping your knee straight, toes close to the ground, as you turn your head to the other side so that you can see your foot again; repeat three times on one side, then three times with the other side. Do six to ten repetitions in all.

12 Standing straight, go up on your toes, then bend your knees slowly half-way or fully, keeping your heels off the floor and your back straight, then rise quickly to stand up again. Repeat five to ten times.

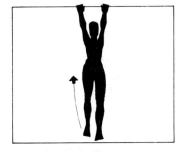

13 Hang from a bar, relaxing your back. Step down when your hands feel tired, even if this is after only a few seconds. Repeat five to ten times.

14 Hanging from a bar, keeping your legs together, swing them from side to side, pendular-fashion. Repeat five to ten times without pause.

15 Hanging from a bar, gently hitch one leg upwards to pull your hip towards your waist, then relax and hitch the other leg. Repeat five to ten times in succession.

RETURNING TO RUNNING AFTER A BACK PROBLEM

- Start with slow- to medium-pace running on a flat, yielding surface such as grass or cinder.
- Avoid running on camber.
- Run the wrong way (i.e. clockwise) round the track.
- Maintain your programme of remedial back exercises.
- Do some remedial back exercises after every running or exercise session.
- Include conditioning training for good body balance in your overall schedule.
- Stop running and seek specialist help at any hint of a recurrence of back twinges or pain.

Running risks and safety factors

1 Over-training The temptation to over-train is by far the biggest risk facing most runners, as it is the single most common cause of overuse injuries. Vary your training by doing different types of running, avoiding running on consecutive days, running on different surfaces, doing background fitness training, and by cross-training.

2 Shoes and kit Choose what suits you and is suitable for the kind of running you do, and the conditions you run in.

3 Running together If you run in a group, do not run in a packed bunch along public highways. Allow room for other road users, whether pedestrians or vehicles. On a track,

Running together should be social and safe.

Andrew on the road on Hvar:
always be visible and run towards
oncoming traffic.

especially when racing, make sure you judge your position in
relation to other runners, to avoid being jostled or spiked.

4 **Running alone** Make sure you know your route, and
that you can cope with it. If you are going for a run in a
strange town or village, check locally whether there are any
places you should avoid. Inform someone of where you are
going. Women, especially, should avoid isolated places, at
any time of day. Carry a mobile telephone and a personal
alarm, if possible, or carry a card or change so that you can
use a public telephone if you need help.

5 **Environmental hazards** Be sure you know the climate
you are running in, the surface you are running on, and
any particular pollution risks. Check whether the weather is
likely to change, and be prepared, by carrying suitable spare
clothing. If your route might take you cross-country, make
sure you know where any specially muddy areas might be, or
any fields with potentially dangerous animals. Try to avoid
areas with obvious air pollution, such as main roads or
factories.

6 **Surface hazards** Choose smooth firm terrain, and avoid
rough, uneven ground. Try to vary between hard and
softer surfaces. Watch out for unexpected dangers, such as
pot-holes, uneven paving, and debris or litter.

7 Traffic hazards When you run along any road, keep to the pavement. In the absence of pavements, take care always to run towards any oncoming traffic, wear bright coloured clothing, and keep well to the side of the road, especially if you hear a lorry or a motorbike approaching.

8 Darkness Women, especially, should avoid running alone after dark, if at all possible. Running in unlit areas, wear reflective clothing, and perhaps carry a torch.

9 Dogs Do not run past an uncontrolled dog: stop and walk slowly away from it. If you take your own dog out running with you, remember that dogs are not natural distance runners, so choose a route where your dog can run at its own pace, stopping and starting at will.

The Author with the family dogs. Pets, like humans, need varied and enjoyable exercise for health and fitness.

10 Smoking and alcohol Any smoking habits are bad for you and reduce your capacity for exercise or athletic activities. If you cannot break the habit, at least allow time between smoking and going out training – you need a good two hours to give your lungs a chance of working slightly better. Moderate consumption of alcohol is not considered harmful, but remember that alcohol should not be taken before exercise, as it can contribute to dehydration and reduce your energy reserves. Whenever you drink alcohol, you should try to take in plenty of plain water at the same time, to maintain a good fluid balance.

11 Illness and injury Always recover fully from any illness or injury before you re-start running or physical training. Do not try to make up for lost training time: always start with little and build up gradually.

12 Demotivation If you are not in the mood, do not force yourself to train just to keep up with a theoretical target schedule. You will not exercise efficiently, and you may push yourself to damaging levels of fatigue.

THE TWIN BENEFITS OF RUNNING AND FITNESS EXERCISE SHOULD BE GOOD HEALTH AND FUN.

Ten golden rules for safer, better running.

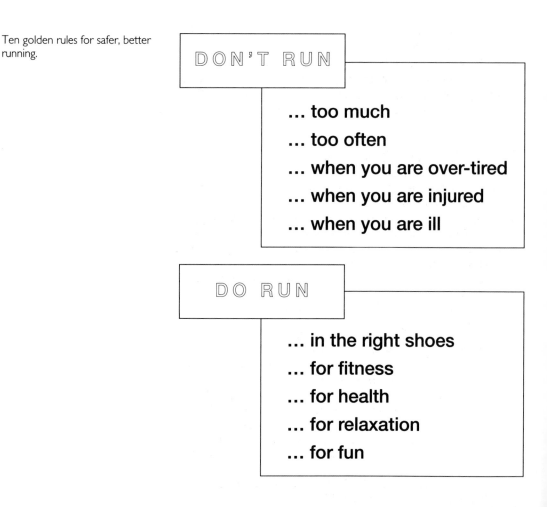

DON'T RUN

... too much

... too often

... when you are over-tired

... when you are injured

... when you are ill

DO RUN

... in the right shoes

... for fitness

... for health

... for relaxation

... for fun

Recommended reading

As this book is intended primarily for a lay audience without medical qualifications, I have not inserted references into the text. However, the following list of books and articles is for those, including any medically or paramedically qualified readers, who may wish to read more. Works which are particularly suitable for lay readers are marked with an asterisk.

TRAINING AND SKILLS

*Alford, J., Holmes, R., Hill, R. and Wilson, H., *Complete Guide to Running*. Sterling Publishing, New York, 1985.

*Benyon, T. and Macey, K., *How to Run a Marathon*. Hodder & Stoughton, New English Library, Sevenoaks, Kent, UK, 1986.

*Costill, D. L., *A Scientific Approach to Distance Running*. Track & Field News, Los Altos, USA, 1979.

*Darden, E., *The Nautilus Book*. Contemporary Books, Chicago, 2nd edn, 1982.

*Dyson, G. H. G., *The Mechanics of Athletics*. University of London Press, London, 4th edn, 1968.

*Fisher, A. G. and Jensen, C. R., *Scientific Basis of Athletic Conditioning*. Lea & Febiger, Philadelphia, 3rd edn, 1990.

Fry, F. W., Morton, A. R. and Keast, D., 'Overtraining in athletes: an update', *Sports Medicine* 12 (1) (1991): 32–65.

Fyfe, I. and Stanish, W. D., 'The use of eccentric training and stretching in the treatment and prevention of tendon injuries', *Clinics in Sports Medicine* 11 (3) (1992): 601–24.

*Gunnari, H., Evjenth, O. and Brady, M., *Sequence Exercise – A Sensible Approach to All-Round Fitness*. Dreyers Forlag, Oslo, 1984.

*Humphreys, J. and Holman, R., *Focus on the Marathon*. EP Publishing, Wakefield, UK, 1983.

Kannus, P., Jozsa, L., Renstrom, P., Jarvinen, M., Kvist, M., Lehto, M., Oja, P. and Vuori, I., 'The effects of training, immobilization and remobilization on musculoskeletal tissue. 2. Remobilization and prevention of immobilization atrophy', *Scandinavian Journal of Medicine and Science in Sports* 2 (1992): 164–76.

*Kirkley, G. and Goodbody, J., *The Manual of Weight-Training*. Stanley Paul, London, 4th edn, 1986.

Lehmann, M., Gastmann, U., Petersen, K. G., Bachl, N., Seidel, A., Khalaf, A. N., Fischer, S. and Keul, J., 'Training – overtraining: performance, and hormone levels, after a defined increase in training volume versus intensity in experienced middle- and long-distance runners', *British Journal of Sports Medicine* 26 (4) (1992): 233–42.

Lundin, P. and Berg, W., 'A review of plyometric training', *National Strength and Conditioning Association Journal* 13 (6) (1991): 22–30.

Macdonald, R. P., 'Physiological changes seen after six weeks' sequence training', *British Journal of Sports Medicine* 17 (2) (1983): 76–83.

McKenzie, D. C. and McLuckie, S. L., 'Running in water as an alternative training method for injured runners', *Clinical Journal of Sport Medicine* 1 (4) (1991): 243–6.

*McNab, T., *The Complete Book of Athletics*. Ward Lock, London, 1980.

*McNab, T., *Successful Track Athletics*. Letts, London, 1982.

*Martin, D. and Coe, P., *Training Distance Runners*. Human Kinetics Publishers, Champaign, Illinois, 1991.

Mero, A., Komi, P. V. and Gregor, R. J., 'The biomechanics of sprint running', *Sports Medicine* 13 (1992): 376–92.

*Myers, L., *Training with Cerutty. Revolutionary Track and Field Techniques*. World Publications, Mountain View, USA, 1977.

*Newsholme, E. and Leech, T., *The Runner. Energy and Endurance*. Walter L. Meagher, Oxford, 1983.

*Peach, S., *Improve Your Running Skills*. Usborne, London, 1988.

Radcliffe, J. C. and Farentinos, R. C., *Plyometrics – Explosive Power Training*. Human Kinetics Publishers, Champaign, Illinois, 1985.

Reilly, T., Secher, N., Snell, P. and Williams, C., *Physiology of Sports*. E. & F. N. Spon, London, 1990.

Safran, M., Garrett, W., Seaber, A., Glisson, R. and Ribbeck, B., 'The role of the warmup in muscular injury prevention', *American Journal of Sports Medicine* 16 (1988): 123–8.

*Stein, S., *The 'Running' Guide to Keeping Fit*. Corgi Books, London, 1986.

*Temple, C., *Cross Country and Road Running*. Stanley Paul, London, 1980.

*Temple, C., *Challenge of the Marathon*. Stanley Paul, London, 1981.

Ting, A., J., 'Running and the older athlete', *Clinics in Sports Medicine* 10 (2) (1991): 319–25.

*Tulloh, B., *The Complete Distance Runner*. Panther Books, London, 1983.

*Tulloh, B., *The Teenage Runner*. Tulloh & Tulloh, Marlborough, Wiltshire, UK, 1984.

Vagenas, G. and Hoshizaki, B., 'Functional asymmetries and lateral dominance in the lower limbs of distance runners', *International Journal of Sport Biomechanics* 7 (4) (1991): 311–29.

*Watson, A. W. S., *Physical Fitness and Athletic Performance*. Longman, London, 1983.

*Watts, D., Wilson, H. and Horwill, F., *The Complete Middle Distance Runner*. Stanley Paul, London, 1982.

SHOES AND INSOLES

Andreasson, G. and Peterson, L., 'Effects of shoe and surface characteristics on lower limb injuries in sports', *International Journal of Sport Biomechanics* 2 (1986): 202–9.

Cook, S. D., Brinker, M. R. and Poche, M., 'Running shoes: their relationship to running injuries', *Sports Medicine* 10 (1) (1990): 1-8.

Frederick, E. C., *Sport Shoes and Playing Surfaces*. Human Kinetics Publishers, Champaign, Illinois, 1984.

Gross, M. L., Davlin, L. B. and Evanski, P. M., 'The effectiveness of orthotic shoe inserts in the long-distance runner', *American Journal of Sports Medicine* 19 (4) (1991): 409–12.

Gross, M. L. and Napoli, R. C., 'Treatment of lower extremity injuries with orthotic shoe inserts: an overview', *Sports Medicine* 15 (1) (1993): 66-70.

Lewis, G., Tan T. and Shiue, Y. S., 'Characterization of the performance of shoe insert materials', *Journal of the American Podiatric Medical Association* 81 (8) (1991): 418–24.

Noakes, T. D., 'Running shoe anaphylaxis – a case report' (Letter), *British Journal of Sports Medicine* 17 (3) (1993): 213.

Stacoff, A., Denoth, J., Kaelin, X. and Stuess, E., 'Running injuries and shoe construction: some possible relationships', *International Journal of Sport Biomechanics* 4 (1988): 342–94.

*Turnbull, A., 'The race for a better running shoe', *New Scientist* 15 July 1989: 42.

SPORTS MEDICINE, INJURIES AND INJURY PREVENTION

Arnheim, D. D. and Anderson, M. K., *Essentials of Athletic Training*. Mosby Year Book, St Louis, Missouri, 1991.

Brunet, B. E., Cook, S. D., Brinker, M. R. and Dickinson, J. A., 'A survey of running injuries in 1505 competitive and recreational runners', *Journal of Sports Medicine and Physical Fitness* 30 (3) (1990): 307–15.

Clement, D., Taunton, J., Smart, G. and McNicol, K., 'A survey of overuse running injuries', *Physician and Sportsmedicine* 9 (1981): 47–58.

*Clews, W., *Sports Massage and Stretching*. Partridge Press, London, 1990.

*Colson, J. H. C. and Armour, W. J. *Sports Injuries and their Treatment*. Stanley Paul, London, 1986.

*Flanagan, X., *Sport First Aid*, Cumann Luthchleas Gael, Dublin, 1989.

*Flegel, M. J., *Sport First Aid*. Human Kinetics Publishers, Champaign, Illinois, 1991.

Fry, F. W., Morton, A. R. and Keast, D., 'Overtraining in athletes: an update', *Sports Medicine* 12 (1) (1991): 32–65.

Graham, J., 'Muscle injuries', *Journal of the Royal College of Surgeons, Edinburgh* 35 (1990): Suppl. S14–S17.

*Grisogono, V. A. L., *Sports Injuries, A Self-Help Guide*. John Murray, London, 1984.

*Grisogono, V. A. L., *Children and Sport. Fitness, Injuries and Diet*. John Murray, London, 1991.

Heil, B., 'Lower limb biomechanics related to running injuries', *Physiotherapy* 78 (6) (1992): 400–6

Hutson, M., *Sports Injuries. Recognition and Management*. Oxford University Press, Oxford, 1990.

Jakobsen, B. W., Nielsen, A. B. Yde, J., Kroner, K., Moller-Madsen, B. and Jensen, J., 'Epidemiology and traumatology of injuries in track athletes', *Scandinavian Journal of Medicine and Science in Sports* 3 (1) (1993): 57–61.

James, S. E. and Bates, B. T., 'Injuries to runners', *American Journal of Sports Medicine* 6 (1978): 40–50.

Jarvinen, M. J. and Lehto, M. U. K., 'The effects of early mobilisation and immobilisation on the healing process following muscle injuries', *Sports Medicine* 15 (2) (1993): 78–89.

Kannus, V. P. A., 'Evaluation of abnormal biomechanics of the foot and ankle in athletes', *British Journal of Sports Medicine* 26 (2) (1992): 83–9.

Kibler, W. B., Chandler, T. J. and Stracener, E. S., 'Musculoskeletal adaptations and injuries due to overtraining', *Exercise and Sport Science Reviews* 20 (1992): 99–126.

Kulund, D. N., *The Injured Athlete*. J. B. Lippincott, Philadelphia, Pennsylvania, 1988.

Macera, C. A., 'Lower extremity injuries in runners: advances in prediction', *Sports Medicine* 13 (1) (1992): 50–57.

O'Donoghue, D. H., *Treatment of Injury to Athletes*. W. B. Saunders, Philadelphia, 1984.

O'Toole, M., 'Prevention and treatment of injuries to runners', *Medicine and Science in Sports and Exercise* 24 (9) (1992): S360–63.

*Peterson, L. and Renstrom, P., *Sports Injuries – Their Prevention and Treatment*. Martin Dunitz, London, 1986.

Roy, S. and Irvin, R., *Sports Medicine. Prevention, Evaluation, Management and Rehabilitation*. Prentice-Hall, Englewood Cliffs, New Jersey, 1983.

Sowinski, J., Golebiewski, J. and Jozwiak, A., 'Minimum age limits for young marathon runners', *New Studies in Athletics* (quarterly publication of the International Amateur Athletics Federation) 4 (1986): 91–100.

*Sperryn, P., *Sport and Medicine*. Butterworths, London, 1983.

*Tippett, S. R., *Coaches' Guide to Sport Rehabilitation*. Human Kinetics Publishers, Champaign, Illinois, 1990.

Warren, B. L. and Davis, V., 'Determining predictor variables for running-related pain', *Physical Therapy* 68 (1988): 647–51.

TREATMENT TECHNIQUES

Dyson, M., 'The use of ultrasound in sports physiotherapy', in V. A. L. Grisogono (ed.) *IPPT Sports Injuries*. Churchill Livingstone, Edinburgh, 1989.

Grimby, G., 'Current aspects of eccentric training for muscle rehabilitation', *Clinical Journal of Sports Medicine* 2 (1) (1992): 1–5.

Knight, K. L., *Cryotherapy. Theory, Technique and Physiology*. Chattanooga Corporation, Tennessee, 1985.

*Phaigh, R. and Perry, P., *Athletic Massage*. Simon & Schuster, New York, 1984.

Windsor, R. E., Lester, J. P. and Herring, S. A., 'Electrical stimulation in clinical practice', *Physician and Sportsmedicine* 21 (2) (1993): 85–93.

*Ylinen, J. and Cash, M., *Sports Massage*. Stanley Paul, London, 1988.

Diet and eating disorders

*Eisenman, P. A., Johnson, S. C. and Benson, J. E., *Coaches Guide to Nutrition and Weight Control*. Human Kinetics Publishers, Champaign, Illinois, 1990.

Gleaves, D. H., Williamson, D. A. and Fuller, R. D., 'Bulimia nervosa symptomatology and body image disturbance associated with distance running and weight loss', *British Journal of Sports Medicine* 26 (3) (1992): 157–60.

*Griffin, J., 'Diet for children', in V. A. L. Grisogono, *Children and Sport, Fitness Injuries and Diet*. John Murray, London, 1991.

Stephenson, J., 'Medical consequences and complications of anorexia nervosa and bulimia nervosa in female athletes', *Athletic Training* 26 (1991): 130–35.

*Wootton, S., *Nutrition for Sport*. Simon & Schuster, London, 1988.

Bone problems

Devas, M., *Stress Fractures*. Churchill Livingstone, Edinburgh, 1975.

Gerrard, D. F., 'Overuse injury and growing bones: the young athlete at risk', *British Journal of Sports Medicine* 27 (1) (1993): 14–18.

Orava, S., Karpakka, J., Hulkko, A., Vaananen, K., Takala, T., Kallinen, M. and Alen, M. 'Diagnosis and treatment of stress fractures located at the mid-tibial shaft in athletes', *International Journal of Sports Medicine* 12 (4) (1991): 419–22.

Pappas, A. M., 'Epiphyseal injuries in sports', *Physician and Sportsmedicine* 11 (6) (1983): 140–8.

Taube, R. R. and Wadsworth, L. T., 'Managing tibial stress fractures', *Physician and Sportsmedicine* 21 (4) (1993): 123–30.

Walter, N. E. and Wolf, M. D., 'Stress fractures in young athletes', *American Journal of Sports Medicine* 5 (4) (1977): 165–70.

Foot injuries

*Arnot, M., *Foot Notes*. Sphere Books, London, 1982.

Bartold, S., 'Heel pain in young athletes', *Sport Health* 10 (4) (1992): 27–8, 40, 43.

Dietzen, C. J., 'Great toe sesamoid injuries in the athlete', *Orthopaedic Review* 19 (11) (1990): 966–72.

Irvine, W. O., 'Feet under force: treating sprains and strains', *Physician and Sportsmedicine* 20 (9) (1992): 132–44.

Kibler, W. B., Goldberg, C. and Chandler, T. J., 'Functional biomechanical deficits in running athletes with plantar fasciitis', *American Journal of Sports Medicine* 19 (1) (1991): 66–71.

Middleton, J. A. and Kolodin, E. L., 'Plantar fasciitis – heel pain in athletes', *Journal of Athletic Training* 27 (1) (1992): 70–75.

Santopietro, F. J., 'Foot and foot-related injuries in the young athlete', *Clinics in Sports Medicine* 7 (3) (1988): 563–89.

Trevino, S. and Baum, J. F., 'Tendon injuries of the foot and ankle', *Clinics in Sports Medicine* 11 (4) (1992): 871–90.

Warren, B. L., 'Plantar fasciitis in runners: treatment and prevention', *Sports Medicine* 10 (5) (1990): 338–45.

ANKLE INJURIES

Firer, P., 'Effectiveness of taping for the prevention of ankle ligament sprains', *British Journal of Sports Medicine* 24 (1) (1990): 47–50.

Lentell, G. L., Katzman, L. L. and Walters, M. R., 'The relationship between muscle function and ankle stability', *Journal of Orthopaedic and Sports Physical Therapy* 11 (1990): 605–11.

McManama, G. B., 'Ankle injuries in the young athlete', *Clinics in Sports Medicine* 7 (3) (1988): 547–62.

Meisterling, R. C., 'Recurrent ankle sprains', *Physician and Sportsmedicine* 21 (3) (1993): 123–32.

Reisberg, S. and Verstraete, M. C., 'Reusable prophylactic ankle support: a review of the literature', *Journal of Sport Rehabilitation* 2 (1) (1993): 43–52.

ACHILLES TENDON INJURIES

Allenmark, C., 'Partial Achilles tendon tears', *Clinics in Sports Medicine* 11 (4) (1992): 759–69.

Cetti, R., 'Ruptured Achilles tendon – preliminary results of a new treatment', *British Journal of Sports Medicine* 22 (1) (1988): 6–8.

Grisogono, V. A. L., 'Physiotherapy treatment for Achilles tendon injuries', *Physiotherapy* 75 (10) (1989): 562–72.

Helal, B., 'Achilles heel (cord)', *Clinical Sports Medicine* 1 (1989): 17–28.

Mahler, F., 'Partial and complete ruptures of the Achilles tendon and local corticosteroid injections', *British Journal of Sports Medicine* 26 (1) (1992): 7–14.

Niesen-Vertommen, S. L., Taunton, J. E., Clement, D. B. and
   Mosher, R. E., 'The effect of eccentric versus concentric
   exercise in the management of Achilles tendonitis', *Clinical
   Journal of Sports Medicine* 2 (1992):109–13.

Shin problems

Bates, P., 'Shin splints – a literature review', *British Journal of
   Sports Medicine* 19 (3) (1985): 132–7.
Black, K. P., Schultz, T. K. and Cheung, N. L., 'Compartment
   syndrome in athletes', *Clinics in Sports Medicine* 9 (2) (1990):
   471–87.
Detmer, D. E., Sharpe, K., Sufit, R. L. and Girdley, F. M., 'Chronic
   compartment syndrome: diagnosis, management and
   outcomes', *American Journal of Sports Medicine* 13
   (1985):162–70.
Kues, J., 'The pathology of shin splints', *Journal of Orthopaedic and
   Sports Physical Therapy* 12 (3) (1990): 115–21.
Morris, R. H., 'Medial tibial syndrome: a treatment protocol using
   electric current', *Chiropractic Sports Medicine* 5 (1) (1991):
   5–8.
Power, R. A. and Greengross, P., 'Acute lower leg compartment
   syndrome', *British Journal of Sports Medicine* 25 (4) (1991):
   218–20.

Knee problems

Anderson, G. S., 'Iliotibial band friction syndrome', *Australian
   Journal of Science and Medicine in Sport* 23 (3) (1991): 81–3.
Blackburn, T., 'Rehabilitation of anterior instability of the knee',
   Journal of Sport Rehabilitation 1 (1992): 132–45.
Engle, R. P. (ed.), *Knee Ligament Rehabilitation*. Churchill
   Livingstone, New York, 1991.
Eisele, S. A., 'A precise approach to anterior knee pain', *Physician
   and Sportsmedicine* 19 (6) (1991): 127–39.
*Fox, J. M. and McGuire, R., *Save Your Knees*. Dell Publishing, New
   York, 1988.
*Grisogono, V. A. L., *Knee Health*. John Murray, London, 1988.
Hilyard, A., 'Recent developments in the management of
   patellofemoral pain: the McConnell programme',
   Physiotherapy 76 (9) (1990): 559–65.
Lucas, C. A., 'Iliotibial band friction syndrome as exhibited in
   athletes', *Journal of Athletic Training* 27 (3) (1992): 250–52.

McConnell, J., The management of chondromalacia patellae: a long term solution', *Australian Journal of Physiotherapy* 32 (4) (1986): 215–23.

McDermott, M. and Freyne, P., 'Osteoarthrosis in runners with knee pain', *British Journal of Sports Medicine* 17 (2) (1983): 84–7.

Macnicol, M. F., *The Problem Knee. Diagnosis and Management in the Younger Patient*. William Heinemann Medical Books, London, 1986.

Noble, N., Hajek, M. and Porter, M., 'Diagnosis and treatment of iliotibial band tightness in runners', *Physician and Sportsmedicine* 10 (1982): 67–74.

Rintala, P., 'Patellofemoral pain syndrome and its treatment in runners', *Athletic Training* 25 (2) (1990): 107–10.

Shelton, G. L., 'Conservative management of patellofemoral dysfunction', *Primary Care* 19 (2) (1992): 331–51.

THIGH MUSCLE AND HAMSTRING INJURIES

Keene, J. S., 'Thigh muscle injuries in athletes', *Sports Medicine Digest* 14 (12) (1992): 1–2, and 15 (1) (1993): 1–2.

Smith, K., 'Study of hamstring injury treatment and rehabilitation management', *Athletics Coach* 24 (1) (1990): 24–7.

Stanton, P. and Purdam, C., 'Hamstring injuries in sprinting – the role of eccentric exercise', *Journal of Orthopaedic and Sports Physical Therapy* 10 (9) (1989): 343–9.

Worrell, T. W. and Perrin, D. H., 'Hamstring muscle injury: the influence of strength, flexibility, warm-up, and fatigue', *Journal of Orthopaedic and Sports Physical Therapy* 16 (1) (1992): 12–18.

GROIN, HIP AND BACK PROBLEMS

*Ferguson, A., *Back and Neck Pain. A Complete Plan for Self-Diagnosis and Treatment*. Pelham Books, London, 1988.

Fields, K. B. *et al.*, 'Osteitis pubis and pelvic stress fracture in an elite female distance runner, *Clinical Sports Medicine* 2 (1990): 173–8.

Garbutt, G., Boocock, M. G., Reilly, T. and Troup, J. D. G., 'Running speed and spinal shrinkage in runners with and without low back pain', *Medicine and Science in Sports and Exercise* 22 (6) (1989): 769–72.

Hackney, R. G., 'The sports hernia: a cause of chronic groin pain', *British Journal of Sports Medicine* 27 (1) (1993): 58–62.

Kahler, D. M., 'Low back pain in athletes', *Journal of Sport Rehabilitation* 2 (1) (1993): 63–78.

*McKenzie, R. A., *Treat Your Own Back*. Spinal Publications, Waikanae, New Zealand, 1980.

McKenzie, R. A., *The Lumbar Spine. Mechanical Diagnosis and Therapy*. Spinal Publications, Waikanae, New Zealand, 1981.

Renstrom, P., 'Tendon and muscle injuries in the groin area', *Clinics in Sports Medicine* 11 (1992): 815–31.

Waters, P. M. and Millis, M. B., 'Hip and pelvic injuries in the young athlete', *Clinics in Sports Medicine* 7 (3) (1988): 513–25.

OSTEOARTHRITIS

Allen, M. E., 'Arthritis and adaptive walking and running', *Rheumatic Disease Clinics of North America* 16 (4) (1990): 887–914.

Felson, D. T., 'Epidemiology of hip and knee osteoarthritis', *Epidemiologic Review* 10 (1988): 1–28.

Graham, G. P. and Fairclough, J. A., 'Early osteoarthritis in young sportsmen with severe anterolateral instability of the knee', *Injury* 19 (4) (1988): 247–8.

McKeag, D. B., 'The relationship of osteoarthritis and exercise', *Clinics in Sports Medicine* 11 (2) (1992): 471–87.

Murray, R. O. and Duncan, C., 'Athletic activity in adolescence as an etiologic factor in degenerative hip disease', *Journal of Bone and Joint Surgery* 53B (1971): 406–19.

Panush, R. S. and Brown, D. G., 'Exercise and arthritis', *Sports Medicine* 4 (1) (1987): 54–64.

Puranen, J., Ala-Ketola, L., Peltokallio, P. and Saarela, J., 'Running and primary osteoarthritis of the hip', *British Medical Journal* 5968 (1975): 424–5.

Index

Abdominal exercises, 214
Abdominal muscles, 38, 226
Abductor muscles (of hip), 211, 219
Accident(s), 71, 97, 110, 141, 167, 219
Achilles peritendinitis, 60
Achilles tendon, 60, 122, 126, 127, 139–51, 153, 198
Achilles tendon friction syndrome, 60, 142–3, 147–9
Achilles tendon rupture, 74, 79, 141
Acupuncture, 81,83, 85
Adductor muscles (inner thigh muscles), 153, 211, 212, 219
Aerobic capacity, 4
Aerobic tests, 27
Aerobic training, 5, 7, 10, 41, 46–7, 146
Aerobics, 194
Aircraft travel, 76, 187
Alcohol, 22, 76, 237
Allergy, 61, 84, 92
Alternative training, 9, 26, 81, 83, 85, 108, 111, 123, 159, 175, 177
Amenorrhoea, 217
American football, 167
Anaerobic training, 5, 7, 41, 45
Ankle, 71, 74, 102, 110, 116, 131–8, 139, 153, 157, 159, 166, 173
Ankle exercises, 138
Ankylosing spondylitis, 118, 228
Anorexia, 4, 18, 104
Anterior knee pain ('runner's knee'), 88
Anterior tibial muscles, 132, 153
Antibiotics, 21

Anti-tetanus injections, 73
Apophyseal avulsion fracture, 99
Apophysitis, 98, 122, 163
Arch supports, 125, 151
Arches (of the foot), 113, 154
Arm(s), 3, 8, 39, 104, 110, 111, 227
Aromatherapy, 83
Arteries, 76
Arthritic conditions, 72
Arthrogram(s), 170
Arthroscopy, 135, 170
Asthma, 4, 21, 82, 84
'Athlete's foot' (tinea pedis), 120
Avulsion fracture(s), 99, 133, 168, 200, 219

Back, 7, 44, 132, 147, 156, 198, 200, 207, 212, 225–36
Back extensor muscles, 226
Background conditioning, exercises, training, 9, 10, 11, 16, 28, 41, 104, 236, 237
Badminton, 106, 141
Balance mechanisms (proprioception), 87, 110, 114, 132, 133, 137, 189, 199, 210
Ballet, 124
Bandaging, 73, 78, 134, 136, 144, 183, 208
Barefoot running, 64, 136
Barefoot exercise(s), 129, 136, 183
Basal pulse, 22
Baseball, 104
Basketball, 106
Bend running, 7, 17, 52, 144, 166, 186, 194, 227
Biceps brachii muscle, 39
Biceps femoris muscle, 196

Big toe (hallux), 113, 123
Big toe stiffness (hallux rigidus), 123
Biomechanical tests, 29–33, 118
Biomechanics, 3, 61–2, 104, 108, 115, 124, 133, 161, 167, 187
Biopsies, 27
Blister(s), 60, 77, 120, 173
Blocks, 52, 123, 124
Blood, 72, 97, 102, 121, 170
Blood clot, 80
Blood pressure, 76
Blood tests, 84, 158, 174, 189, 213, 228
Body balance, 3, 8, 9, 41
Body conditioning, 1, 47, 71, 83
Body fat, 18, 217
Bodyweight, 4, 8, 110, 119
Bone(s), 72, 80, 97–112, 118, 121–3, 131, 133, 167, 208, 213
Bone density, 104
Bone growth, 98, 100, 101, 122
Bone scan(s), 106, 108, 121, 135, 142, 159, 174, 213, 232
Boots, 55, 136
Bouncer (mini-trampoline), 40, 48
Bounding, 45, 99, 106, 186, 198, 204, 207, 210
Bow legs (genu varum), 173
Brain, 72, 97, 132
Bruise, bruising, 61, 76, 105, 124, 126, 134, 141, 144, 168, 198, 207
'Bum bag', 66
Bunion (hallux valgus), 124
'Burn-out', 15
Bursa (cyst), 124, 141, 173
Bursitis, 126, 220

Calcanean tendon, 139

Calcaneus (heel), 98, 113, 121, 122, 139
Calf, 3, 36, 74, 113, 126, 132, 139–51, 153, 163, 187, 198
Calluses, 117, 119, 121
Camber running, 141, 173, 186, 194, 227
Cancer, 228
Candidiasis, 72
Carbohydrates, 20
Cardiac massage, 72
Cardiorespiratory fitness, system, training, 2, 9, 47
Cartilage (bone), 165, 168, 170, 188
Cartilage (meniscus), 82, 165, 167, 168, 170, 187
Casualty department, 80, 110, 144, 160, 169
Charity, 66
'Charley-horse' thigh injury, 207
Chartered physiotherapist (physical therapist), 26, 28, 41, 60, 76, 83, 87, 90, 100, 105, 110, 146, 161, 171, 173, 199, 200, 201, 208, 218
Chest infection, 21
Chest pains, 72
Chest specialist, 82
Childbirth, 226
Children, 15, 24, 67, 83, 97, 100, 164, 173, 229
Chilblains, 76
Chinese iron balls, 78
Chiropodist (podiatrist), 26, 57, 83, 108, 118, 119, 120, 121, 147, 148, 156, 161, 191
Chiropractor(s), 26, 83
Cholesterol, 76
Chondromalacia patellae, 185, 188
Chronic injury, 71
Cigarette(s), 41
'Cinema (moviegoer's) sign', 186
Circuit training, 11
Circulation, 12, 34, 45, 75, 104, 146
Circulatory care programme, 75–8, 106, 107, 108, 110, 136, 151
Circulatory problems, 76, 108, 110, 132, 147, 156, 160, 207
'Clarke's sign', 190
Clothing, 64–70, 237
Club officials, 73
Coach(es), 2, 14, 19, 24, 41, 51, 73
Coffee, 22

Cold compress(es), 77, 134, 144, 170
Colds, 21, 33, 35
Compartment syndrome, 160–1
Competition, 5, 177
Competitor(s), 13, 15, 41, 47, 48
Computerized muscle testing, 27
Concentration, 51, 70
Concentric muscle work, 27, 86, 87, 201
Contact (stance) phase, 115
Contraceptive pill, 231
Contracture, 85
Contrast baths, 122
Cool-down (warm-down), 33–40
Co-ordination, 33, 85, 88, 110, 111, 136, 169, 198, 204, 208, 223
'Corked thigh', 207
Corn(s), 120
Corset, 233
Cramp(s), 80, 144, 197, 207
Cricketers, 104
Cross-country running, 55, 105
Cross-training, 9, 110, 142, 177, 216, 237
Cruciate ligament(s), 165, 167, 168, 171, 184
Crutches, 74, 106, 110, 144
Cryotherapy, 77, 159, 191
Cuboid bone, 113
Cybex, 43
Cycling, 6, 9, 10, 40, 47, 102, 106, 141, 159, 161, 163, 175, 177, 187, 193
Cyst (bursa), 124, 141, 170, 173

David exercise equipment, 44
Deep vein thrombosis, 80
Deformity, 101
Dehydration, 20, 73
Diabetes, 82, 84
Diadynamic therapy, 78, 86, 107, 126, 134, 146, 148, 158, 159, 191, 200, 220
Diapulse, 78, 86, 174
Diarrhoea, 20, 72
Diary, 28, 84, 95, 105
Diet, 18, 21, 84, 93, 101, 103, 177, 217
Dietician, 21, 26, 82, 91, 108, 217
Digestive problems, 231
Disc(s), 226, 229, 230
Dislocation, 97, 167, 187
Diseases, 72, 84, 94, 99, 100, 101, 106, 156, 228
Dizziness, 72

Doctor, 21, 22, 25, 26, 35, 41, 60, 73, 76, 79, 80, 82, 85, 95, 100, 105, 107, 110, 112, 119, 123, 125, 126, 128, 148, 158, 159, 160, 169, 171, 173, 188, 199, 201, 208, 213, 215, 217, 220, 230
Dogs, 237
Dorsiflexion, 132, 135, 155, 157
Double-leg-raises, 214, 234
Driving, 74, 144, 193
Drug testing, 14
Drugs, 14, 80, 100
Dynamometer, 28

Ear, nose and throat consultant, 82
Eccentric muscle work, 27, 44, 87, 187, 191, 195, 201, 205, 208
Elbow, 76, 92
Electrical muscle stimulation, 78, 86, 102, 106, 123, 124, 135, 158, 159, 163, 171, 174, 191–4, 200, 208, 218, 220, 233
Electrolytes, 80, 144, 197
Electrotherapy, 77, 80, 82, 85, 100, 106, 122, 125, 126, 127, 134, 145, 146, 148, 163, 171, 200, 220, 233
Electromagnetic energy, 107, 158, 159, 200
Elite athlete(s), 2, 14, 68, 149
Embolus (embolism), 80
Emergency, 110, 160, 169
Emergency services, 74
Endorphins, 4
Endurance, 6, 11
Energy, 18
Energy depletion, 19
Epilepsy, 82
Eversion, 116
Exercise bicycle, 10, 27, 187
Exercise-induced asthma, 4
Exercise tests, 27
Exostosis (spur), 99
Extrinsic injuries, 71
Eye protection, 67

Facet joint injury, 232
'Fallen arches', 115
Family doctor (general practitioner), 25, 71, 81, 90
Fancy dress, 66, 68
Faradic muscle stimulation, 86
Fashion, 58, 64
Fast-twitch muscle, 3, 27, 139
Fat percentage measurements, 28

Fatigue, 9, 41, 43, 51, 94, 196, 197, 228, 237
'Fatigue fractures' (stress fractures), 49, 102–9, 121–2, 157–9, 163, 168, 188, 207, 216–17, 219, 230
Fell running, 55, 142
Female runner(s), 65, 68, 82, 84, 104, 144, 217, 226, 228, 231, 237
Femur (thigh-bone), 165, 173, 188, 196, 205–7, 211
Fencing, 194
Fibula (outer leg-bone), 85, 104, 106, 108, 131, 140, 153–9, 171
Field hockey, 6, 51, 141, 194
Fingers, 92
First-aid, 72–4
Fitness, 1
Fitness monitoring, testing, 27–33, 88
Fitness training, 1, 5–17, 40–9
Fixed flexion deformity, 177
Fixed-weights machines, 47
Flat feet, 57, 115, 155
Flexibility, 3, 9, 12, 47, 103
'Flick-ups', 204
Flu, 33
Fluids, 144, 207
Focal core degeneration, 143
Food intolerance, 82, 91–6, 101, 147, 156, 170, 215
Foot, 36, 49, 60, 76, 99, 104, 143, 159, 166
Foot exercises, 129–30
Foot injuries, 113–30
Foot massage machine (vibrator), 79, 158
Foot strike, 49, 115
Football, 141
Forearm, 39
Forefoot, 49, 116, 117, 123
'Fowler's position', 231
Fracture(s), 49, 97–112, 121–2, 134, 167
Freiberg's disease, 99, 123
Friction, 72, 118, 120, 124, 125, 127, 128, 141, 143, 165, 171-176
Front-thigh muscles, 3, 37, 99, 163, 187, 195, 197, 205–210
Functional electrical muscle stimulation (FES), 160–1
Functional recovery, 85, 100, 147, 176
Fungal infection, 120
Fun-runner(s), 1, 41, 66

Galvanism, 78
Gastrocnemius, 139, 153
General practitioner (family doctor), 25, 71, 81, 90
Genu valgum, 177
Genu varum (bow legs), 173, 177
Glandular fever, 22
Glands, 213
Gluteal muscles, 198, 211
Golf, 78, 135
'Good morning' exercise, 44, 234
Gout, 118, 132, 147
Gracilis muscle, 205
Grass running, 115
Grip strength, 28
Groin, 37, 105, 211–24
'Growing pains', 207
Growth spurt(s), 103, 104, 164, 187
Gymnastics, 124
Gynaecologist, 82

Hallux (big toe), 113, 123
Hallux rigidus (big toe stiffness), 123
Hallux valgus (bunion), 124
Hammer toes, 125
Hamstring-emphasis programme for cruciate ligament deficiency, 171, 182
Hamstrings, 3, 10, 36, 71, 99, 139, 143, 153, 163, 187, 195–204, 211
Hands, 76
Headaches, 71, 73, 92
Healing, 85, 100, 107–8, 112, 158
Heart, 2, 4, 5, 17, 21, 27, 41, 47, 72, 75, 97
Heart failure, 14
Heat dissipation, 1
Heat exhaustion, 73
Heat rub(s), treatments, 76
Heel (calcaneus), 98, 113, 121, 122, 139, 160, 191
Heel bruise, 61, 126
Heel-kick, 49–54, 195
Heel spur, 127–8
Heel strike, 116, 195
Heel-toe motion, 115, 117, 141
Heel tab(s), 56, 60
Height, 28
Hernia, 213–14
High arch (pes cavus), 115
High blood pressure, 76
High-jumper(s), 121
Hill running, 141, 175, 186, 187, 194, 198, 206, 207, 218, 227

Hip, 37, 61, 99, 102, 116, 132, 143, 147, 156, 164, 166, 171, 173, 184, 187, 188, 190, 195, 198, 205, 207, 211–24
Hip flexor muscles, 3, 37, 211, 217-219
Hip joint problems, 215–16
Hip replacement operation, 102, 177, 216
HLA-B27, 228
Hockey, 6, 51, 141,
Hopping, 45, 106, 123, 138, 183, 186, 198, 207, 210
Hormone(s) 84, 103, 108, 228, 231
Hormone Replacement Therapy (HRT), 217, 228
Hospital, 73, 169
Hot-and-cold therapy, 77
Hurdling, 52, 99, 121, 207
Hydrafitness exercise equipment, 44, 204, 223
Hydrotherapy, 101
Hygiene, 67–8, 72,
Hypothermia (over-cooling, over-chilling), 73

Ice, 73, 77, 81, 108, 122, 134, 144, 148, 158, 159, 160, 170, 174, 191, 200, 208, 218, 220, 230
Iliac crest, 99, 225
Iliotibial tract (band), 169, 171–6, 187, 191
Iliotibial tract exercises, 175–6
Illness, 4, 13, 24, 27, 40, 84, 94, 231, 237
Immediate (phase of) injury, 71
Immune system, 21
Impotence, 14
Infection, 20, 35, 110, 120, 132, 146, 188, 213
Inflammation, 99, 100, 123, 126, 128, 158, 163, 171, 172, 217
Inflammatory joint condition(s) (inflammatory arthritis), 101, 118, 132, 188, 213, 228
Ingrowing toe-nails, 118
Injection, 85, 125, 126, 127, 128, 148, 190, 217, 220
Injury prevention, 9, 11, 12, 22–3, 33, 42, 44, 57, 71
Inner thigh muscles (adductor muscles), 153, 211, 212
Insole(s), 55, 155, 174
Interdigital neuroma, 125
Interferential therapy, 78, 86, 107, 158, 159, 174, 218

Interphalangeal joints, 125
Intertrigo, 71
Interval training, 16, 45
Intrinsic injuries, 71
Intrinsic muscles (of the foot), 113
Inversion, 115, 157
Ischial tuberosity, 99, 195, 225
Isokinetic machines, 43
Isometric exercises, 87, 171, 201

Jarring stresses, 14, 16, 103, 107, 122, 123, 124
'Jockstrap itch' (tinea cruris), 70
Jogger(s), 1, 41, 47, 61, 116
Jogging, 47, 186
'Jumper's knee' (Sinding-Larsen-Johansson 'disease'), 99–100
Jumping, 106, 122, 132, 163, 165

'Kick-backs', 204
Kicking, 163
Kin Com, 43
Knee, 44, 61, 92, 98, 102, 116, 139, 143, 153, 165–94, 195, 196, 198, 205, 212
Knee brace, 171, 183, 184
Knee cartilage (meniscus), 82, 165, 187
Knee exercises, 163, 171, 177
Knee injuries, 167–94
Knee pick-up, 49–54, 195, 206
Knee replacement operation, 102, 177
Kneecap (patella), 104, 165, 185
Kneecap (patellofemoral) joint, 163, 165, 176
Kneecap joint pain ('runner's knee'), 88, 164
Kohler's disease, 99, 123

Lactic acid, 6, 45
Laser therapy, 25
Lateral release operation, 191
Lay-off, 13, 103
Leg length differences, 231, 233
Legg-Calvé-Perthes disease, 99
Lido, 43
Life-saving techniques, 72
Lifting, 214, 229
Ligaments, 72, 85, 99, 113, 131, 133, 153, 165, 167, 168, 169, 187, 211, 226
Limp, 23, 24, 111
Liver damage, 14
'Locked' knee, 169
London Marathon, 65–7
Long-distance runners, 6, 47, 50, 121, 197

Long distance running, 3, 124
Long toe flexors, 153
Loose bodies, 99
Lordosis, 227
Low-frequency electrical currents, 77, 107
Lower back (lumbar spine), 7, 226–36
Lumbago, 232
Lumbar traction, 200, 232
Lungs, 2, 5, 17, 27, 41, 45, 47, 97
Lymph, 75

'Ma technique', 146
McConnell technique, 191
Magnetic field therapy, 78
Magnetic Resonance Imaging (MRI), 170
Malleolus, 131, 133, 140
Manipulation(s), 25, 83, 85, 86, 123, 200, 233
Marathon, 8, 15, 103, 177
Marathoner(s), 3, 7, 47, 50
'March fracture', 121
Massage, 76, 80, 81, 85, 86, 99, 106, 122, 126, 127, 145, 146, 148, 158, 159, 174, 191, 208, 218, 220, 233
Medial ligament (of the knee), 99, 166, 167, 169
Meniscus (knee cartilage), 85
Menopause, 104, 217
Menstrual cycle, 84, 104, 144, 228
Mental concentration, rehearsal, 34
Metatarsal(s), 99, 108, 113, 121, 123, 124
Metatarsalgia, 61, 125
Middle back (thoracic spine), 226
Middle-distance running, 3, 50
Midfoot, 132
Mileage, 16, 103, 105, 109, 173
'Military press' exercise, 44
Minerals, 95, 103, 217
Mini-trampoline (bouncer), 40, 48
Misuse injuries, 71, 118, 156, 213
Mobility, 1, 3
Mobility, mobilizing exercises, 34, 36–9, 41, 42–3, 222
Morton's foot, 115, 121
Motorcycling, 167
'Moviegoer's (cinema) sign', 186
Muscle biopsies, 27
Muscle endurance, 3, 44, 47
Muscle injury, 48,
Myalgic encephalomyelitis, 22
Myelogram, 232

Myositis ossificans, 77, 99–100, 208

National Health Service, 81
Nausea, 92
Nautilus exercise equipment, 43, 44
Navicular bone, 99, 113, 121, 123
Neck, 111
Nerve(s), 98, 110, 113, 125, 136, 200
Neuroma, 125
Noble's test, 174
Non-steroidal anti-inflammatory drugs (NSAID), 85
Norsk exercise equipment, 44, 47
Novice runner(s), 103
Nutritionist, 82, 91, 95

Ober's test, 174
Oedema, 75
'One-repetition maximum', 45
Operation (surgery), 80, 89, 90, 92, 100, 102, 108, 123, 124, 125, 127, 134, 146, 148, 161, 163, 174, 177, 191, 200, 208, 214, 217, 219, 220, 232
Organ(s), 72, 97, 225
Orthopaedic specialist (surgeon), 26, 82, 100, 108, 109, 123, 125, 135, 170, 171
Orthotics, 57, 105, 108, 116, 124, 125, 126, 147, 148, 151, 156, 161, 177, 191
Osgood-Schlatter's 'disease', 98, 163
Osteitis pubis, 217
Osteoarthritis, osteoarthrosis, 101–2, 112, 168, 170, 173, 176–8, 188, 215, 228
Osteochondral fracture(s), 98, 135
Osteochondritis, 99, 123, 168, 188
Osteochondritis dissecans, 98
Osteopath, 26, 83
Osteoporosis, 80, 104, 217
Outer leg-bone (fibula), 85, 104, 106, 108, 131, 140, 153–9, 171
Overcooling, 67, 73, 77
Overheating, 67
'Overload' training, 7, 43, 198
Over-pronation, 116, 117, 133, 143, 155, 157, 167, 187
Over-stretching, 12, 201
Over-striding, 197
Over-supination, 117, 121, 133, 143, 155, 157, 167, 173

Over-training, 8, 41, 71, 121, 141, 144, 157, 207, 213, 218, 237
Overuse injuries, 9, 71, 97, 118, 122, 142, 156, 160, 167, 199, 207, 213, 219
Overweight, 6, 13, 177

Paediatric specialist, 100, 215
Paralysis, 230
Paramedical treatment, 82
Paratendinitis, 143
Parents, 19
Patella (kneecap), 104, 165, 185
Patellar strap, 193
Patellar tendon, 153, 163, 165, 169, 185, 191, 205
Patellofemoral (kneecap) joint, 163, 165, 176
Pellegrini-Stieda's 'disease', 99
Pelvic joints, 212
Pelvis, 7, 104, 211, 225
Performance-enhancing drugs, 14
Pericarditis, 21
Periostitis, 158
Peritendinitis (peritendonitis), 143
Peronei muscles, 153
Personal alarm, 68, 237
Perthes disease, 99
Pes anserinus, 167, 169, 205
Pes cavus (high arch), 115
Pes planus, 115
Phalanges (toes), 113
Physical therapist (chartered physiotherapist), 26, 28, 41, 60, 76, 83, 87, 90, 100, 105, 110, 146, 161, 171, 173, 199, 200, 201, 208, 218
Physiological capacity, 3, 14, 49
Physiological testing, 27–8
Physiologist, 28
Plantar fasciitis, 61, 99, 113, 118, 126
Plantar ligament, 99, 113, 127
Plantarflexion, 132, 135, 139, 155
Plaster cast(s), 78, 103, 107, 109, 134, 146
Plyometric training, 43
Pneumatic leg brace, 106
Podiatrist (chiropodist), 26, 57, 83, 108, 118, 119, 120, 121, 147, 148, 156, 161, 191
'Policeman's heel', 127
Pollution, 4, 237
Pool exercises, 48, 101, 110, 204
Positive thinking, 81, 92
Posture, 212, 229, 233
Power, 11, 41, 45, 47
Pregnancy, 82, 226, 228, 231

Pronation, 116
Proprioception (balance mechanisms), 87, 110, 114, 132, 133, 137, 169
Proprioceptive neuromuscular facilitation (PNF), 219
Propulsion, 3, 45, 111, 115, 132, 165
Protective exercises, 28, 42, 47, 102, 111, 136, 164, 178, 216, 234–6
Pruritus ani, 69
Psychology, 14, 19
Pubic ramus, 105, 216
Pulse, 22, 35, 40
Pulsed high-frequency electromagnetic energy, 78
Pulsed short-wave therapy, 78
'Pump bump', 61, 127
Push-off phase, 49–52, 115, 205

Quadriceps muscles, 99, 153, 185, 198, 205-210

Race organisers, 73
Racing, 15, 35, 52, 144
Racket games, 6, 116
Racquetball, 106
Rainwear, 66
Rape, 68
Recent injury, 71
Rectus femoris muscle, 205
Referred pain, 156, 188, 198, 200, 207, 214, 219, 229
Reflective clothing, 68
Reflexology, 83
Relaxation, 81, 96
Remedial exercises, 9, 13, 28, 42, 78, 86–8, 101, 110, 111, 124, 125, 126, 127, 129-130, 136–8, 146, 149–51, 156, 162, 171, 174, 177, 178-83, 184, 192, 200, 202–4, 208, 216, 220, 221–4, 234–6
Removable cast, 79, 146
Resuscitation, 72
Retropatellar, pain
Rheumatoid arthritis, 101
Rheumatologist, 82
Rib(s), 104
Road running, 6, 16, 105, 237
Rocker board, 136
Rowers, 6, 104
Rowing, 9, 46
Rugby, 167
Runner's 'high', 4
'Runner's knee', 88, 171, 185–94
Running drills, 51–4

Running skills, 16, 47, 49
Running style, 8, 23, 117, 227
Running technique, 8, 16, 49

Sacroiliac joint(s), 218, 225
Sartorius muscle, 205
Schnell exercise equipment, 44
Scoliosis, 227
Semimembranosus muscle, 196
Semitendinosus muscle, 196
Sesamoid bones, 113
Sesamoiditis, 123–4
Sever's 'disease', 98, 122
Shiatsu, 83
Shin, 153–64
Shin-bone (tibia), 85, 104, 106, 108, 131, 140, 153-9, 165, 171, 205
Shin soreness, splints, 61, 157
Shock-absorbing insoles, 102, 132, 177
Shoes, 22, 28, 55–64, 79, 83, 99, 102, 103, 105, 116, 120–1, 123, 124, 125, 126, 128, 132, 136, 142, 147, 155, 167, 173, 174, 177, 233, 237
Shoulder(s), 3, 39, 227
Shuttle runs, 6, 27, 45
Simmonds' test, 145
Sinding-Larsen-Johansson syndrome, 'disease', ('Jumper's knee'), 99–100
Skiing, 167
Skin, 72, 78, 79, 92, 117, 119–21, 156
Skipping, 45, 47, 106, 138
Sling, 78, 111
Slipped epiphysis, 215
Slow-twitch muscle(s), 3, 27, 139, 161
Smoking, 41, 237
'Snapping hip', 220
Soccer, 167
Socks, 69, 121
Soleus, 139, 153
Specialization, 15, 216
Speed, 1, 5, 6, 11, 16, 41, 45, 47
Spikes (spiked shoes), 55, 73, 156
Spinal cord, 97, 226
Spinal joints, 226
Splint(s), 136, 158
Spondylolisthesis, 230
Spondylolysis, 230
Sportesse exercise equipment, 44
Sports clinic(s), 61
'Spring' ligament, 113, 126
Sprint(s), 3, 5, 45, 49, 109, 123, 126, 141, 195, 199, 227

Sprint starts, 7, 16, 123, 124
Sprinter(s), 3, 11, 45, 47, 52, 65, 116, 197
Spur(s) (exostosis), 99
Squash, 51, 64, 106, 141, 159, 194
Squats, 35, 184, 186, 189, 198, 205
Staleness, 9, 15, 41, 48
Stamina, 1, 3, 6
Stance (contact) phase, 115
Starting blocks, 52, 123, 124
Step machine, 204
Stirrup splint, 136
Stitch, 19
Stomach upsets, 72
Strapping (taping), 134, 135, 200
Strength, 1, 6, 9, 41, 43–4, 47, 87, 103, 111, 145, 159, 181, 201, 203, 208, 210, 219, 223
Stress(es), 14, 16, 24, 92, 94, 96, 102
Stress fracture(s) ('fatigue fractures'), 49, 102–9, 121–2, 157–9, 163, 168, 188, 207, 216–17, 219, 230
Stress tests, 27, 160
Stretching exercises, 12, 13, 17, 33, 36–9, 41, 42–3, 46, 47, 87, 145, 159, 201, 202, 208, 209, 219, 221
Stride length, patterns, 52–3, 204
Subluxation, 187
Subtalar joint, 115, 132
Sudeck's atrophy, 80–1
Supination, 116
Support stockings, 79
Supports, 102, 136
Surgeon, 85, 89, 107, 110, 123, 146, 170, 173, 191
Surgery (operation), 80, 89, 90, 92, 100, 102, 108, 123, 124, 125, 127, 134, 146, 148, 161, 163, 169, 174, 177, 191, 200, 208, 214, 217, 219, 220, 232
'Sweat-promotion' elements, 34, 39–40
Swelling, 75, 76, 80, 85, 86, 91, 101, 105, 120, 144, 158, 160, 167, 169, 170, 171, 176, 186, 189, 191, 207
Swimming, 9, 10, 47, 48, 102, 106, 110, 159, 161, 163, 175, 177
Swing phase, 115, 213

Sympathetic nervous system, 80
Syndesmosis, 132
Synovial fluid, 75, 139, 165, 211
Synthetic tracks, 115

Talus, 116, 135, 140
Taping (strapping), 134, 135, 200
Tarsal bones, 113
Teachers, 2, 19, 73
Telephone, 68, 74, 237
Temperature, 22, 40
Tendo calcaneus, 139
Tendon(s), 72, 97, 99, 113, 118, 125, 127, 128, 135, 139–51, 153, 159, 163, 219
Tendonitis, 143
Tennis, 51, 64, 104, 106
Tenosynovitis, 61, 128
Thigh, 110, 155, 164, 191, 195, 207
Thigh-bone (femur), 165, 173, 185, 188, 196, 205–7, 211
Thompson's sign, 145
Thoracic spine (middle back), 226
Tibia (shin-bone), 85, 104, 106, 108, 131, 140, 153–9, 165, 171, 205
Tibial tubercle (tuberosity), 99, 153, 163–4, 165, 185, 206
Tibialis posterior muscle, 153
Tibiofemoral (knee) joint, 165–84, 187
Tibiofibular joints, 131–2, 133, 135
Tinea cruris ('jockstrap itch'), 70
Tinea pedis ('athlete's foot'), 120
Toe(s) (phalanges), 92, 113
Toe-nails, 60, 118–19
Toe-strike, 195
Toe-touching, 234
Tooth abscess, 22
Track running, 6, 16, 47, 48, 52, 56, 105, 166, 186, 194, 216, 237
Training, 3, 14, 17, 27, 40, 47–9, 103, 186, 198, 207
Training diary, 28, 84, 95, 105
'Trapped nerve', 207
Traumatic fractures, 103, 109–11, 230
Traumatic injuries, 71, 97, 118, 141, 156, 167, 200, 207
Treadmill, 27, 48, 57, 106, 115, 118
Triathlon, 9, 20

Trunk, 3, 38
Tuberculosis, 213, 228
Tumour, 24, 156, 207

Ultra-distance runners, 7, 20
Ultrasound, 25, 86, 100, 122, 126, 134, 145, 148, 159, 163, 171, 174, 190, 200, 220
Underwear, 69
Urinary problems, 231
Urologist, 82

Varicose veins, 75, 104, 156
Vaseline, 69, 121
Vastus medialis obliquus, 163, 169, 171, 174, 185–8, 191–4
Verruca(e), 120
Vertebra(e), 218, 226
Veteran runner(s), 177
Video, 51, 57, 118, 228
Virus infection, 21, 72, 94, 120
Vitamins, 22, 95
Vomiting, 92

Walkie-talkie radios, 74
Walking, 2, 49, 115, 132, 135, 142, 165, 213, 233
Walking stick, 75
Warming-down (cooling-down), 17–18, 33–40, 42
Warming-up, 17–18, 33–40, 42, 144, 197
Wart(s), 120
Washing, 66, 71
Water, 67, 73, 79, 197
Waterproof suit(s), 66, 69
Weather, 66, 237
Weight, 18, 28
Weight-lifting, 11
Weight training, 11, 43, 161
'Wet-vest', 10, 48, 106, 204
Wobble board, 136, 137, 210
Wobbler, 137
World records, 16
Wrist(s), 92

X-rays, 80, 84, 101, 106, 108, 121, 122, 123, 128, 134, 135, 170, 174, 188, 213, 232

Young runner(s), 28, 97, 122, 123, 163, 187, 188, 207, 213, 215, 220, 228, 229